HEAVY

WEATHER

BOATING

EMERGENCIES

**Other
Marlor Press
Books**

Boat Log & Record

Call of the North Wind

Guest Afloat

In the Teeth of the Northeaster

The Stormy Voyage of Father's Day

The Other Side of Sydney

London for the Independent Traveler

Going Abroad

*New York for the Independent Traveler**

*Winner of the Best Travel Guidebook Award
from *Publisher's Marketing Association*

HEAVY WEATHER BOATING EMERGENCIES

The survival guide for freshwater
powerboat operators.
What to do when
everything goes wrong

CHUCK LUTTRELL
with Jean Luttrell

MARLOR PRESS
Saint Paul, Minnesota

HEAVY WEATHER
BOATING EMERGENCIES

A Marlin Bree Book

Copyright 1998 by Chuck Luttrell and Jean Luttrell
Illustrations by Matthew Carter and Chuck Luttrell
Printed in the United States of America
ISBN 0-943400-97-X

Library of Congress Cataloging-in-Publication Data

Luttrell, Chuck, 1957
Heavy weather boating emergencies : the survival guide for freshwater powerboat operators : what to do when everything goes wrong / Chuck Luttrell with Jean Luttrell.
  p.   cm.
Includes index.
ISBN 0-943400-97-X
1. Boats and boating--Safety measures. 2. Marine meteorology. 3. Boating accidents. I. Luttrell, Jean, 1932- . II. Title.
VK200.L93   1998   98-7274
623.88'8--dc21   CIP

MARLOR PRESS, INC
4304 Brigadoon Drive   Saint Paul, MN 55126

CONTENTS

ACKNOWLEDGMENTS

First, we thank those people who believed we could write this book even before we undertook the project: At the top of the list is Bob McKeever, Assistant Chief Ranger in charge of water activities at Lake Mead Recreation Area and President of the National Water Safety Congress. Also we thank writing instructors Anne Serzow and Everett Chase for their encouragement.

Second, we thank Marlin Bree, the publisher, who believed in the need for this book and had faith in our ability to write it.

Third, since *Heavy Weather Boating Emergencies* could not have grown from a training manual to a comprehensive text without information, we thank all the people who gave us the benefit of their insight, experience and education.

Notably:

United States Coast Guard personnel: Chief Petty Officer Peter W. Hocking, Cleveland Rescue Coordination Center; Lt. Robert Patton, Annapolis, Maryland; Bruce Schmidt, Jack O'Dell, and Richard Todd, US Coast Guard Headquarters, Washington, D.C.

National Park Service employees: Ranger Bob Whaley, Isle Royale National Park; Rangers David Evans and Bob Wilson, Lake Meredith National Recreation Area; Ranger Lawrence Olsen, Lake Mead Recreation Area; Bill Hanrahan, Captain of Ranger III, Isle Royale; and Karen Whitney, public information officer at Lake Mead Recreation Area

Army Corps of Engineers: Frank Trent and David W. Hewitt, Safety Office, Washington, D.C.; Bob Rentschler and Don Williams, Vicksburg, Mississippi; Farris Chamberlin, St. Paul, Minnesota; Tom Holden, Assistant Director and C. Patrick Labadie, Director Lake Superior Maritime Visitors Center

State Boating Officers: Bill Engfer, Wisconsin Department of Natural Resources; Mark Richardson, Missouri State Water Patrol; John Rudd, Florida Game & Freshwater Fish Commission; Tim Smalley and Kim Elverum, Minnesota Department of Natural Resources

National Weather Service: Larry Jensen and Ron McQueen, Las Vegas, Nevada; Ed Fenelon, Negaunee, Michigan; Jose Garcia, Amarillo, Texas

American Red Cross: Carolyn Fielding, Las Vegas, Nevada

Experienced boaters: Cornie Paauwe, Grand Rapids, Michigan; William King, Naubinway, Michigan; Curtis and Ruth Johnson, Bayfield, Wisconsin; Captain Bill Bowell, St. Paul, Minnesota; Mary K. Allen, Washington, Utah; and from Las Vegas, Nevada -- Cactus McHarg, Philip Rennert, Patricia Seevers, C.R. Bud Cleland, and Ray Eicher

Research Librarian: Abigail Noland, Boulder City, Nevada

Internet research: Kent and Diane Etteldorf

In addition to those who helped make this project a reality, Chuck acknowledges the people who taught him boating safety, starting with his dad. Chuck says, "He taught me the right stuff by word and example, and some of it even had to do with boating." Chuck's first formal training came from Rangers Bill Sherman and Keith Eland.

Others who added to his boating education were: Carlie Ross of the Army Corps of Engineers, and Bob McKeever, Bob Wilson, Barney Turner, John Batzer and Jim Kosa — all National Park Service employees.

But not every lesson came from his teachers. Chuck has worked with many fine operators and alongside outstanding instructors from the Department of the Interior motorboat training program. Chuck says, "I cannot list them all, but I must mention my first patrol boat crew: Rod Goodwin, Nancy Hildreth and Mike Smith.

"And last but not least, James 'Jimbo' Sanborn, my friend and one of the finest boatmen around."

FOREWORD

With a few quick and easy lessons almost anyone can learn to operate a small powerboat on open water. I did. On open, calm water, that is. I found a few challenges such as the Rules of the Road and trailering, learning how to maintain and properly equip a boat, and handling a boat around a dock and in close quarters with other boats. But most of boat operation seems deceptively easy.

When the wind builds to the point where whitecaps appear, then many, if not most small boat operators find an environment that they are not prepared to deal with safely and effectively. I did. Most modern powerboats and their engines, if well maintained, can weather storms far beyond the capability of their owner or operator. Mine did. This book will help narrow that gap and offers a great deal of information designed to help the small-boat skipper navigate wind and waves on inland lakes. This book would have helped me too!

As I reviewed the manuscript I was reminded of many lessons in rough water boat handling I learned through trial and error during my years as a Park Ranger operating a patrol-res-cue boat on Lake Mead in Nevada and Arizona. I remembered hundreds of swamped, capsized or sunken boats. I remembered finding pieces of boats or boats being beaten into pieces on the rocks. I remembered people stranded ashore, people in sinking boats, people in the water, and sometimes people drowned or missing. I remembered how ill prepared I was for this job at first and remembered mistakes I had made. I had a few close calls but somehow always managed to do what needed to be done; I often wonder how.

This book has information that can help the boater on inland waters deal with wind and rough water without having to negotiate the years of trial and error that both Chuck Luttrell and I have experienced.

As you will see and perhaps already appreciate, avoiding rough water is your first, best option. For those times when you can't avoid the wind and waves, this book can help make the difference between an exciting but uneventful trip or a trip that shows up in the Coast Guard accident statistics with all the pain that it can mean to you and yours.

—**Bob McKeever**
President
National Water Safety Congress

Chuck Luttrell with search-and-rescue boat

INTRODUCTION

Fourteen years ago when I began my professional boating career, I found myself in the uncomfortable and unsafe position of being asked to perform a job for which I had no training. Assigned to a maintenance crew that used boats on a daily basis, I was handed the keys and told to go to work. I had my hands full just getting away from the dock. Fortunately, it was a calm day. Had it been foul weather, I would have been in real trouble.

A year later I became a boat patrol ranger at Lake Meredith National Recreation Area in Texas. That's where I got real on-the-job training in heavy weather seamanship. Being a rookie, I falsely believed that stormy days were shore duty days. However, the chief boating officer quickly set me straight: "We go out when others are coming in, because that's when we'll be needed."

I learned a lot — sometimes the hard way — at Lake Meredith. In 1989, I transferred to Lake Mead National Recreation Area in Nevada. As District Boating Officer I was involved in lake patrol, rescue and boating instruction.

When asked to prepare and teach a supplementary module on heavy weather seamanship for the Department of Interior's Motorboat Operators Course, I discovered very little had been written on this subject for the inland power boater. Forced to rely on experience and information gleaned from many sources, I developed my own teaching materials — the seed from which this book has grown.

Although boat patrol is no longer my job, I've written this book to give operators of freshwater power boats the benefit of my experience.

This book is intended to provide you with the knowledge and skills needed to manage and control heavy weather emergencies. It is a practical how-to guide with a serious message that could save your life.

— **Chuck Luttrell**

HEAVY WEATHER

BOATING

EMERGENCIES

AUTHORS' NOTES AND DISCLAIMER

This book was written for the small motorboat operator who boats on lakes, reservoirs and slow-moving or calm rivers. It is not intended for the ocean, coastal or white-water settings.

Additionally, it is intended for the recreational boat user. While boating is fun, it can also be dangerous — especially dangerous when the weather goes bad.

This book has attempted to compile commonly accepted basic information on operating in heavy weather and handling related emergencies. Every attempt was made to check the text for completeness and accuracy. However, the reader must recognize that procedures and technology change. While the information contained herein is the present recommendations of such authorities as the U.S. Coast Guard, it is the reader's responsibility to stay informed and maintain his or her boating skills.

Unfortunately, because of litigious society, we must give this disclaimer: the authors and the publisher disclaim responsibility for any adverse effect resulting from the use of information contained herein. Readers are strongly advised to attend a formal boating class, do further reading on the subject, and practice their skills. No two situations are alike and the events are dynamic.

In the end it is the captain who must use his or her judgement and take responsibility.

—Chuck Luttrell and Jean Luttrell

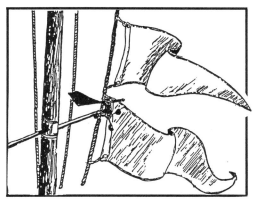

Two red flags signal gale-force winds forecast

Chapter 1

HEAVY WEATHER

Why weather consciousness is vital
to the boater's survival

At Lake Meredith, Texas, on a windy day in June 1993, a man, his two-year-old son and a friend cast off in a 14-foot boat powered by a 55 h.p. motor intending to check their "jug lines." They had only one adult life jacket, which they put on the toddler.

Soon realizing this was no day to be out on the lake, they tried to return to the dock. But this maneuver presented the stern to a following sea and made the situation worse. Then one of the men moved to the back of the boat — already weighted down by the large motor and gas cans. The added weight lowered the transom. Water surged over the stern. The boat, a 1967 model without proper flotation, swamped and sank, and the little boy came out of the too-large life jacket.

At 11:30 that night, searchers found the child's body lying on the beach next to an empty gas can. The boy and the can had floated two and a half miles from the scene of the accident.

Investigating officers concluded the father died trying to save his son — probably had given the child the empty gas can to cling to.

For David Evans and Bob Wilson, the rangers who investigated this accident — 555 deaths from drowning in 1993 was not a meaningless statistic — it was a baby clutching a gas can tossed by angry waves multiplied by 555.

Tragedies that might have been prevented — if only a properly fitted life jacket had been worn. If only the vulnerable stern had not been turned toward a following sea. If only the boat operator had understood the dangers of heavy weather.

Coast Guard statistics show:

- Approximately **90 percent** of all boating accidents involve motorboats.
- **Fifty percent** of these catastrophes are on lakes or freshwater reservoirs.
- **Weather** is a contributing factor in a **third** of all reported accidents.

In spite of these alarming statistics, which clearly show the dangers of heavy weather for the inland boater, most texts on this subject describe typhoons, hurricanes and huge ocean waves of 70 feet or more. The boater on Lake Okeechobee in Florida, Lake Mead in Nevada or any other large inland body of water will not encounter these conditions.

Nevertheless these small boat skippers do experience heavy weather. While the magnitude of a lake storm does not compare to that of an ocean tempest, the cost and lives lost are not insignificant. For the typical recreational boater out for a weekend of fun with his family in a 20-foot boat, a storm that generates six-foot waves creates no less fear, no less risk than a big blow on the high seas.

The difference is nobody told the small boat captain about the dangers of wind and waves.

According to a 1997 survey conducted for the International Association of Fish & Wildlife Agencies, there are an estimated 19.6 million recreational boats in the United States. Seventy-three percent of these boats are being used on freshwater lakes.

In simple terms this means there are a lot of people who are not being warned of the very real hazards of weather on lakes and reservoirs.

Low thick clouds indicate the approach of a cold front,
with possible wind and rain

Boating under conditions of heavy weather is serious business. Even the cautious boater should have a clear understanding of how to handle rough water, because sooner or later, he or she is likely to be caught out, unable to reach shelter.

During my boating career I've learned many things about weather and seamanship. I've learned how to handle a boat tossed by savage waves. I've learned how to overcome and survive adversities.

My purpose in writing this book is to give other boaters the benefit of my experience — starting with a knowledge of weather — what creates it, how it behaves and the destruction it can cause.

But first, even before weather knowledge, comes weather consciousness. Your survival begins with awareness of and respect for weather.

I have three basic rules:
1. You can't ignore the weather.
2. You can't gamble against the weather.
3. You can't beat the weather.

You can't ignore the weather

You must know your adversary. That is why it is important to learn about weather, find out what it is capable of doing in your boating area and then never take your eyes off it.

I'm always amazed by how many boaters launch their vessels in the shadows of flapping storm flags. As a ranger I often wished I had the power to tell a captain that he or she couldn't go out on a bad day. I certainly agree with Larry Jensen, Meteorologist in Charge of the Las Vegas National Weather Service, who says, "People don't look at the consequences of their actions."

He explains that when boaters ignore the forecast and disregard a prediction of foul weather, they never think: "I might capsize the boat. I'll be sitting out there for three or four hours drifting around in water that is 68 degrees — that's really cold. I might die."

Unfortunately, it seems once some boaters get an idea like let's go fishing, or let's water ski — they're going to do it even if it kills them.

I remember just such a case. It happened on a windy summer day at Lake Meredith, Texas. Due to a three-foot chop there were very few boats on the lake. Even though it was not a day for pleasure boating, my deckhand spotted a boat in the open

This daycruiser has small cabin under the bow and an inboard/outdrive engine. A relatively stable vessel with built-in floatation, this design is middle America's favorite recreational boat.

Going out for a weekend, want a place to eat and sleep, and want to water ski? This may be the boat for you because it combines some amenities — small head, galley and a bunk in the cabin — with a planing hull for speed.

water. It wasn't moving and we suspected it was disabled and adrift. Why else would a boat be dead in the water in the middle of the lake on this windy day?

But as we motored closer we saw that there was a man in the water attempting to water ski. I thought, "You've gotta be kidding!" It was unbelievable — but not illegal.

When we came close enough I shouted advice. I reminded them of the weather forecast and suggested they seek a sheltered area. The operator seemed to agree, but he said they were going to try "just one more time."

As we pulled away, still watching, we saw them try to pull the skier up — he fell. Instead of helping the skier back into the boat, they circled around to try again. Since they had not heeded our advice and apparently were not going to, we motored away.

Later, we learned that shortly after we left the skier got in trouble, the three people on board moved to the same side of the boat and it capsized. One person drowned immediately; the others clung to the hull and floated across the lake to shore. Sometime after dark one of them hiked to a nearby community and called for help.

This accident happened because these people went out in bad weather and attempted an activity that was not safe in a three-foot chop. They ignored the weather.

Before you put your boat in the water:

- Get an up-to-date weather forecast.
- Ask about the weather in your boating area.
- Check the marine weather warning flags.

Weather forecast

Experienced, safety-conscious boaters check the Weather Channel on cable TV, the weather segment of the news or the weather page in the newspaper before heading for the lake.

These sources show the national weather picture. You can see storms that are moving in your direction. Also many television weather reports show the location of the jet stream — that band of strong wind which flows from west to east in the upper troposphere.

At times this river of air aloft bends to the north, at other times it dips southward. These fluctuations are important because storms tend to move along its path and a hard blow aloft usually means a hard blow below.

After checking newspaper and television to get the overall picture, the weatherwise boater monitors NOAA (National Oceanic and Atmospheric Administration) weather on the VHF marine radio. The most current forecast is broadcast continuously by the National Weather Service from 400 locations on seven frequencies in the VHF band, ranging from 162.400 to 162.550 megahertz. These broadcasts are updated every 1 to 3 hours and focus on the weather information needed locally. For instance, in southern Nevada, a Lake Mead forecast is included in every broadcast. This means if you have a weather radio (a radio designed to receive only NOAA Weather) or a VHF marine radio you can hear the latest forecast for your area any time of the day or night.

Most marinas also receive NOAA Weather. If you don't have a radio, ask someone at the marina to let you listen to the latest forecast.

Local weather variations

Every lake is different. The mountains, canyons, valleys and other physical features surrounding a lake can greatly affect its weather.

Ron McQueen, a meteorologist at NWS in Las Vegas, offers this advice to boaters: "Know the local effects ... There are a lot of people who come in from other areas, who don't know the waters around here. I would hope that they would ask. Say, 'Hey, right now the winds are really light, the Weather Service is saying 20 to 30 miles per hour, what does that mean for the lake?' Or, 'What does that mean for this arm that I want to go up?' I would hope that they would go in and talk to (someone) at the marina."

Weather warning flags

Check the marine weather warning flags that you will usually see at marinas and boat docks. But do not depend entirely on these flags, pennants or lights for your weather information. Warning flags should supplement the weather forecast, not replace it. See Sidebar 1.1.

You can't gamble against the weather

"That's an ugly-looking thunderhead."
"Think it'll get us? "
"Don't know."
"Should we head in?"
"Naw, it'll probably bypass us."

How many times has some form of this conversation taken place on board and how many times has it been the prelude to disaster? We'll never know.

But I do know of one time when two young men had a discussion similar to this, bet against the weather and lost.

It happened at Lake Mead on September 3, 1990. The National Weather Service had forecast afternoon thunderstorms. The storm arrived right on schedule and was clearly visible long before it reached the lake.

I was one of the two rangers patrolling the lake that day. In separate boats, going opposite directions, we warned as many small vessels as we could of the approaching storm and told people to head for shelter. Shortly before the storm reached my patrol boat, I saw a large sailboat and thought, Oh man! They're going to get a good ride.

I wasn't concerned. Sailboats are seaworthy vessels and, unlike most powerboat operators, the captain and crew of a sailboat are usually well trained and know how to handle heavy weather.

As I expected, the wind hit hard and was quickly followed by driving rain. A good chop soon became 6- to 7-foot seas and it felt as if my boat were being heaved up, only to be dropped again in a world of gray-green water that washed over the deck. Like the sailboaters, I was getting a good ride.

After about 30 minutes, almost as suddenly as it had started, the rain and wind slacked off. Now my 31-foot patrol boat settled into a rhythmic pitching motion. That's when I heard the dispatcher on the radio:

Weather Warnings

SMALL CRAFT ADVISORY

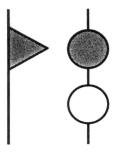

Wind up to 38 miles per hour
Hazardous wave conditions

Daytime: One red pennant

Nighttime: One red light over
           one white light

GALE WARNING

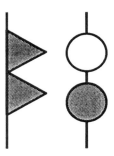

Sustained winds of 39 to 54 mph

Daytime: Two red pennants

Nighttime: One white light over
           one red light

STORM WARNING

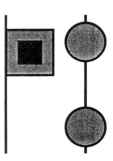

Sustained winds of 55 to 73 mph

Daytime: Black square in center of
          a square red flag

Nighttime: Two red lights

Sidebar 1.1

"416 (my number) respond to Lake Mead Marina area, boat accident, one survivor coming into Lake Mead Harbor."

The report was confusing. At first I didn't even know the location of the accident. I started toward the marina before being redirected by radio to the area west of Burro Point where I'd been during the storm.

There I met the sailboat I'd seen before the bad weather hit us. From radio transmissions and the sailboat crew I learned the storm had capsized a small 14-foot fishing vessel.

Two young men had been in the boat. One of the victims was picked up by the sailboaters and then transferred to a powerboat for transport to the marina; the other man was still missing.

Immediately I began searching for the victim still in the water. Unfortunately, he was never found.

Later that evening, I interviewed the survivor. He told me water surged over the transom, that waves lifted the bow and capsized his boat. The heavy motor pulled the vessel into an almost vertical position in the water, trapping an air bubble in the bow.

As the survivor described the scene, I visualized the two young men desperately clutching the slippery surface of the bow, protruding no more than two feet above the water.

Waves pitched and rolled the submerged craft and slowly the air which gave it buoyancy escaped. The boat, an older model without flotation, sank.

One of the men found a floating cushion and clung to it until he was sighted and rescued by the crew of the sailboat.

I asked the survivor if they had seen the storm coming.

Yes. They had watched it for an hour or more, had discussed the possibility of returning to the marina, but had decided instead to avoid the storm by moving farther out in the lake.

The lesson to be learned from this tragedy is: never try to outguess the weather, especially a thunderstorm.

Local weathermen tell me they have tracked thunderstorms moving at 50 to 60 miles per hour.

This means in a race with a fast moving thunderstorm the boater is going to lose.

You can't beat the weather

Overconfidence may have killed as many boaters as ignorance. The uneducated operator ignores the weather or, unaware of the stakes, gambles against it. The overconfident operator knows about heavy weather, but says, *This boat can handle it. I've been in worse.*

Mother nature has a way of slapping down the cocky skipper. And when it comes to boats, there has never been one built that couldn't be sunk, or at least capsized.

I once deliberately drove my boat into a thunderstorm under the guise of training. What I was really doing was trying to be a hotshot captain, showing off. I came very close to paying the big price for my bravado.

I was in a patrol boat with a flying bridge. Sitting eight feet above the water in my big boat, I felt invincible. I saw the gust front coming and decided to show the rookies on board how to handle weather.

Because the storm was moving fast and the waves had not yet had time to build, I felt confident as I charged into the storm. The wind howled, blew the tops off the waves and drove the spray against us. It felt like we were being peppered with buckshot.

The flat-bottomed fishing pram "bass boat" is designed with moveable fishing chairs on a pedestal for casting. It's powered by a small outboard in a cutout transom.

A fun boat for zipping to choice fishing holes in placid waters, this boat design sometimes can take on water in waves greater than two feet in height. Chairs should be vacated when the boat is under power.

Things were bad and getting worse fast. Now I didn't feel like such a hotshot. I decided to save face by making a hasty retreat.

As I brought the vessel around, the wind struck our high broadside with gale force. The boat heeled over. It rolled. And kept rolling. Gear, crew, everything slid across the deck.

I gripped the wheel to keep from loosing my seat. The starboard gunwale dipped closer and closer to the water.

Suddenly, I was no longer eight feet above the water, but close enough to reach out and touch the bow wake. Water poured onto the deck.

I thought, *We are going to roll over!* The entire maneuver lasted less than ten seconds — a long, long ten seconds.

I'm not sure what my students learned, but I learned my lesson that day. You can't beat the weather. Unfortunately some operators never get a chance to benefit from their mistakes.

I've heard that people in dangerous jobs begin to worry about their safety when they become complacent and no longer feel afraid. This also applies to the dangers of heavy weather. You should strive to improve your boating skill and build confidence, because confidence is good, but overconfidence can kill you.

A final word of advice

When I was a kid, I used to look forward all week to our family's weekend outing on Lake Mead. I can still remember my great disappointment when weather canceled our plans. I would say, "Dad, the wind is dying. It's going to be a perfect day on the lake."

However, my dad, always mindful of our safety, was never influenced by my weather predictions based on wishful thinking.

Now that I know what can happen, I'm thankful I had a dad who was weather conscious and I wish there were more skippers like him. Being disappointed is not the worst thing that can happen to you.

Weather information, like boat maintenance, should be an essential element of your boating experience. Just as you wouldn't go out in a leaky boat, you shouldn't cast off without obtaining the most up-to-date weather forecast possible. Better yet, purchase an inexpensive weather radio and monitor the National Weather Service broadcasts. Conditions can change and a weather report that is twenty-four (or even twelve) hours old may be completely outdated.

But don't rely solely on forecasts. Keep an eye to the sky. Failure to obtain a weather forecast before venturing out, or not heeding the warning of an approaching thunderstorm, can spell disaster.

Remember: in more than half of all motorboat accidents on lakes or reservoirs, weather is a contributing factor.

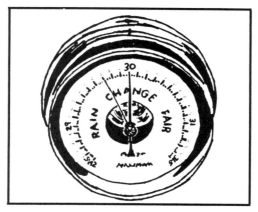

Barometer: A valued boater's weather indicator

Chapter 2

WEATHER KNOWLEDGE

What every boat operator
should know about weather

"I was out of port heading into the open lake and, as I usually do, listening to weather radio," Marlin Bree, author of *In the Teeth of the Northeaster* and *Call of the North Wind*, begins his story. The forecast was for moderate weather, moderate wind, a fine day for boating.

But Marlin's weather sense told him the forecast was wrong. He could feel a storm brewing. He explains, "Boaters have an inveterate sense — painfully acquired at times — about weather."

Deferring to the judgment of the National Weather Service, he continued out into the lake. First he ran into fog — not unusual on Lake Superior. Then as he came out of the fog he noticed a red tint to the sky, reminding him of the weather adage, "Red sky at morning, Sailor take warning."

Marlin turned on his weather radio again, the forecast had not changed: "moderate winds, moderate weather." Still trusting the forecast, and ignoring his intuition, he proceeded north under power.

"All of a sudden," he says, "I looked up and saw clouds

coming at me. They resembled bowling balls. I felt the wind switching — not from the forecast direction — but from the northeast. A northeaster."

He turned, headed back toward the harbor, but the savage storm caught him — hit his small craft like a violent explosion. He battled gale force winds and huge waves, and barely made it back to safety.

In port, when he again turned on his radio, it was still forecasting fine weather. Marlin ended his story with this advice, "When you go out, no matter what the forecast is, always use your own judgment. Always keep an eye out for weather. One heavy weather bashing will make a believer — and a weather watcher — out of anyone."

It is important to obtain the latest weather report before going out on the water, but you should be able to supplement the forecast with your own observations of local conditions because:

- Weather can change suddenly.
- Radio, television and newspaper forecasts are not specifically aimed at boaters and may not cover your boating area.
- Weather in your boating area may differ from the forecast due to local geography that can deflect the wind or, by channeling, intensify it.

Boaters need to develop their weather sense. This chapter details what boaters should know about weather, describes storm indicators and tells you how to recognize weather hazards.

The inland, small boat operator does not need to study meteorology; what he or she needs to do is obtain an up-to-date forecast and watch the sky. Clouds can tell you a great deal about the weather. To make your own local predictions you need to become a cloud watcher.

Clouds

Clouds are formed when the water vapor in warm expanded air rises and then condenses in the colder, higher altitudes. There are three basic cloud forms:

1. Cirrus — high clouds, sometimes called mares' tails.
2. Cumulus — billowy clouds, often with flat bottoms.
3. Stratus — sheets of clouds that cover much of the sky.

In addition to these three basic cloud forms there are various combinations of shapes and locations (low or high altitude) that make up a list of seven more possible cloud types:

1. Cirrocumulus — Cirrus clouds combine with cumulus. These clouds look like rippling sand, an effect sometimes called a mackerel sky.

2. Cirrostratus — These are the lowest of the high clouds. They are often found four or five miles above the earth and look like a veil over the sky. It is the cirrostratus clouds that cause halos around the sun or moon. If they become low and thick, rain can usually be expected within twenty-four hours. (This generalization doesn't necessarily hold true in the dry Southwest where I live.)

3. Altostratus — The prefix "alto " is given to clouds of middle level altitudes or clouds averaging an altitude of 10,000 feet. Altostratus clouds give the sky an overcast, frosted look.

4. Altocumulus — These clouds look much like altostratus clouds except they are puffier, and they are commonly referred to as sheepy sky.

5. Stratocumulus — These are low, layers or patches of gray with some darker parts. They are not rain clouds, although they may indicate that rain is coming.

6. Cumulonimbus — This is a tall cumulus cloud — the common thunderhead. These clouds can grow to a height of 30,000 to 50,000 feet and develop an anvil-shaped top.

7. Nimbostratus — These are dark, shapeless rain clouds. Nimbostratus are low level (from ground level to 6,500 feet) and are the typical rain clouds. They can produce steady rain over an extended period of time.

Since clouds usually are seen in combinations of the three basic types, it can be difficult to remember exactly what they mean.

Here is a simplified, easier to remember, explanation:

- If clouds are high, thin, white or sparse they usually mean fair weather.
- If clouds are thick and low they indicate the approach of

low pressure with possible wind and rain.

When watching the sky, notice the types of clouds and the direction they are moving. Are the clouds increasing or decreasing? Are they lowering or lifting? How are the cloud patterns changing? Also take note of the color of the sky. When there is low humidity the sky is bright blue. A yellow cast to the sky is caused by moisture, which acts like a prism breaking up the sun's rays, turning aside the blue and allowing the long-wave reds and yellows to dominate.

While I'm on the subject of clouds, let me say a few words about fog, which is a cloud on or near the surface of the earth. Fog, however, is quite different in the way it is formed. A cloud is the result of warm moist air rising and cooling. Fog occurs when moist air remains close to the ground or water. If this air becomes saturated and cools, its moisture condenses into small droplets. The temperature when this happens is called the dew point.

Fog

Kinds of fog the inland boater might encounter:

- Advection fog
- Precipitation fog
- Radiation fog
- Steam fog

Advection Fog — The type of fog that is most likely to be a problem for boaters is advection fog. This fog forms when warm air from land moves across cold water. For this fog to form, the air at about 100 feet above the water must be warmer than the air just above the water and the water must become progressively cooler in the direction the air is moving. The fog moves in a bank that can overtake an unsuspecting boater and completely obscure his or her view of surrounding landmarks.

Advection fog is the most common type of fog and does not dissipate as easily as other types. Sunshine does not affect it, and it usually does not lift until the wind stops, changes direction or increases to more than 15 miles per hour.

Precipitation Fog — This is sometimes called frontal fog because it is associated with the passage of a warm front. When the warm rain of a warm front falls through a layer of cold air near the surface, it begins to evaporate, the cold air becomes saturated and fog forms.

Radiation Fog — This fog forms on clear nights, often in late summer and early autumn in valleys near lakes and rivers. It is created when heat radiates from the earth's surface into space. The ground becomes cool and by conduction the air near the ground is cooled to its dew point. As a light breeze brings warmer air into contact with the cold surface, it increases the fog, which forms over the land and then spreads over nearby water. Radiation fog evaporates shortly after sunrise and usually signals fair weather for the boater.

Steam Fog — This fog is formed when very cold air passes over warmer water. By conduction the air near the water picks up both heat and water vapor, creating fog that rises like the steam from a hot-tub on a cold patio deck. Steam fog, or sea smoke as it is sometimes called, occurs only in very cold weather — the kind of weather when one would not normally go out for a day on the lake.

A Final Word about Fog — It can be predicted by measuring the dew point with a hygrometer or monitoring a National Weather Service broadcast which will report the dew point as well as temperature changes.

Fortunately, fog is generally not a major problem for boaters on most inland bodies of water. The exceptions are the Great Lakes, and the Mississippi and Ohio rivers (See Chapter 12).

Temperature and barometric pressure

Two additional indicators of local weather are temperature and barometric pressure.

While I don't advocate purchasing a lot of weather instruments, I have found that a thermometer and an inexpensive barometer are helpful, but not absolutely necessary. I have a thermometer and an aneroid barometer fastened to a porch post outside my house, which is only a few miles from the lake where I boat.

The evening before going out on the water I begin checking the barometer about once an hour before going to bed and again the next morning before heading for the lake. I note the position of the needle on the barometer to see if it is rising or falling and the rate of change.

Some barometers have the words Fair — Change — Rain on them. These words are meaningless, because one reading of a barometer means very little. It is the amount and rate of change that enables one to forecast the weather. Some change in barometric pressure during the day is normal, but continued and steady falling or rising is significant.

The changes in air pressure signaled by a barometer, spell changes in the weather. High pressure usually means good weather, while low pressure brings unsettled conditions and wind.

Wind

Heavy weather for the small craft operator means wind and rough water. Although temperature (extreme heat or cold) and precipitation can be significant factors, it is wind and its mate — waves — that are the essence of heavy weather.

The atmosphere is constantly in motion in a never-ending struggle to equalize temperature differences. As air at the earth's surface warms, it becomes lighter.

The lighter air rises (weathermen call this convection) and the result is decreased air pressure — a low pressure cell.

The opposite of low pressure is high pressure, which occurs when air cools and contracts causing a downdraft (a subsidence).

The boater with a basic knowledge of this motion is better off than the boater who relies only on daily weather reports. The weather map on television or in a daily newspaper gives an overall view of the weather on that day.

Knowing what makes the highs, lows, and fronts shown on the map, together with your observations while on the water, can help you sense an approaching storm.

We all know weather conditions can change suddenly. To avoid being taken by surprise (to develop your weather sense), you need to understand what causes these changes — starting with air pressure.

Highs and lows

Even though this is not an entirely accurate analogy, I tend to think of high pressure areas as mountains of air and low pressure areas as valleys. Associated with these highs and lows are winds which circulate clockwise around the center of high pressure — or the peak of the air mountain — and counter clockwise around a center of low pressure.

When a high pressure (air mountain) and a low pressure (valley in the air) are close together the gradient (or slope) between them is steep. The steeper the gradient, the stronger the winds. Regional high and low pressure areas with steep gradients can create strong, sustained winds.

On the Nevada desert, where I live, it is common for these winds to blow 25 to 30 miles an hour for several days at a time. This makes big waves.

Fronts

Due to heating and cooling on the earth, air masses of roughly uniform temperature form. These air masses are characterized as either warm or cold.

Vilhelm Bjerknes and his son Jakob, two Norwegian meteorologists of the early 20th century, described weather as a battle between warm and cold air masses. Using military terminology from World War I, these scientists named the point of contact between air masses a front.

This term, which denotes a battle zone, is exactly what a front is — a battle zone. The exchange of warm and cold air causes storms which move roughly from west to east across our continent.

Watching these storms is, of course, a major concern of the NWS. But when you are out on the water, you also need to be able to identify the signs of approaching bad weather. See Sidebar 2.1. (You might want to make a laminated machine copy of this chart for a quick on-board reference.)

When using this chart to forecast weather, remember that one indicator by itself doesn't tell you much. The more indicators pointing to a change in the weather; the more reliable the prediction.

INDICATORS OF POSSIBLE WEATHER CHANGES

Indicators	Weather Observed	Possible Change
Clouds	High, thin, white or sparse	Fair weather
	Thick and low	Wind & rain
	Cumulus on horizon	Cold front approaching
	Cirrostratus	Warm front, rain
	Rapid formation of stratocumulus	Thunderstorms
	Nimbostratus	Steady rain
Sky Color	Bright blue	Fair weather
	Yellow cast	High humidity, rain
Barometric Pressure	Slow upward movement	Continued fair
	Slow downward movement	Unsettled, possible rain
	Rapid downward movement	Stormy weather
	Rapid upward movement	Clearing with gusty winds
Wind	Increasing steadily	Front approaching
	Southerly winds	Cold front approaching
	Weak winds	Warm front approaching
	Shifting winds	Squally weather
Temperature	Little change	Stable weather
	Rising slowly	Approach of a warm front
	Falling	Approach of a cold front

Sidebar 2.1

For instance, if there are cumulus clouds on the horizon, a downward movement in barometric pressure, an increasing southerly wind and a falling temperature; you can be fairly certain that a cold front is approaching.

Warm fronts

When a warm air mass bumps into a colder air mass, it rides up and over the cooler air, creating a warm front (See Figure 2.1). Typically there will be a drop in air pressure as the warm air moves in.

Cirrus clouds change to stratus, then to cumulus and finally to nimbostratus and there is a steady rain over an extended period of time, accompanied by weak winds. As the front passes, the clouds begin to break up and the wind shifts, although some drizzle may continue as the sky gradually clears.

Warm fronts are not as dangerous for boaters as cold fronts.

Cold fronts

On the morning of December 14, 1996, a man and his three sons — ages eight, nine and eleven — set out in their 14-foot aluminum boat on Lake Meredith, Texas. They were going duck hunting. With four people (the smallest weighing about 50 pounds) plus guns, decoys and camouflage net, the small boat was overloaded. However, the wind was calm and the water smooth; they were able to cross the lake to their hunting area without any trouble.

About 11 a.m. a cold front moved in. Soon the lake developed two-to-three-foot waves. The father called his wife on a cellular phone, to tell her the lake was getting rough and they were coming home.

At about 5 p.m. the Park Service was notified that the father and boys had not returned. Rangers immediately began searching.

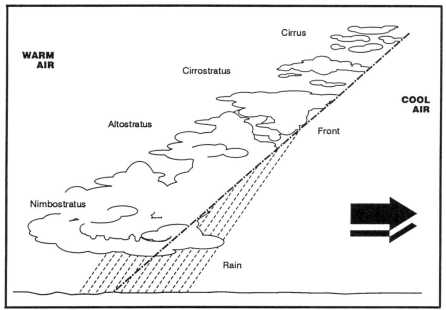

Figure 2.1   Warm front

The capsized boat and the body of the eleven-year-old were located that evening. The boy was floating about 50 feet from the boat with his life jacket over one arm.The next day the father's body (without a life jacket, but buoyed up by hip waders) was found. Several weeks later the nine-year-old was sighted, partially submerged in the backwater surrounding a grove of trees. The eight-year-old's body was found nearly five months later.

Rangers can only guess what happened. One theory based on the evidence is: Returning to the marina the father and boys crossed the lake with the waves on the boat's stern. As they turned to approach the dock, a beam wave swamped the boat from the port side. One life jacket was found under the boat, which indicates the father was not wearing a PFD. All life jackets on board were adult size and searchers theorize that the eight-year-old came out of his PFD when he was thrown from the vessel.

I have seen the NOAA daily weather maps for the day of this accident and the following day and there is no doubt in my mind that a fast-moving cold front coming out of Colorado and crossing the panhandle of Texas was a contributing cause of this accident.

Cold fronts form when a cold air mass pushes up against and under a warm air mass. The cold air close to the ground is slowed by friction, making the leading edge of a cold front very steep (See Figure 2.2).

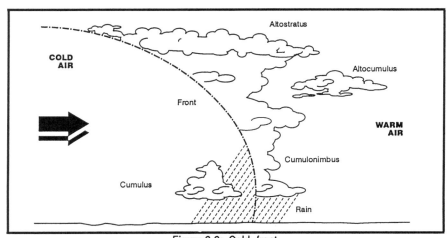

Figure 2.2: Cold front

A cold front normally moves faster than the warm air it is overtaking and forces the warm air up. Wind increases in the warm air ahead of the front as it approaches. This sudden, sometimes violent uplifting of warm air causes a cloud line to build rapidly. Cumulus clouds signal the arrival of a cold front.

Cumulus clouds may build to towering heights and become cumulonimbus. With a cold front the band of weather is usually narrower, more severe, and of shorter duration than with a warm front. Often a southerly wind precedes a cold front and shifts to westerly or northwesterly as the front passes over.

Normally, the heaviest precipitation occurs as the front passes over. However, if the warm air ahead of the cold front is moist and unstable, the heaviest precipitation may be a few miles ahead of the cold front.

This line of showers and thunderstorms ahead of a cold front is called a squall line. This squall line can be more severe than the weather along the actual cold front.

The alert boat operator will see a wall of boiling low, black clouds. (Remember Marlin Bree's story at the beginning of this chapter?) When you see a squall line you should do what Marlin did: Head for shelter immediately.

Unfortunately, because of changing local conditions, the NWS broadcasts are not always able to warn of an approaching squall line. This is one of the reasons why it is important for boaters to understand weather.

A variation of the cold front is the dry front. This is a cold front without moisture. Meteorologists describe it as a " wind event." There are no clouds, but the wind increases, air pressure drops and, as the front moves through, the wind will usually shift from southerly to westerly or northwesterly.

Cold fronts are dangerous because they produce strong, gusty and shifting winds. But the most dangerous weather phenomenon for the freshwater boater is the thunderstorm.

Thunderstorms

One sunny day as I drifted in calm water, I noticed a huge thunderhead several miles away moving in my direction. From my tranquil vantage point, I watched the cloud come closer with the water under it churning into whitecaps.

Neither water nor air stirred around my little boat; I felt safe and secure — as if I were in a theater viewing a storm on the big screen. Almost mesmerized, I watched this boiling, churning water race toward me.

Suddenly, the wind hit. Powerful blasts and angry waves pummeled my small vessel. Moments later the wind slammed into a 30-foot sailboat a quarter of a mile away, knocking it over. As quickly as it had come, the wind subsided.

I hurried to assist the people on the sailboat. When I reached them, I stared in amazement. Hanging by its rigging, the boat's aluminum mast was bent into a nearly perfect N shape.

What I had witnessed was not a tornado or some other rare phenomenon. It was a downburst.

When rain in a thunderstorm cell falls, it creates a significant downdraft with wind speed sometimes in excess of 70 miles per hour. Wind pours out of the bottom of the thunderhead, hits the ground (or water) and spreads out in all directions.

It is possible — as I was — to be hit by these strong gusty winds even when the thunderstorm is several miles away.

Neither the sailboaters nor I were injured by this downburst, but many boaters have not been so lucky.

On August 4, 1996, a small group of people drifting in a pontoon boat on the Missouri River, enjoying the warm afternoon weather (and not watching the clouds) were suddenly hit by a thunderstorm. Since there was not enough time to reach the bank, one woman and two children put on PFDs and crowded into a small closet-type bathroom for protection. High winds from the thunderstorm overturned the boat, trapping these three people in the closet.

Washington, Missouri, fire department personnel cut a hole in the floor of the boat in an attempted rescue, but the victims had already drowned.

It has been estimated that 40,000 thunderstorms occur on earth every day and more than 100,000 thunderstorms occur in the United States each year, causing millions of dollars in damage and hundreds of deaths.

In my boating career I have seen the power of thunderstorms many times. I have seen a storm of less than 20 minutes' duration rip apart a marina — swamping, capsizing and sinking dozens of vessels.

As a meteorological event, thunderstorms are short-lived, isolated, rapidly changing and fast-moving storms. One authority calls the thunderstorm "the most powerful weather phenomenon on earth."

There are several types of thunderstorms, but all are formed when warm, moist air is lifted or forced upward. The two that are of most concern to boaters are:

    1. Thunderstorms that occur with the arrival of a cold front.

    2. Convection-type thunderstorms that are local in origin and occur on hot summer afternoons and evenings.

Cold front and squall line thunderstorms

On the afternoon of July 12, 1995, a stationary front across North Dakota to the Great Lakes, an area of low pressure over eastern Montana and a strong southerly flow of warm, moist air sweeping across the plains came together to create a gigantic thunderstorm.

Photo courtesy of C. (Bud) Cleland, Marine Salvage

Vessel aground on the leeward shore after a thunderstorm July 11, 1984.
at Callville Bay, Nevada.

Meteorologist Ed Fenelon of Marquette, Michigan, called it a derecho (a big cluster of thunderstorms producing very strong winds). Unlike a winter cold front, this front was driven by subtle changes in temperature and high moisture levels. The storm began moving during the early evening hours of July 12, traveled across North Dakota, northern Minnesota, Lake Superior, the upper peninsula of Michigan, Lake Michigan, Lake Huron, Lake Erie and Ohio, ending up in West Virginia.

Ed Fenelon says, "This was really a unique case because it is very rare for a derecho to have the lifetime that this one did. And to cover so much of the country. It lasted 24 hours and traveled from eastern Montana all the way to West Virginia."

Tropical storms and hurricanes have names. This storm went unnamed, but not unremembered.

Weathermen, ship captains and Coast Guard rescue personnel remember the Big Storm of July 13, 1995. Bill Hanrahan, captain of the Park Service ship Ranger III (a 165-foot vessel that services Isle Royale National Park from its home port, Houghton, Michigan) recalls, "I actually broke the speed limits going out of the canal (Portage Canal, bisecting the Keweenaw Peninsula) to get onto the lake. I didn't want to get hit with the storm in the channel. I had it on the radar ... I think it hit us about three or four minutes after we got outside the break wall."

A typical pontoon patio boat has a large deck space and is powered by inboard / outdrive or outboard engine.

A picnic on the deck of this boat makes a pleasant family outing as long as you stay close to shore and avoid rough water. Built-in floatation and natural buoyancy make it almost impossible to sink this type of vessel.

With gusts of 70 miles per hour forecast, small vessels scurried to reach safe harbors, big ships ran for deep water and the Coast Guard stood by ready to rescue those that didn't make it.

"The skies grew very dark," meteorologist Ed Fenelon remembers. "There were a lot of low-hanging scud (fragmented, shredded) clouds out ahead of the gust front, and a wedge-shaped, ominous-looking shelf cloud stretched across the horizon, dominating the sky as the leading line of thunderstorms came through."

Peter W. Hocking, Chief Quartermaster at the Cleveland Coast Guard Rescue Coordination Center, which received more than 200 requests for assistance, reported that the storm slammed in with winds in excess of 60 miles per hour, golf-ball-size hail and torrential rains.

This was a once in a lifetime thunderstorm — an ordinary squall line storm magnified many times. Because of its ominous scope, it was tracked by NOAA, which issued severe storm warnings, and most boat operators were able to reach the comparative safety of protected harbors.

But even relatively small squall line storms tend to be more severe than isolated thunderstorms. These storms can occur in various stages of development along a squall line or cold front, and the storm may last for several hours as new individual cells develop while old cells are dissipating. Also due to individual cell development, the storm may seem to split, back into the wind, turn to one side or move rapidly forward.

Your warning that a squall-line thunderstorm is approaching is the appearance of low, dark, boiling clouds. This is a squall line. When you see these dramatic scud clouds, get off the water. The lake is no place to be during the passage of a cold front or squall line thunderstorm.

Convection thunderstorms

These thunderstorms are usually not as severe as cold front or squall line thunderstorms, but are more dangerous because they seem to spring out of nowhere.

The convection thunderstorm usually occurs on hot muggy summer afternoons, covers a small area and lasts about an hour.

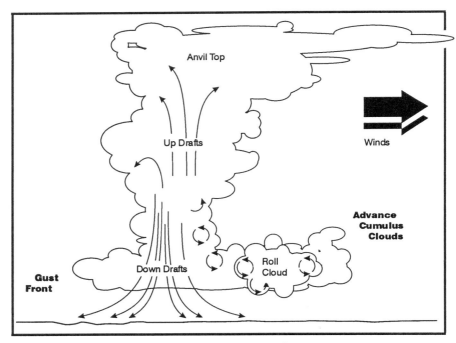

Figure 2.3: Thunder Head

It was this type of thunderstorm, created by temperature imbalance, which overturned the pontoon boat on the Missouri River.

Warm, moist surface air rises and cools. A strong updraft develops and the cloud reaches heights where the surrounding air is below freezing. At an altitude of about 40,000 feet, moisture-laden air meets a strong current of cold upper troposphere air, which stops its upward flow and spreads it out. The result is the characteristic anvil-shaped cloud.

Raindrops and snowflakes form, which can no longer be supported by the updraft. Rain begins to fall, creating a strong downdraft. Downdrafts and updrafts exist side by side until finally the downdrafts overpower the updrafts and the cloud releases its water in a heavy downpour (See Figure 2.3).

A thunderhead should be viewed by all boat operators as a big, flashing sign in the sky that says, DANGER. Thunderheads, or cumulonimbus clouds, are easy to recognize.

Distinct features of thunderheads:

• Rapid formation or growth

- Smooth anvil-shaped tops, which conveniently point in the direction the storm is moving
- Towering height — often 40,000 feet or more, with cauliflower sides
- Dark interiors
- Relatively flat bases
- Often accompanied by a rolling, churning cloud at the leading edge of the cumulonimbus cloud

When you spot a thunderhead while boating it is time to head for shelter. If you are on a protected beach — stay where you are.

You can estimate your distance from the thunderstorm if you remember that sound travels at a rate of one mile every five seconds. When you see a flash of lightning, count slowly: one thousand, two thousand, etc.

If you count to five this way before you hear the thunder, the storm is one mile away. However, sometimes when there are multiple lightning strikes, it is difficult to tell which strike produced which thunder clap.

The two hazards of thunderstorms are lightning and strong gusty winds.

Lightning — It can and does strike boats. When you are on a vessel in open water, you are a target. The period of greatest danger is immediately before the storm and as the rain starts. Although lightning protection can be installed and will offer some defense for the crew, the absolute best course of action is to avoid areas of lightning activity. Seek shelter.

If lightning does strike your vessel, it is important to remember that persons who appear to have been killed may be revived if prompt action is taken.

A National Oceanic and Atmospheric Administration pamphlet gives this advice for victims of a lightning strike: Immediately begin mouth-to-mouth resuscitation. Citing the American Red Cross as the source of its advice the NOAA pamphlet also suggests that, if the victim has no pulse, a properly trained person should administer CPR (cardiopulmonary resuscitation). Every skipper should have an approved first-aid manual on board and be prepared to follow its instructions.

Strong Gusty Winds — While it is possible to be struck by lightning in a small boat, you are more apt to suffer damage from wind. Rapid wind shifts can create dangerous, confused seas and the downdrafts caused by thunderstorms can whip up huge waves in a matter of minutes. This danger from strong, gusty wind is often underestimated by novice operators.

An additional word of caution: thunderstorms can produce tornadoes, waterspouts and microbursts.

- A tornado is a whirlpool of air that looks like a funnel with a long spout. Scientists estimate the wind velocity of the strongest tornadoes to be in excess of 250 miles per hour.
- A waterspout is a tornado over water.
- A microburst is a highly accelerated downdraft.
- Microbursts have wind speeds of more than 135 miles per hour and have been known to capsize large boats.

A boater's only defense against a tornado, waterspout or microburst is avoidance.

Remember this:

Thunderstorms are potentially the most dangerous weather for the recreational boater.

These storms are difficult to forecast.

Recently, my brother took his children and a neighbor child to a protected beach on the lake for an afternoon of boating, swimming and picnicking. Being a careful boater, he kept an eye on the clouds.

When he noticed a thunderstorm forming on the other side of the lake, he quickly loaded the kids in the boat and headed for the launch ramp. But — this was a mistake.

Wind from the storm caught him out in open water and five-foot waves put his seamanship to a real test. Though he and his passengers were shaken, they survived.

The moral is clear: You cannot outrun a fast-moving thunderstorm.

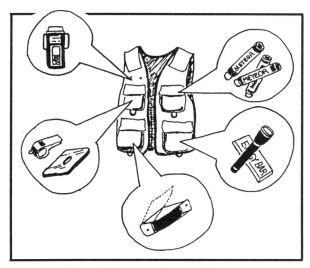

PFD with heavy weather survival gear

Chapter 3

PREPARATION

How to prepare for heavy weather

When I began my boating career as patrol officer at Lake Meredith, Texas, I'd heard about and read about heavy weather, but never experienced it. I listened to heroic stories told by veteran rescuers about their small patrol boats battling wind and sea in the dead of night and I anxiously waited for the time when I would be called upon to save a helpless boater.

For the first few weeks the lake remained calm and my patrols were routine. Then came the night I'd been waiting for. A severe thunderstorm was forecast.

After receiving the message of the approaching storm, I and my equally inexperienced deckhand hurried out on the lake. Quickly we maneuvered our patrol boat in and out of coves and inlets in the dark as lightning winked in the distance. Wherever we found campers or fishermen, we shouted out a warning — told them to stay off the lake.

Intent on our task, I gave no thought to our own safety. I failed to give orders to rig the boat for heavy weather.

Suddenly, the storm hit and we were battered by its full

fury. The boat tossed and rolled. Rain stung our faces. Water soaked our clothes and poured into the cockpit. The wind roared so loud I had to shout my orders to the deckhand standing next to me.

Now I remembered all the things I'd learned about getting the boat and crew ready for heavy weather. Even though we were both cold and wet, I sent my deckhand below to put on her storm gear. As my grandmother would say, I decided to lock the barn door after the horse was stolen.

In less than five minutes my crew person was back on deck, but her short stay in the rolling cabin had made her violently seasick. We tried to zip and snap the weather curtains in place around the cockpit, but my assistant was too sick to be much help, and I had to keep one hand on the helm. The wind ripped away the curtains, shredding the zippers.

Not only were we wet and cold, but in the downpour I couldn't see where we were going. The cockpit radio was damaged by water; medical gear that we failed to lash down fell to the deck and broke.

This type of patrol boat, with enclosed cockpit and inboard / outdrive, is designed and built for search-and-rescue work.

In this boat, a fire department, sheriff's department or a state boat patrol agency can hurry to the scene of an accident. Though small, this patrol boat is tough and seaworthy.

By far the most serious consequence of our lack of preparation was that our effectiveness as a rescue unit was seriously compromised. During the storm we completely forgot about our original mission while we focused on our own survival. We were in no shape to help others — and without radio contact we couldn't even hear a distress call.

Fortunately, the storm passed quickly. I have been in many storms — far worse storms — since that night; but I've never been as frightened. I still shudder when I think what might have happened if our engines had failed. We were so completely unprepared that we could have been blown aground on nearby rocky reefs before we could have dropped anchor.

That experience taught me a lesson. I learned that the stories I'd heard of small patrol boats battling wind and waves to save helpless mariners gave only half the facts. The other half — not nearly so dramatic, but equally important — was preparation.

Preparation starts long before the storm. It involves your general competence, the type of vessel you operate, the equipment you carry on board and how you maintain it. Part of being prepared (and the focus of this book) is to imagine every possible heavy weather emergency and how you can deal with it. This will enable you to avoid panic, which is a great liability in dealing with life-threatening emergencies.

Another aspect of being prepared is making sure you have the equipment and safety gear on board to deal with an emergency.

Before you say, "but I'm not going out in stormy weather," let me remind you: weather can turn foul, even when fair weather has been predicted.

Every boater should be prepared for heavy weather.

Operator competency

According to a Red Cross study, 91 percent of all life-threatening emergencies are handled by the boat operator.

The skipper is morally, and often legally, responsible for the safety of his crew and passengers. With the sue-happy attitude of recent years, the operator can be held legally responsible should injured crew or guests contend that he or she did not exercise reasonable care for their safety.

Liability insurance, which every boat owner should have, may help protect you from some monetary damages, but only careful preparation and competence will abrogate your moral responsibility.

You should be prepared not only to deal with your own vessel's emergencies, but also to assist others in life-threatening situations. The skipper in many states is afforded some liability protection by Good Samaritan laws. However, this Good Samaritan protection covers the rescuer only so long as he or she exercises reasonable care and does not cause damage. In other words, you still need to know what you are doing (See Chapter 9).

The skipper must understand and be competent in all basic boating skills, including such things as ordinary docking maneuvers and knowing the Rules of the Road, which apply to his or her boating circumstances. This fact is recognized by most boaters.

Eighty-one percent of boaters surveyed by the Red Cross favored boater safety education and two-thirds of those questioned favored licensing requirements for boat operators.

State governments and federal agencies are getting the message: Responsible boaters want mandatory boating safety instruction and operator licensing. In 1998, 20 states required boating safety education for youths, and several states have passed laws requiring boat operators to be licensed. This is a start in the right direction.

Indeed it is strange that we have driver's licenses and pilot's licenses, but in most states, any adult — without any training — can operate a boat.

Organizations that offer boater education

U.S. Coast Guard Auxiliary
2100 Second St. SW
Washington , D.C. 20593
Telephone: 202-267-1077

U.S. Power Squadron
P.O. Box 30423
Raleigh, NC 27622

Telephone: 919-821-0281

American Red Cross
431 18th St. NW
Washington, D.C. 20006-202
Telephone: 202-737-8300

Also, state boating agencies, resource/wildlife departments, county sheriff's departments, community colleges and other public safety organizations often present safe-boating classes. Many of these same organizations offer classes in basic emergency engine repairs, First Aid and CPR, and swimming. If the boat operator is deficient in any of these important skills, he or she should acquire them.

The American Red Cross, U.S. Power Squadrons and U.S. Coast Guard Auxiliary will gladly provide information about their boating and safety instruction and furnish telephone numbers of the local chapters where classes are given.

After learning basics skills, practice them. On days when the water is calm, maneuver the boat in and out of a slip, pull into and away from a dock and test your anchor. Next go out on a windy day when the water is choppy.

Remember to start in safe water and build your competence slowly. Then practice at night. Get the feel of the water when visibility is limited. Believe me, it seems rougher at night. Finally, conduct special drills such as man overboard.

Make sure that more than one person can operate the boat in case something happens to the skipper. I learned the wisdom of this when I was only five years old.

My family was on a camping and boating vacation with a group on Lake Powell in Arizona. One night as my mother and I slept on the fold-down seats in our boat, we were suddenly awakened by a thump, scrape. I raised up and looked over the side. Our camp was gone! My mother beamed the flashlight at the beach — no camp. The wind had pulled our boat from its mooring and pushed us across a cove. I asked my mother if she could drive the boat. She couldn't. But she sure could yell. A good quarter mile away, my dad and the other boaters were awakened by her shouting.

The next day both Mother and I received our first lesson in boat operation.

While drifting across a cove posed no threat to our safety, this experience pointed up the fact that someone other than the skipper should know how to operate the boat. What would my mother have done if my dad had fallen overboard? There are times when shouting does not solve the problem.

Vessel seaworthiness

Hand-in-hand with operator competence is vessel seaworthiness. Preparation also means making certain your boat is appropriate for the water where it will be used. For instance, a Jon boat might be exactly the vessel needed for a river or small lake, but would be a foolish choice for a large lake (See Chapter 11).

Just as there is a limit to your capabilities, there is also a limit to your vessel's capabilities, not only on fair days, but also in foul weather. Know these limits and stay within them.

Assuming the boat is the right vessel for the boating environment, the skipper needs to become familiar with its characteristics. Every boat is different. A manual for U.S. Coast Guard crews advises, "...know the characteristics of your boat in all types of weather so you will be able to tell how it will respond in virtually every condition." Good advice for Coast Guard crews and all boaters.

What you should know about your boat

- **Responsiveness** — Know what the boat can and cannot do. Find out how it reacts to various power settings and helm commands.
- **Drift Angle** — Every boat has its own angle of drift in relation to the wind.
- **Operational Range** — Know how far the boat will go on a tank of fuel and the boat's average fuel consumption per hour at cruising speed.
- **Sea Keeping** — Learn how the boat feels and reacts as it takes waves from various directions.
- **Load Capacity** - Boats less than 20 feet in length, manufactured after November 1972, are required to have attached metal tags stating carrying capacity. Do not overload the boat.

Overloading can have serious consequences. First of all you might be subject to a fine depending on local laws. Second, it may void your insurance if overloading is found to be the cause of an accident. Third, and most important, it will certainly affect your boat's handling. This is especially true in heavy weather, when weight should be kept well below the maximum limit.

While getting acquainted with the boat's characteristics and capabilities, you can also gain valuable knowledge about your boating area. Just as every boat is different, every lake is different.

On fair days use a chart to explore the water. Mark the chart to show good natural harbors, dangerous reefs and rocky shores, because there may come a time when you'll be glad you did. When wind and waves are high and you need to find shelter, it is nice to remember a protected cove or inlet and you certainly will want to know where the reefs and rocks are.

Bob McKeever, program coordinator for the Department of Interior Motorboat Operator's Instructor Training Program at Lake Mead, says, "Local knowledge is the single most critical piece of information you can give to people. That is, they need (to know) the operating environment they are in."

He points out that boaters should understand the particular buoy system used in their area, know how the water changes color where reefs are near the surface and talk to experienced boaters about local hazards.

As McKeever says, "Everybody knows about these (hazards). People have been wrecking their boats on them since the seventeen hundreds."

Survival equipment

Survival gear means life. The Congress of the United States recognized this fact when it passed the Federal Boat Safety Act of 1971, which authorized the U.S. Coast Guard to set minimal equipment standards.

Minimum safety equipment required by law:

- **One PFD (Personal Flotation Device) Type I, II, III, or** V for each person onboard. See sidebar 3-1. Boats 16 feet

Personal Floatation Devices

Type I Jacket

Type I Bib

Type I
Offshore Lifejackets:

- 22 pounds buoyancy • 2 sizes
- **Advantages**: Most buoyancy & Turns most unconscious victims face up
- **Disadvantages**: Bulky & cumbersome

Type II
Near Shore Buoyant Vest

- 15.5 pounds buoyancy • 3 sizes
- **Advantages**: Usually floats victim face up & is less bulky than Type I
- **Disadvantages**: Not as buoyant as Type I

Type III Sport Vest

Type III Float Coat

Type III
Floatation Aid

- 15.5 pounds buoyancy • Many sizes
- **Advantages**: Not bulky, comfortable fit, variety of colors & styles, can be worn at all times & allows wearer freedom of movement
- **Disadvantages**: Not as buoyant as Type I & does not float victim face up

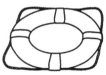

Type IV Ring Buoy

Type IV Horseshoe Buoy

Type IV
Throwable Device

- **Advantages**: Can be thrown to victim, immediately available, makes quick rescue possible
- **Disadvantages**: Does not give protection at all times, can float away during emergency & will not aid unconscious victim

Type V Whitewater Jacket

Type V
Special Use Device

- **Advantages**: High floatation when inflated, combines floatation with other types of protection i.e. Cold weather, cold water
- **Disadvantages**: Must be worn to comply with Coast Guard requirements, must be properly cared for & checked often to assure serviceability of inflation chamber

Sidebar 3.1

to 65 feet must have — in addition to a wearable PFD for each person — one Type IV (throwable) PFD.

- **A Whistle or Horn** — Boats up to 39.4 feet in length must have a device that will make an efficient sound signal. Boats 39.4 feet to 65 feet in length require a sound device that can be heard a distance of one half mile and a bell with a sound pressure level not less than 110 dB at one meter.
- **Flame Arrestor** — An acceptable means of backfire control is required for all gasoline engines, except outboard motors.
- **Ventilation Blowers** — On vessels that can entrap gasoline fumes within the hull a ventilation system and blowers are required. These must be free of obstructions and operating properly.
- **Distress Signals** — Visual distress signals are not required on boats operating on inland waters, except the Great Lakes and mouths of rivers that are two miles wide. Although not required in most inland waters, visual distress signals are still an excellent safety measure. Where they are required, you must have some combination of either pyrotechnic or non-pyrotechnic devices that give you 3 day signals and 3 night signals, for example: 3 hand-held red flares meet the legal requirements. Distress flares must be less than 3 years old.
- **Fire Extinguishers** — All vessels must have at least one B-1 type approved hand-portable fire extinguisher, except outboard motorboats less than 26 feet in length and not carrying passengers for hire. If the boat is constructed in such a way that gases or vapors can be trapped on board, it will require one or more fire extinguishers.
- **Navigation Lights** — Navigation lights are required for all boats operated at night. The exact configuration of lights depends on the size and type of vessel, its propulsion, its activity, and where it is operated. (For more information on requirements consult U.S. Coast Guard regulations, available from the Superintendent of Documents, United States Government Printing Office, Washington, D.C. 20402)

The Coast Guard requirements listed here are minimal, and

additional equipment may be required in the state in which the vessel is operated. The boat operator must check to be sure the boat complies with the state regulations where it is used.

All the equipment listed above is important, but if I had to single out one item as the most important it would be the PFD. Coast Guard figures for 1996 show that:

- Out of 500 drownings, 440 victims were not wearing a PFD.
- Approximately 84 percent of those involved in fatal boating accidents were not wearing PFDs.

Adults require 10 to 12 pounds of additional buoyancy to stay afloat. Type I PFDs provide 22 pounds of buoyancy and Type II & III have 15 pounds of buoyancy.

Like all equipment on the boat, PFDs require maintenance. Air dry them after use and check periodically for mildew, leaks and frayed straps. Kapok-filled PFDs must be checked to see that the kapok has not become hard and that there are no holes in the covering. Remember PFDs are safety equipment — do not use them as fenders or abuse them.

It is interesting to note that life jackets now come in a variety of colors and sport styles. Even though color or logo will not improve your chances of survival, they give the wearer the option of being style conscious, as well as safety conscious. Now you can have a PFD that matches your boat or your activity, i.e. fishing, water skiing or hunting.

The Coast Guard requirements are the bare minimum for boater safety and survival. But every experienced boater knows you need more — much more — for the safety of the boat and passengers.

Minimum additional gear

- **Knife** — All crew members should carry folding or sheathed knives. The knife should be easily accessible, because being able to quickly cut yourself free in the event of capsizing or cut a tow or anchor line can save your life.

Almost every boating instructor I know has a story about the importance of carrying a knife. The one I remember most vividly was told to me on a raft trip down the Colorado River. As we approached Upset Rapid our boat operator pointed to a pie tin on the river bank at the spot where Jessie "Shorty" Burton's raft overturned on June 14, 1967. Burton's life jacket became tangled with the boat line and because he did not have an accessible knife, he drowned. Because Burton was a baker before becoming a boatman, he is remembered with a simple pie tin beside the rapid which was named (Upset) for the accident.

- **Boat Shoes** — Nonskid soles are important.
- **Foul Weather Gear** — Exposure to cold temperatures can cause fatigue and even hypothermia, two enemies of survival. Remember to include a hat and gloves along with the rain coat and waterproof coveralls.
- **Bailing Scoop** — A bailer can be purchased for less than $5. The bailer I use has a square bottom, making it efficient and easy to manipulate. If you don't have a commercial bailing scoop, you can make one from a gallon plastic jug with a handle. Cut the bottom out of the jug on an angle, tightly screw on the cap and you will have an inexpensive piece of survival equipment.
- **Ground Tackle** — This is so important I can not understand why it is not included in the Coast Guard minimum requirements. There are many times during heavy weather when you will need an anchor (or two anchors) — engine failure, keeping away from breaking surf, holding your position for any reason.

There are many different types of anchors for different kinds of situations. An excellent general purpose anchor is the Danforth (fluke type). It works well for sand or mud bottoms. And you will, of course, need anchor line — at least 100 feet. Small boat owners prefer nylon line, which is easy to handle.

A sea anchor is another piece of equipment that experienced boat handlers have found useful in heavy weather.

- **Buoyant Cushions** — In addition to the one Type IV PFD required by the Coast Guard, every boat longer than 16 feet should have several buoyant cushions. These immediately available flotation devices are extremely important in the event of a man overboard emergency (See Chapter 6).
- **Auxiliary Power** — Two engines are better than one. But lacking a small emergency motor, a paddle or oar is next

best. Every small motorboat should have a 7- to 9-foot oar that can be used as a push pole, a pry bar or as an oar.

- **Extra Fuel** — Carry a spare approved container of fuel. Standard advice: 1/3 fuel for passage to destination, 1/3 for return and 1/3 for reserve. To make estimates of fuel consumption you should know how much fuel your engine uses per hour at normal throttle settings.

- **Navigation Equipment** — At a bare minimum, the boat operator needs a magnetic compass to determine the boat's heading and a local chart (map). Binoculars, a watch and a speedometer are recommended. A Global Positioning System (GPS) is the most accurate and easy-to-use navigation system available. Also, small-boat radar systems are becoming more affordable and are very useful.

- **Lights** — In addition to the navigation lights required by the Coast Guard, the boater should carry a waterproof flashlight and a hand-held spotlight. A flashlight or a high-intensity strobe flasher can signal your position in the event of an emergency.

- **Depth Sounder** — This tells how much water is underneath your hull for safety and is also useful for navigation. In a pinch a lead line will do the job of telling you depth. In fact, even if the boat is equipped with an electronic depth sounder it is a good idea to have a lead line as a backup in case the electronics fail. However, if you don't have a lead line you can check the depth of the water by lowering the anchor.

- **Basic Tools** — The tool box should include wrenches, pliers, screwdrivers, adjustable end wrench, hammer, vise-grip pliers, a file, jumper cables, duct tape and electrical tape.

- **Spare Parts** — You can't run to the store for a part when you are dead in the water in the middle of the lake. You should have extra filters, belts, spark plugs, propeller, propeller nut, light bulbs, hose clamps, cotter pins, shear pins, fuses, starter rope and any other parts suggested in the owner's manual for your boat. You might want to have on board assorted wooden plugs for quick repair of failed through-hull fittings.

- **Dead Man Key** — If the boat is equipped with a dead man key, you should also have an extra key in the tool box. A dead man key is a safety device attached by a lanyard to the operator. This device stops the engine in the event of an accident that causes the operator to leave the helm unattended, such as a fall overboard. But how could a skipper in the water be rescued, if those left in the boat couldn't restart the engine?

• **Fenders** — Fenders should be appropriate in size and sufficient in number. They protect the vessel from damaging bumps with fixed objects or with other boats when close maneuvering is required.

• **Docking Lines** — The need for docking lines will become apparent the first time you attempt to dock or leave a dock when the wind is blowing. Aside from docking there are many emergency situations such as man overboard rescues and towing when lines are needed. It is a good idea to carry at least 4 docking lines of 15 to 20 feet and one long line no less than 100 feet for towing and tying up to beaches.

• **Boat Hook** — A boat hook is a useful tool for maneuvering and docking. With a six-foot boat hook a deckhand can pull the boat closer to or push away from another boat or fixed object. Once you get used to having a boat hook you won't want to be without one.

• **Boarding Device** — Don't forget a ladder or some boarding device. Getting a person out of the water and on board is difficult (in some cases impossible) without the aid of a boarding device.

• **First Aid Kit** — This should include bandages, antiseptic lotions, sun block, seasick medicine, aspirin, antibiotic ointment and a CPR mask — as well as a first aid manual.

• **Radios** — a VHF radio for receiving and transmitting emergency messages could save a life. A less expensive alternative to a VHF radio is a cellular telephone. Cellular telephones, which can be carried and used almost anywhere, offer practical, affordable protection. Ideally a boater should have both a cellular phone and a VHF radio. The advantage of the radio: the distress message is broadcast to all boaters monitoring channel 16 in the area and will probably bring help quicker than a cellular call to a person or agency on shore. A Citizen Band (CB) radio is another option. The disadvantage of the CB radio is that you can't be sure someone will be monitoring the frequency (See Chapter 10).

Another useful radio is the VHF/FM single band (SSB) weather radio. The National Weather Service continually updates and repeats weather information. This radio is inexpensive and available at most radio stores.

- **Safety Harness** — This is a wide belt with shoulder straps and a line less than 6-feet long, with a stainless steel snap which can be fastened to a secure fitting on the vessel. Although safety harnesses have long been used by sailboat crews, powerboaters have been slow to realized their value (Figure 3.1).

- **Emergency Food, Water and Blanket** — You probably won't starve or die of thirst when stranded on a lake, but if you have a little food and safe drinking water you'll feel better. A blanket, on the other hand, could save a life. In the event of hypothermia or other medical emergency, a blanket can be very important. Some boaters carry a space-age reflective metallic blanket, which reflects heat quickly and warms a victim. It takes up very little space.

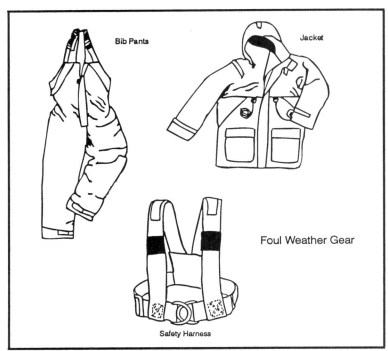

Figure 3.1

I believe in having good equipment and as complete an outfit as possible. I have seen numerous fatal accidents caused in part because the boaters did not have the right gear or their gear wasn't serviceable.

Be prepared. Good equipment is insurance. Believe me, it is much better to have the means of solving a problem than to experience its conclusion.

Maintenance of vessel and equipment

In a storm — when you need it most — poorly maintained equipment is apt to fail. That's why a routine inspection and service program is an important part of heavy weather preparation.

- Study the manufacturer's operating manual for the vessel and follow service recommendations.
- Test run a vessel that has been stored for a long time and thoroughly inspect it before taking it out on open water away from docking and repair facilities.
- Have your boat and motor inspected and serviced by a qualified mechanic at least once a year.
- Keep a log of routine inspection and service.

Inspection and service checklist

___ Helm, shifting lever and throttle functioning properly
___ No fluid leaks (water, oil etc.)
___ Temperature & oil warning lights and alarms functioning
___ Spark plugs, anodes, water intakes and pumps, and fuel filters clean and in good condition
___ Moving parts lubricated and fluid levels (oil, gear case, power trim reservoir, coolant, power steering, etc.) checked
___ Battery terminals clean
___ Drive belts and steering cables in good condition
___ Vessel's fittings and deck hardware in good condition, tight and free of corrosion
___ Hull fittings free of corrosion
___ Fiberglass hull free of cracks and blisters

Pre-trip Inspection

___ Fuel tanks topped off
___ Bilge area clean and well ventilated; bilge blowers functioning
___ PFDs and ring buoy available and in good condition
___ All lights functioning
___ Fire extinguishers working properly
___ Horn functioning properly
___ Visual distress signals available
___ Marine radio working properly
___ All electronic equipment — depth sounder, GPS, radar — functioning properly
___ Anchor and line ready for use

In addition to this yearly inspection, the responsible boat owner gives careful and scrupulous attention to maintenance before every outing.

Remember: The best way to avoid emergencies in heavy weather is to be careful and meticulous about maintenance. When you are caught in a storm, far from supply and service facilities, you don't want the motor to quit because you forgot about the yearly inspection or discover some vital piece of equipment, such as the marine radio, is not working.

Steps to take before every trip

Get a weather forecast.

Obtaining a weather forecast should be part of the routine before any boat trip, but on days when the weather is unsettled it is imperative.

File a float plan

This is not just a heavy weather precaution, but a precaution for every time you take your boat out. Before you leave home, tell some responsible person where you are going, how many are in your party and when you expect to be back.

In my family this was part of my early training. Now I'm an adult and while I don't tell someone where I'm going every time I take a trip, I do tell someone if I'm going out on the lake.

In my job I've seen the disastrous results of searches that started too late. The person you file the float plan with should know who to contact if you do not return soon after you are expected. They might notify the sheriff department, the National Park Service, the Coast Guard or another public safety agency, depending on where you are boating.

Prepare the crew

New crew members and guests should be told where to find emergency equipment and how to use it. Part of being prepared is knowing what to expect. Tell passengers who have never experienced heavy weather how the boat will behave. Warn them that the boat will bounce around and some water will splash on board. Explain that this is normal.

Steps to prepare for heavy weather

The specific steps taken to prepare for heavy weather may vary from vessel to vessel. However, for most situations the following list will be applicable:

Figure 3.2: Survival Coverall and worksuit

Put on survival gear

At the first sign of approaching heavy weather, all persons on board must put on PFDs of Type I, II, III or V. Any crew member who will be working on exposed decks should also wear a safety harness and foul weather gear. When the weather is cold Type V coveralls or float coats are preferable. A Type V survival coverall and worksuit will keep you warm and dry while on the boat and if you have to abandon ship in cold water you will survive longer (Figure 3.2).

Remember that when cold and wet, the crew's efficiency rapidly diminishes. That's why the skipper and crew should put on rain gear, gloves and hats before feeling cold. If the water is below 60 degrees, immersion suits should be easily accessible for quick donning if you have to abandon ship.

Prepare gear that may be needed

Prepare before the storm hits. It is easy to get the boat's gear out and set up in calm weather, but it's almost impossible to perform the same task when your vessel is pitching and rolling. Before heavy weather hits, have all the equipment you might need out and ready.

The ground tackle should be accessible for immediate deployment. Search lights should be plugged in and tested, if darkness is a possibility. Man-overboard rescue lines and Type IV PFDs must be ready for use. Any other gear you anticipate needing, such as towlines, should be located and ready.

Stow gear not needed

After getting out what you might need, stow or lash down everything else. Gear not properly put away or secured could shift during a storm. Gear not lashed down can cause damage, be damaged or create a hazard for the boater.

Rig lifelines

If your crew will have to work on exposed decks that are not adequately protected with handrails, then lifelines should be rigged. This line will provide a hand hold or a place where crew safety lanyards can be attached. On small vessels, a lifeline might be rigged in advance, if crew members must walk narrow gunwales to get around the cockpit or wheelhouse to reach the bow deck.

Batten the hatches

The vessel should be made as watertight and dry as its construction allows. All hatches, ports, windows, doors and ventilators must be closed. I learned from experience why this is important. One day, I rescued a family from a swamped boat. I sent them below deck where they would be safe and dry, but I left the cabin door open so I could talk to them. As I brought my vessel around, a huge wave broke over the transom. Water ran across the deck and poured down into the cabin. Already unnerved from their swamping, they panicked at this new flood and eight people tried to come through the small hatch at once. If I had closed the hatch before the incident, I would have avoided a minor flood and a major stampede.

Lower the center of gravity & trim the boat

Any heavy, movable objects or gear should be moved and secured in as low a place as possible. In small boats, passenger weight should also be distributed to trim the boat.

It is generally preferable to concentrate any adjustable weight low in the vessel, along the center line, near amidships. Too much weight forward can cause the bow to plunge into waves. Too much weight aft can cause the boat to be pooped. Avoid lowering the transom, especially if a heavy outboard is attached to it.

Remove any free water

Pump the bilges dry. Any free water on board is dangerous. It adds extra weight, which causes the vessel to ride lower in the water and be more susceptible to waves breaking on board. Also, water is shifting weight that can exaggerate the rolling and pitching motions of the boat. Once all water is pumped overboard, keep the bilges dry by closely monitoring them or setting the pumps to automatic.

Rig weather curtains

Depending on the vessel, sturdy weather curtains and canvas tops should be rigged in place and reinforced with lashings. Generally speaking, curtains and canvas tops of good marine quality should be in place to keep you and the boat dry, but there is an exception. On some small boats, certain types of canvas tops have flimsy supports and are really meant only as sunshades. These large sheets of canvas can act as sails and capsize a vessel in a strong wind. The whole thing can come crashing down, adding to the problems you already have. These sunshades should be taken down and stored.

Turn on the marine electronics

Turn on the vessel's navigation lights, radios, depth sounders, radar and navigation systems, if they are available. All of this equipment will aid you in monitoring your position and your relationship to nearby hazards.

There is a school of thought that during thunderstorms marine electronics should be turned off because if lightning strikes the vessel, any electrical equipment turned on may be damaged. It's my belief that it does not matter whether the electronics are on or off — if lightning strikes the boat they will be damaged anyway, and that won't be your biggest problem. My advice: Use your equipment to keep your boat out of shallow water and away from dangerous reefs and shorelines.

Get a position fix

Before the storm hits, get a good position fix. Once the weather is upon you, especially at night, you may lose sight of land or other visual reference points.

Nothing is more frightening than to be in zero visibility during a storm with a rocky shoreline close at hand. In this situation you will be much better off if you have a GPS and a depth sounder.

However, if you don't have these electronic aids or they are not functioning, you can navigate by dead reckoning with a compass, a watch, a speedometer or a tachometer and a chart.

Loss of position is uncomfortable at any time, but during a storm when you might be forced to make a distress call, it could be disastrous. Remember, the most important part of a mayday call is knowing where you are.

There are many things to do to prepare yourself, your vessel and your crew for heavy weather. Whether you have several hours to get ready or only a few minutes, the best way to ensure that you have done everything is to use a checklist.

I used one when I was a boating officer, and I strongly recommend it. On the next page is an example of a storm checklist taken from a small patrol boat log book.

HEAVY WEATHER CHECKLIST

1. Crew in PFDs.. ☐

2. As Appropriate: Float Coats, Survival Coveralls, and
   Safety Harness On... ☐

3. Gear Ready: Anchor & Line Ready...................................... ☐
                 Towline Rigged.. ☐
                 Search Light Tested & Ready......................... ☐
                 Rescue Line & Ring Buoy Ready.................... ☐

4. Loose Gear Secured/Stowed... ☐

5. Trim Tabs & Engine Trimmed to Level............................... ☐

6. Batten Hatches   Bow Hatch Closed.................................. ☐
                     Cabin Ports (2) Closed............................. ☐
                     Cabin Hatch Closed.................................. ☐
                     Cabin Ventilators Closed.......................... ☐

7. Weather Curtains Rigged.. ☐

8. Bilge Pump Set to Automatic .... ☐

9. Navigation Lights On.. ☐

10. Marine Electronics On: GPS On..................................... ☐
                             Radar On..................................... ☐
                             Depth Sounder On........................ ☐
                             Marine Radio On (Channel 16)....... ☐

11. Fuel Amount Checked, Both Tanks On.............................. ☐

12. Weather Forecast Checked.. ☐

13. Speed Reduced to Safe Passage.. ☐

14. Position Fix Obtained.. ☐

15. Compass Heading Determined, Course Set......................... ☐

Head for shelter

The best way to deal with heavy weather is to avoid it. If time and circumstances allow, move out of the storm's path or head for shelter. If the marina is too far away, duck into the closest protected cove.

Once you are in a sheltered area don't become impatient. Be prepared to wait hours or even overnight if need be. I have had to work on several vessel sinkings and capsizings because people left a safe cove in an ill-advised attempt to run for home.

The skipper's number one priority is to protect human lives. Saving the boat is secondary. With that in mind, here are some tips for protecting the boat during a storm.

- If you have a small trailerable boat, usually the best option is to get the boat off the water and onto the trailer. But don't risk lives trying to get to the marina to save the boat.
- If caught out on a small lake, adjust your speed for wave conditions and head into the wind toward a protected cove or bay. In heavy seas it is usually best to take the waves at a slight angle on the bow, and by heading into the wind you will be approaching a shore protected by land.
- When you reach the windward shore (the shore protected from wind by land) either anchor or beach the boat.
  — If you beach be sure to tie the boat to a strong, fixed object.
  — If you anchor, monitor your position closely to be sure your anchor is not dragging.
- If you cannot make progress because of heavy pounding by steep, high waves, consider heaving to. In a powerboat this means turning into the waves and reducing throttle to hold your position or make a little headway. Maintain steerage and take waves at a slight angle — experiment to find the angle and side for best handling of your boat. When the storm abates, head for safety.
- While waiting for a storm to pass in a protected area, do not anchor or tie up close to other vessels. During heavy

weather, boats may drag anchor or come loose from their moorings and batter each other.

• If forced onto a leeward shore (the shore the wind is blowing toward) expect damage. Anchor the boat with two anchors and bow into the wind.

If a vessel is caught with its transom into the seas or allowed to broach (turn sideways to the beach) it is at great risk of being swamped or damaged. Driving your bow into the seas offers the only hope of weathering the storm.

Remember — A lee shore is a dangerous place for boats in heavy weather.

Avoid the lee shore whenever possible.

• Check anchor lines frequently during a storm for chafing and check your position in relation to a fixed object on shore to make sure your boat is not dragging anchor.

Final words of caution

First, stay within the limits of your ability and your vessel's seaworthiness. When you try to operate outside these limits accidents happen.

Second, once you are on the water don't forget about the weather. Always keep an eye to the sky. There is no excuse for allowing a storm to take you by surprise.

Even a quick-moving thunderstorm will provide ample preparation time if you are alert. The best policy is to immediately rig for heavy weather any time you have a doubt or concern about the weather.

Don't *hesitate!*

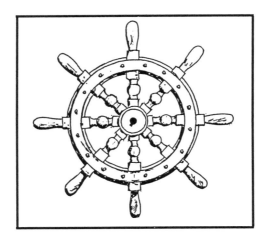

Chapter 4

BASIC PRINCIPLES
OF HEAVY WEATHER BOATING

What to do when the wind is strong and the waves are high

There are many variables in the heavy weather equation. Each vessel has its own handling characteristics and sea-keeping integrity. Each body of water has its own challenges and dimensions and each crew has its own abilities and limitations. In short, heavy weather is not the same for all vessels nor all boat operators.

I worked an accident in which a 42-foot houseboat flooded and sank — while in the same seas, spray barely wet the deck of my 22-foot patrol boat. This happened on Lake Meredith, Texas, when a duck hunter drove his houseboat too fast into oncoming waves. With its windows opening onto the bow at deck level, the vessel clearly had not been designed for heavy weather.

Waves broke over the bow, smashed the windows and flooded the forward compartment. The boater, probably a better duck hunter than boat operator, immediately aimed the vessel full throttle for the nearest shore. Unfortunately, the closest land was the leeward shore (the side the wind blows toward) — not a place to be in heavy weather. In a state of panic he leaped off the boat and watched helplessly as the boat continued on, crashing into a rocky beach. Surf and wind battered the vessel. A short time later, it sank.

This 42-foot houseboat was not seaworthy in heavy weather. Even though it is a commonly held belief that the bigger the vessel, the more seaworthy it is, that is not always the case (See Chapter 11).

The story could have had a happy ending if the operator had not made a series of mistakes: (1) drove the boat too fast into oncoming waves, (2) left windows unprotected, (3) steered toward the leeward shore and (4) allowed the boat to crash onto a rocky beach.

Waves caused this accident and sank the boat. It's important for every boat operator to have a basic understanding of wind and waves. Knowing what makes waves, how they behave and what can be done in an emergency will help you avoid unwise actions caused by panic.

This type of houseboat is both a recreational-type house and boat. It is a big boat with a lot of windage.

Invite family and friends to come along for an adventure on the water. Sightsee from the deck, pull into protected coves for swimming and fishing. In heavy weather, take special care and head for shelter.

Wind and waves

Wind interacts with water to create heavy seas. To build waves, three wind elements must come together:

- Speed — how fast the wind is blowing
- Duration — how long the wind has blown
- Fetch — distance the wind has traveled over water

Waves begin as ripples. As wind increases the waves grow. The harder the wind blows, the larger the wave. It is easy to understand this relationship of wind speed to wave size. It is also reasonable to assume that waves are not created instantly when the wind blows; therefore, wind duration is necessary for waves to grow to their maximum size. It is the third element, fetch, that is most often misunderstood.

I rescued a young wind surfer one day who learned the concept of fetch the hard way. With wind blowing from land out across the water, the surfer saw only ripples along the shore.

He thought the stiff breeze would make for ideal sailing. He didn't realize the waves grew larger farther out and they were moving away from shore. He sailed his board out into the lake like a bullet, but when he tried to return he had a problem. He couldn't sail back because those ripples had turned into big breaking waves. Fortunately, I came along and picked him up.

The important thing for a boater to remember is: The farther the wind blows across the water the bigger the waves will be. And while fetch is finite — that is, waves do not get bigger and bigger forever — for the inland boater, this is almost a moot point. Ripples along the shore can, a short distance out, turn into huge waves.

Whether it is a ripple or a tsunami, all waves have these same features (Figure 4.1): A crest is the highest point and a trough the lowest point.

Waves are described by:

- Wave length — the distance between crests
- Height — vertical distance from trough to crest
- Period — the time it takes for two successive crests to pass a fixed point

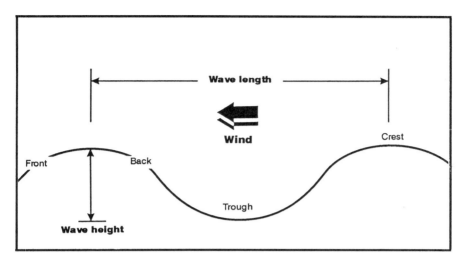

Figure 4.1   Waves

Wave length, height, and period are related to and dependent on wind speed, duration and fetch.

There are two general types of waves: swells and chop. Swells are large with long wave lengths, rounded crests and troughs, and gently sloping sides. They are wind generated, caused by storms many miles away. Because swells have left the area where they were created, they can be encountered on a fair day when winds are gentle. Generally speaking, swells are ocean waves, and therefore are of little or no concern for the inland boater.

The big problem for freshwater boaters is choppy waves. Created when the wind begins to blow, these waves have short lengths, sharp crests, narrow troughs and steep sides. They move in the direction of the wind, in more or less regular patterns called wave trains.

Because the wind tears at their crests, they usually have breaking tops or whitecaps. As the name, chop, implies these close-ranked waves (often with periods of less than five seconds) can give the boater a rough, sometimes dangerous ride.

It is well to keep in mind that passing fronts and thunderstorms can not only create severe sea conditions, but also waves that come from more than one direction. This condition, called confused seas, can also be produced by waves reflected off breakwaters, canyon walls or other solid vertical surfaces.

The interesting and dangerous thing about confused seas is that when two wave crests collide they tend to combine to produce a much larger wave. And when two troughs collide the new trough will be much deeper than the original ones.

When a crest combines with a trough they cancel each other producing flat water. In confused seas, the boat operator must watch out and be prepared for occasional monster waves.

Which brings us to the subject of wave height. When your boat is pitching wildly it is almost impossible to estimate wave height.

But if you need to make a distress call or warn others of the conditions, you should estimate wave height. Also when telling about your heavy weather experience, you will want to describe the wave height. In the latter case you are allowed to exaggerate a little; almost everyone does.

But for a fairly accurate estimate, compare the known height of your boat with the waves which pass it. For instance, if you are on even keel in a trough and the horizon is obscured by a wave, then the height of the wave is greater than the distance from the waterline of your vessel to your eyes.

Danger of waves in shallow water

People tend to think of waves as moving horizontally downwind. Actually there is very little forward movement due to wind.

A wave is better described as an undulation. A particle of water moves upward as the wave crest approaches, forward as the crest passes, downward as the crest moves on and backward as the trough passes.

Energy is created, then absorbed as the water rises and falls in an elliptical motion. The action of wind on water is similar to the action created by wind blowing over a field of grain. The grain moves (waves) yet remains in one spot.

This rising and falling action in deep water is dangerous, as anyone who has had his boat tossed by angry waves will tell you. But when a wave moves into shallow water it becomes far more dangerous.

Photo courtesy of C. R. (Bud) Cleland, Marine Salvage
Callville Bay Marina hit by thunderstorm on July 11, 1984

If the water depth is less than 1.3 times the wave height, the top of the wave starts to outrun its base. The water piles up; the wave becomes steep and unstable.

The orbiting particles of water can no longer complete their elliptical orbit and eventually the unsupported crest topples forward. The energy that deeper water would have absorbed becomes a dangerous, destructive force.

The energy of waves in shallow water can best be illustrated by the damage they have been known to cause.

On July 11, 1984, a thunderstorm moved across Lake Mead, Nevada, and hit the Callville Bay Marina. Waves generated by this fast-moving storm sank boats in what was considered to be a safe harbor.

According to Bud Cleland, a salvager who helped in the clean up, it destroyed Callville Bay. He worked for three months raising boats that were sunk. There were 40 boats sunk and the Marina was trashed.

This destruction was caused by the devastating force of waves breaking in shallow water onto a leeward shore during a storm that lasted less than two hours.

Remember the breaker zone is the danger zone. Stay out! Large, tumbling waves jeopardize small craft.

Motions of vessels in waves

Depending on their size, all vessels are affected to some degree by waves. A sea that violently tosses around a 14-foot Jon boat may hardly be noticeable on a 40-foot cruiser. Yet both are subject to the same three motions: pitch, roll and yaw (Figure 4.2).

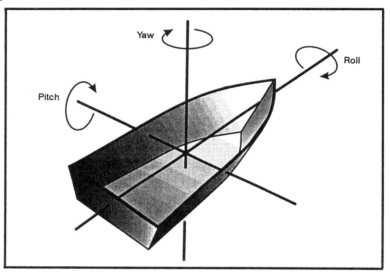

Figure 4.2   Vessel motions

Pitch

Pitch is a movement or partial rotation on a horizontal axis that runs from beam to beam. It causes the bow and stern to rise and fall. A wave lifts the bow, passes under it and drops the bow as it lifts the stern.

Pitch is the motion most people visualize when they think of a boat going through waves. It occurs when the vessel is meeting the seas head on or nearly so, or when being overtaken by following seas. In certain conditions, pitching can be very hard on crew members and damaging to the vessel.

For example, during the summer of 1997 a 28-foot Park Service patrol boat operated out of Cottonwood Cove on Lake Mohave damaged its radar receiving unit when the mast assembly broke off due to constant pitching.

The combination towing tower and radar mast shuddered

with every slamming wave. Over a long period of time this caused metal fatigue.

Eventually as a ranger responded to an emergency call, when the boat was pitching and pounding through the waves, the mast assembly crashed to the deck. The towing tower snapped off, pulling radar cables out and damaging an expensive radar unit.

Roll

Roll is a movement or partial rotation about a horizontal axis that runs from the bow to the stern. It causes the boat to rock from side to side and occurs when the waves are striking a vessel on the beam.

Rolling is very uncomfortable for the crew. This is the motion that often causes seasickness.

But more important, rolling can be dangerous. When a vessel rolls, it becomes unstable. In waves greater than boat width, this may cause the vessel to capsize or sink.

Patrol boat with radar unit mounted on its towing tower. A collision bar on the rear protects the engine; a screen on the towing assembly protects operator and crew from the possible whiplash of a snapped towline.

Towing can be dangerous, but ample deck space aft and proper equipment mitigates the danger.

Yaw

Yaw is a movement or turning on a vertical axis extending up through a point on the center line of the vessel, which causes it to slip or turn sideways. It occurs most often in following seas and is the motion most boat operators are least familiar with.

Yawing is dangerous, because it can trigger situations which jeopardize both vessel and crew. When the boat goes over the front of a wave, the propeller and rudder become less effective because highly aerated water reduces performance and the rudder or propeller may even be lifted out of the water. This can result in an out-of-control side slip, or yaw.

A vessel yawing in a following sea may broach; this often leads to a capsizing.

Drift Angle

When a boat is under power, it can move any direction in relation to the seas. But what happens to a vessel in heavy weather when there is no propulsion?

As all boat operators know, when there is no power the boat drifts. What most operators have not noticed is that the vessel aligns itself at a relatively constant angle to the wind and waves. This alignment is unique to each vessel and is called the drift angle (Figure 4.3).

Drift angle depends on several variables, the most significant of which are the topside windage and the below-water hull configuration.

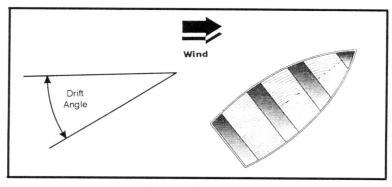

Fig. 4.3   Drift angle

Drift angles can range from parallel to perpendicular to the seas.

However, most small power-driven vessels will drift with their stern quarter into the wind and waves.

Basic heavy weather operations

Ray Eicher, who writes a weekly newspaper column on local boating activities and safety, tells this story about his initial experience with heavy weather: After purchasing a 12-foot aluminum boat with a 6 h.p. motor, he and a friend drove to Las Vegas Bay on Lake Mead to try it out.

They cruised along the shoreline, in and out of coves, for about 20 minutes and gained some valuable experience in boat handling. Then feeling that they were ready for open water, they trailered the boat, drove to another launch ramp and headed out into the main body of the lake to see the back side of Hoover Dam.

In the channel leading to the dam, they were rewarded with a spectacular view. The sheer canyon walls, the concrete dam and intake towers rising out of the clear, calm water made an awe-inspiring sight. It was one of those rare moments a person never forgets.

But this peaceful, never-to-be-forgotten experience was followed by another not so peaceful and never-to-be-forgotten experience when they left the protection of the narrow gorge and headed back to the launch ramp.

Suddenly, the water became a mass of whitecaps. The tiny boat bucked over and through the waves. Spray drenched the two men as they aimed full throttle for the shore.

Ray Eicher remembers they were wearing PFDs and that he directed his friend to sit in the bottom of the boat to help stabilize it. And he says, "After what seemed like a lifetime, we entered the shelter of the bay."

This happened a long time ago. The experience didn't deter Ray's love for boating, but it did teach him the importance of safety.

They did many right things: wore PFDs, moved to the center of the boat and headed into the oncoming waves. In fact, their only mistake (other than not checking the weather forecast before going out) was to make such a desperate run for the harbor.

Pounding the boat into the seas in a wild attempt to make it to the marina often is not the answer. There are a lot of options and one of the best on an inland body of water is to slow down and angle into oncoming waves.

Once in the protection of a windward shoreline, you can make your way slowly and cautiously toward the harbor and launch ramp.

Staying to windward

On most inland bodies of water, the windward shore is close and a smart boat operator will use it to the best advantage. To illustrate: One cold, windy day as I patrolled Lake Meredith in the Texas Panhandle, I received a report of a small boat drifting about eight miles away. Lake Meredith is a long lake and the wind that day was blowing at a slight angle across the lake and toward me.

The ranger who sighted the disabled craft from the shore doubted a rescue could be made in time to save the vessel from crashing into the leeward shore.

I quickly assessed the situation and decided battling a fierce head sea would take almost an hour. Instead, I turned beam to the sea and crossed the lake. Once in the shelter of the windward shoreline I cruised at planing speed in nearly calm water to a point above the disabled vessel. Running with the waves, I swooped in and made the rescue. Although I had traveled farther than if I had taken a direct route, I completed the rescue in less than 30 minutes.

The moral of this story is: Although a straight line is the shortest distance between two points, it is not always the fastest, safest or most comfortable route. Whenever possible, operate near the windward shore and stay away from the leeward shore.

While it is generally best to take waves on your bow, an experienced operator in a large boat may at times decide to run parallel to the waves or even with the waves on his stern (as I did in the above incident). Under these conditions waves may strike you from the side or chase you.

The skipper must understand all three basic sea conditions when making an operational choice. Each sea — a head sea, a beam sea or a following sea — has its own characteristics and dangers. Each requires different operational maneuvers and techniques.

Head seas

When you are meeting the waves on your bow you are running into a head sea. Generally speaking, this usually poses little immediate danger to the average power boat. However, open-bow boats (referred to by lake patrol rangers as "water scoops" for the obvious reason) are at greater risk than closed-bow boats. In fact, most small, open-bow boats and boats with low freeboards should not be operated in heavy weather on large bodies of water.

Most larger vessels have a bow designed to meet waves, and as long as trim and speed are correctly set, they can be operated by an experienced skipper in moderate to severe conditions.

Trim

In a small boat, the passengers and heavy objects should be moved in heavy weather to the center of the vessel. Gas cans, ice chests and heavy gear need to be secured near the center and low in the boat. Loose gear tumbling about can cause injury. In heavy weather you have enough to worry about without dodging flying gas cans. And, of course, you want to lower the vessel's center of gravity to increase stability. List, the side-to-side canting of the vessel, also reduces stability and is very dangerous.

Vessels equipped with adjustable trim tabs or planes and engine trim provide the operator with options for improving the boat's ride and performance in heavy seas. As a general rule, trim tabs should be adjusted so the vessel rides as nearly level as possible. Too much list to either side, or a bow that is too high or too low, is bad.

Correct bow position is not always well understood. A bow trimmed too low will cause the boat to plow through the water.

This results in poor fuel economy and unfavorable handling characteristics. Additionally, the bow will plunge into and under oncoming waves, giving everyone a wet ride and possibly allowing a dangerous accumulation of water.

The reverse condition, a bow trimmed too high, is almost as bad. First, a high bow means a low stern. The stern is already a vulnerable area which should not be compromised further. Second, while a high bow will provide a drier ride, it will give a rougher, pounding ride.

Engine trim should be adjusted so the propellers do not cavitate as the boat pitches, rolls or makes sharp maneuvers. Generally, this means the outboard or outdrives should be in the full down position.

Proper Speed

Failure to operate at a proper speed is the most common heavy weather boating mistake. Almost everyone tries to go too fast.

Pounding is hard on the vessel and crew and should be avoided. I remember the condition of one boat after it had been operated on a choppy day for only a few hours by an inexperienced Park Service employee. This vessel looked as if it had been in combat. Pounding through waves had stripped screws and loosened the cabin bulkhead; the dash was held in place only by the instrument wiring.

When moving through chop, the vessel's speed should be adjusted to allow the boat to ride up and down with each wave. Never try to fly through the wave crests. Never operate at such a high speed as to cause the propellers to clear the water. If your propeller comes out of the water as you pitch over a crest, throttle back to avoid excessive racing of the engine. Operating in head seas requires constant tending to the helm and throttle. Slow down and angle into and through each crest, then resume course and speed up.

The speed rule for heavy weather is: The bigger the chop, the slower the speed. In choppy seas over four feet, you will probably just barely make headway when meeting the seas on your bow.

Too much speed can result in the bow plunging under

waves as the vessel pitches over the crest into a trough. I have seen good, seaworthy boats flooded or sunk because the operator did not slow down and let the bow rise with each wave. Remember: Heavy weather boating is displacement boating. Don't even think about planing.

One of my worst experiences with a head sea occurred one winter day when I was dispatched to rescue a sinking vessel in the main body of the lake. I headed out of a protected cove into mountainous seas. I know that some water over the bow is to be expected in heavy weather, but these combers were the largest I had ever seen. As each successive wave struck, it buried the forward half of the boat in swirling, foaming water. What I did next is what you should do if caught in these conditions. I slowed down and began tacking into the seas.

Tacking in head seas

Tacking is purposeful zigzagging to keep the seas roughly on the bow or stern quarters (Figure 4.4). By taking the waves at an angle somewhere between 15 to 45 degrees you will convert some of the severe pitching motion to rolling motion.

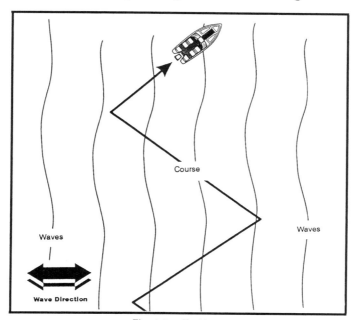

Fig. 4.4   Tacking

This gives a more comfortable ride and often lets you operate at a slightly faster speed.

To tack in a head sea, select a course that meets the seas at an angle of about 45 degrees. After traveling in one direction for awhile, change direction 90 degrees to take the seas at roughly 45 degrees from the other side. How long you stay on one course before changing direction to the other angle is a judgment call.

Because turning in high seas presents some risk and requires an alert, skillful operator, you probably should travel as far as you can in one direction before changing course.

On the other hand a shoreline, narrow channel or obstacle in the water might make frequent course changes necessary. How far you should tack in each direction is one of the many boating decisions you will need to make based on common sense.

However, there comes a point when the seas grow so large that it is no longer practical to try to make headway. When this happens, you can heave to.

Heaving to

Head into the waves, reduce speed while maintaining steerageway and hold your position. Heaving to under power allows you to wait for the storm to pass while taking the seas from a relatively safe direction. This survival technique will reduce pitching and reduce or eliminate rolling, the motion that frequently causes seasickness. As one wit put it, Heave to or your crew will heave too!

I have not often used the technique of heaving to. Once, however, when operating during a storm at night near a shoreline with reefs, I decided it was better to heave to than risk going aground. After the storm, which impaired visibility, passed I reestablished my position and again made headway.

A sailor, Gerry Spiess, tells of a similar experience in the book *Alone Against the Atlantic* by Gerry Spiess with Marlin Bree. He was under power on White Bear Lake, Minnesota, testing his sailboat *Yankee Girl* in a lake storm before attempting a North Atlantic crossing. After some difficulty bringing down the sails in screaming wind and pouring rain, Gerry scrambled into the safety of the boat's cabin and heaved to. He says, "I needed power to maintain my position in the center of the lake...I headed *Yankee Girl* directly into the jaws of the wind. We seemed to be blowing backwards, so I turned the throttle up to three-quarters power. Even with the added boost *Yankee Girl* made barely enough speed to give us steerageway. Still, she was holding her own."

Gerry concludes his account of heaving to with, "In spite of the ferocity of the storm, I was in no real danger as long as I held my heading, kept the motor running, and maintained my mid-lake position."

In summary, when operating in head seas:

- **Adjust trim and lower your center of gravity** — Place your crew and heavy objects near the center of the boat and as low as possible.
- **Try tacking** — As waves get higher and rougher, take them at an angle.
- **Slow down** — Let the bow rise with each wave.
- **Heave to** — In extreme seas or low visibility reduce speed and hold your position.

Beam seas

In a beam sea the vessel is broadside to oncoming waves. These waves strike the craft's sides and cause it to roll or rock from side to side. The effect of a beam sea depends on the vessel: its width, how top-heavy it is, its freeboard and hull design. Generally speaking, it is not practical or safe to operate in beam seas when the waves are high. In my 21-foot patrol boat, for example, I avoid taking the sea on the beam any time the waves are higher than four to five feet.

Beam seas cause two problems. First, the rolling motion is very uncomfortable for passengers and crew. Because boats are narrower in width than length, they roll their beams through a greater angle than they would pitch through. This side-to-side roll makes performing any task, even standing, difficult or dangerous. A rolling motion almost always requires a person to hold on with one hand, leaving only one hand to do the work.

Second, there is the danger of a rollover. When wave height equals or exceeds boat width there is a very real danger of capsizing. On large lakes, such as Lake Mead, waves become close ranked and steep sided in winds of 30 miles per hour or more. If these waves strike the side of a vessel in a rhythm that matches or nearly matches the boat's natural period of roll, the energy of each successive wave will be added to the wave before it. Eventually the boat may capsize.

Even though a large boat can be operated by an experienced helmsman in a moderate beam sea, successful maneuvering requires constant attention. The operator must watch for big waves and turn to meet them on the forward quarter.

At this point it is a good idea to begin tacking.

Tacking in beam seas

Get the seas off your beam by using the zigzag tacking maneuver described in the section under Head Seas. When you tack in a head sea, you angle into the wind, taking the sea first on one side of the bow and then the other.

When you tack in a beam sea, you angle first into the wind and then angle away from the wind. First take the seas on your bow quarter, then change course approximately 90 degrees to take the seas on your stern quarter.

In most cases you should make the tacks as long as possible and be extra vigilant when the seas are on the stern quarter. A combination of slowing and turning to meet the waves at an angle will reduce your risk of capsizing.

Tacking is a slow way to get where you are going, but it is more comfortable and safer than being hammered on the beam.

Following seas

In a following sea, both the vessel and the waves move in the same direction. If the waves are moderate, a following sea presents only a small risk for larger power-driven craft.

But a following sea harbors several serious dangers. In fact, for small boats a following sea is potentially the most dangerous situation, because of the possibilities of broaching, pitchpoling and surfing.

Fig. 4.5 Broaching

Broaching

Most modern small power boats have broad, flat transoms. Unlike the bow, which cleaves the water, the transom is a wall that catches waves.

When a large wave lifts the flat transom, the bow is pushed forward, causing a resistance against the hull. In effect, the stern tries to overtake the bow and the vessel begins to side slip or yaw. At the same time, the propeller or rudder is apt to come out of the water. When this happens — yawing together with little or no propeller or rudder influence — the vessel is out of control. As the boat plunges down the front of the wave it turns sideways to the oncoming waves (Figure 4.5).

Once a broach begins, it is difficult to stop and the result is likely to be a capsizing.

Pitchpoling

A second possible accident in extreme following seas is a pitchpole. If the vessel is allowed to race or surf down the front of a large wave it can bury its bow under the water in a trough or the base of the next wave.

Fig. 4.6   Pitchpoling

With the weight of the seas slowing and holding the bow down, the following wave can lift the stern and flip the boat end over end (Figure 4.6).

The severe sea conditions which cause broaching and pitchpoling are not common on small inland bodies of water, with the notable exception of the Great Lakes, but can be found more often along coastal areas and in the open ocean.

The classic example of a following sea that might cause a pitchpole is a coastal inlet. Here a vessel returning to port can be presented with waves that are much higher and steeper than anything you will encounter inland, except on the Great Lakes.

Surfing

On an inland lake, waves seldom become large enough to cause either a broach or pitchpole. You are in greater danger of surfing.

When you are moving at the right speed relative to the speed of a wave, you can get on it and ride it. If you don't take corrective action you may find yourself on the front of a wave and ride it right into a beach or maybe a canyon wall, depending on your boating area.

The danger of surfing is that you have no control of your boat. It is similar in many respects to broaching. Suddenly the boat feels squishy and helm response is poor. When this happens you must get off the front of the wave by speeding up or slowing down.

The disasters inherent in a following sea — broaching, pitchpoling and surfing — can occur in seconds.

Operational Tactics in a Following Sea

Running

This requires careful attention by the helmsman and constant use of throttle and rudder. It is hard work. In fact, one Coast Guard manual warns boat operators that running before heavy seas is potentially their most dangerous option.

But should you find yourself in this dangerous position, try to stay on the back side of a wave. Through controlled use of power you may be able to ride the back of a wave and this is the best place to be. The worst place to be is surfing down the front of a wave. Going too fast down a wave will cause the bow to bury into the trough. If you find yourself racing down the front of a wave, immediately throttle back. Should the stern start to yaw, counter this tendency by turning slightly to that side. It is important to correct a side slip as soon as it happens before it's too late!

Most small planing boats, capable of going faster than the waves, can easily stay on the back of a wave. Displacement vessels, such as sailboats under power and houseboats, may not be able to outrun the waves. When the seas are running faster than you are, slow down as the following wave approaches and let the wave pass quickly under the boat, then increase power and chase it until the next wave approaches.

And never, never stop in a following sea. When a boat stops, the wave following it hits the transom and splashes up and over into the boat. One big wave can swamp a small boat. The next wave can capsize or sink it.

Turning

Many seamanship texts devote several pages to turning in heavy seas, but for most inland boaters it is rarely that big a deal. For the majority of small power-driven boats in heavy weather, a smartly executed maneuver is all that is required. The only time I found myself in a situation where I judged a turn to be imperative, I found it relatively easy.

In extreme conditions, however, it is important to avoid being caught broadside to the seas, where you will be faced with a possible rollover. The critical factor is timing. Execute the maneuver on the crest of a wave. As your vessel comes up on the crest, put the helm over hard and punctuate the turn with a burst of power. With most small boats this will bring you about quick enough to avoid a rollover.

Now for the final heavy weather operation. You've weathered the storm, you've made it back to the marina. But, how do you come alongside a dock or maneuver into a slip when the water is rough and a strong breeze is blowing?

Docking maneuvers in strong winds

There are some important things to keep in mind when maneuvering around docks and piers in a strong wind.

First, before you attempt to come alongside a dock, pier or another vessel in a stiff breeze, stop and analyze the problem. Anticipate how the wind will affect your boat and plan your moves to deal with it. Whenever you have the option, always work bow into the wind. Make all moves at the slowest possible speed while still maintaining good steerage control.

If you have a deck hand, you have a lot more maneuvering options using spring lines. For example: with a spring line (a short 20- to 30-foot line used to secure the boat) you can hold the bow in place while the stern is maneuvered toward the dock with a small burst of power. And finally, don't forget to rig fenders and have mooring lines and a boat hook ready for use well before you approach the dock.

Sidebars 4-1 show the recommended maneuvering steps in five docking scenarios. Although there are many more possibilities, these five diagrams will cover the most common problems.

Final safety tips

- Wear a properly fitted PFD.
- Avoid operating small boats with low freeboard and transoms, or with open bows in heavy weather.
- Head when possible for the nearest windward shore when caught by a storm.
- Take the waves on the bow whenever possible.

Remember it is much better to spend the night in a protected cove or on a windward shore than to never make it home at all.

Having issued these words of warning, let me add that generally speaking you are safer than you may think you are. Don't panic. Most boats are seaworthy. In fact, your vessel will most likely be able to ride out even the worst of storms. There are many stories of disabled boats being found, while the passengers and crew that abandoned them during a storm were never seen again.

It is at this point that most books on heavy weather end. But this is where this book's most important message begins. The first four chapters have reviewed the basics of weather, preparation and operations; the remainder of this book details how to manage and control emergencies which occur during adverse weather. Heavy weather in itself may not be a life-threatening crisis, but heavy weather together with flooding, sinking or man overboard is a crisis indeed. The following chapters will prepare you to deal with these emergencies on your vessel and give you useful information for the job of aiding other boaters in distress.

Basic Boat Handling

**Single outboard docking with the wind or current
parallel to the dock**

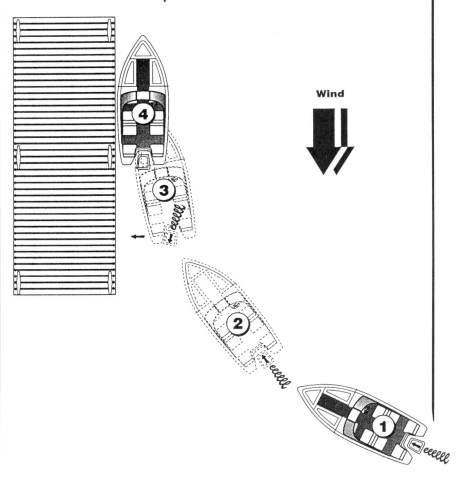

1. Approach the dock by heading into the wind or current.
2. Turn parallel to the dock. Judge the turn to place the boat roughly 2 to 3 feet from the dock when the turn is complete.
3, Apply reverse power and turn the engine toward the dock to stop the vessel and to pull the stern toward the dock
4. Shift to neutral when the boat comes to a stop

Sidebar 4.1

Single outboard docking
with the wind blowing onto the dock

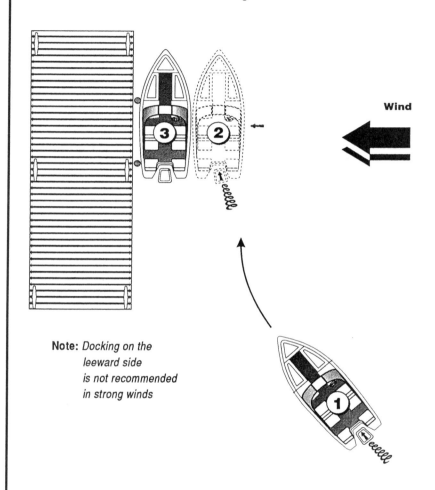

Note: *Docking on the*
leeward side
is not recommended
in strong winds

1. Approach and turn parallel to the dock, roughly 4 or 5 feet from the dock.
2. Come to a complete stop and deploy fenders.
3. Allow the wind to drift the vessel to the dock.

Sidebar 4.1

Single outboard docking
with the windblowing off the dock

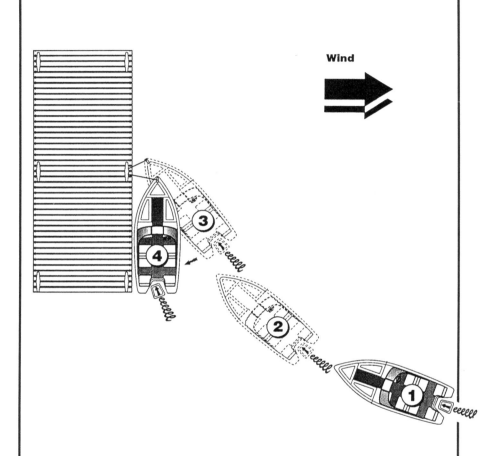

1. Approach the dock at a steep angle, almost directly into the wind.
2. Turn sharply to come parallel to the dock. Note: that the boat will fall off rapidly with the wind, so delay the turn until the last possible moment.
3. In a light breeze you may be able to stop next to the dock. In stronger winds a bowline should be made fast to the dock immediately.
4. Turn the engine toward the dock and power the stern over to the dock. The bowline will hold the vessel's bow close aboard the dock.

Sidebar 4.1

Single outboard leaving a dock
with wind or current holding vessel to dock

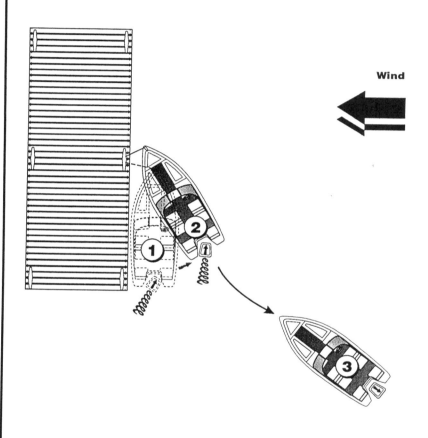

1. Cast off all lines except the bow line.
2. Turn engine toward the dock and motor forward until the stern of the boat is well clear of the dock.
3. Cast off the bow line and back away from the dock.

Sidebar 4.1

Single outboard slipping
with cross wind or current (yawing)

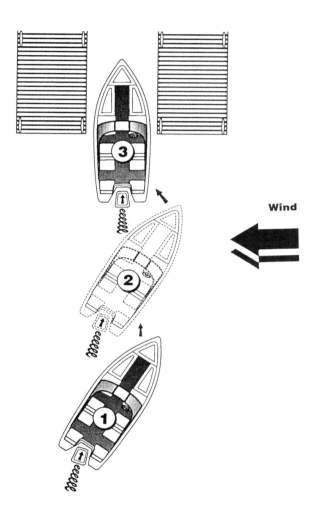

1. Approach the dock, allowing sufficient room to make your turn and to position the boat directly in front of the slip.

2. Turn the vessel into the wind or current. Adjust the yaw angle to allow the vessel's line of travel to be straight toward the slip.

3. Just before reaching the slip, turn the vessel to align with the slip and motor in.

Sidebar 4.1

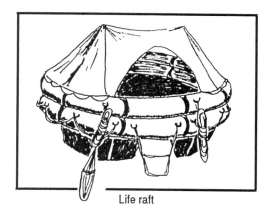

Life raft

Chapter 5

FLOODING, CAPSIZING AND SINKING

What to do when the water is in the boat instead of under it

On November 16, 1996, two men and two boys set out in an 18-foot flat-bottom boat to go duck hunting on Truman Lake, Missouri. When the group did not return home that night, authorities were notified and shortly after midnight began a search for the overdue boat.

About 2 hours later, the duck hunters and their dog, a Labrador retriever, were found on top of the capsized boat. All four were suffering from hypothermia and were taken by ambulance to a nearby hospital.

The operator of the boat told the investigating officer that around 5:30 in the afternoon the craft, caught in very rough water with winds to 25 miles per hour, had started taking on water over the bow and stern. The small boat and 15 h.p. outboard motor were not able to combat the forces of wind and waves.

When the boat suddenly rolled to starboard and the two young boys fell overboard, their fathers dove into the water to help them. The boat continued to broach, the motor stalled and the vessel capsized. Fortunately all four passengers and the dog were able to scramble onto the capsized craft.

In darkness and cold (50 degrees fahrenheit) they clung to the hull for nine hours waiting for help to arrive.

These people can consider themselves lucky. Lucky that they were able to get back on top of the boat and lucky that searchers found them before they succumbed to hypothermia. Although capsizing accounts for only 11 percent of all small-boat accidents, it results in more than one-third of all boating fatalities.

And what is the number one cause of these accidents? Wind and weather. Bob McKeever, watercraft program coordinator for the Department of the Interior, says, "In the history of our park (Lake Mead National Recreation Area) since 1937 to date the single biggest cause of small-boat accidents that lead to fatalities is wind and weather."

I might amend this statement and say, "The single biggest cause of small-boat accidents that lead to fatalities is wind and weather and operator mistakes." An 18-foot flat-bottom boat is not made for heavy weather, and when a wave surges over the gunwale of one of these small boats, it's the beginning of a serious emergency.

But larger, more seaworthy runabouts and cruisers can easily handle moderately rough water. In fact, on bigger boats you expect to get wet during heavy weather; it's inevitable that some water will splash over the sides.

It is flooding, not discomforting spray, that is hazardous. There are several causes of flooding — a damaged through-hull fitting, a hole in the hull or waves surging over the gunwale or transom. Heavy weather can be an indirect cause of the first two conditions and definitely compounds the problem, and heavy weather is almost always a direct cause of waves surging over the gunwale or transom.

Flooding

When a vessel is pitching and rolling wildly in heavy seas, things often go wrong. A boat driven too fast through waves can be severely damaged. But engine vibration and pounding seas can cause failures in even a properly operated boat.

Photo courtesy of C. R. (Bud) Cleland, Marine Salvage
Swamped houseboat

Hull leaks

One cause of hull leaks is failure of through-hull fittings. Large vessels have many through-hull fittings: hoses, shafts, underwater exhausts and rudder posts, to name a few. Often the skipper's first warning that one of these is leaking is when an automatic bilge pump comes on and doesn't shut off.

Ordinarily, on a runabout or cruiser the skipper is alerted to the problem by the sound of the pump running. However, a quiet pump on a large vessel cannot be heard; in heavy weather, wind and wave noise block out all other sounds.

Installation of an audio or visual bilge pump alarm is an excellent precaution. With a warning light or noise that comes on every time the automatic bilge pump is activated, the skipper will notice if the pump is running more often than normal. Frequent pumping alerts the operator to the possibility of a major leak. If you know you have a problem you can usually fix it before it becomes an emergency.

If you don't have an automatic bilge pump you may be alerted to the problem when you notice that the boat feels heavy in the water. One skipper reported that he was alerted to water in the bilge by a thumping noise made by an empty plastic bottle which had risen with the water and was bumping against the floorboards. Since then he has kept tightly capped, empty bleach-type bottles in the bilge. In heavy weather he listens for his "audible bilge warning system." It's certainly better to be alerted to the problem than to find water below deck.

At any rate, one of the first things to do when you discover water on board is to turn on the bilge pump.

Sometimes a measure as simple as closing a sea cock can correct the situation. Other times repairs can be made quickly by tightening a nut or wrapping a hose with waterproof or duct tape. On large boats with many hull openings, shutting off any sea cocks not being used during heavy weather is a wise precaution.

A once-a-year visual inspection of through-hull fittings for corrosion as recommended in Chapter 3 is a good deterrent to failure of fittings, but may not detect corrosion induced by a stray electric current. Electrolytic corrosion involves an interaction of dissimilar metals in brackish water and is usually the result of faulty wiring. It can also be caused by stray electrical currents in a marina. Because it only takes a few weeks for this rapid corrosion to weaken fittings, even the most careful boater can suddenly find water pouring in through a hole where there should have been a pipe or a shaft.

Cabin cruiser with flying bridge, high freeboard, electronics and a diesel engine. A swim step on the stern offers easy boarding.

This type of powerboat is an excellent vacation or weekend-get-away craft. Large cruisers are not required by law to have built-in floatation; however some manufacturers do install floatation. Typically, these vessels have several through-hull fittings. Proper maintenance should include a once-a-year inspection of these fittings for corrosion.

In a storm-tossed boat that is taking on water, you must find the leak quickly. Remove whatever is blocking your view of the bilge area. Knock down berths, rip up decking, do whatever is necessary to get to the source of the leak.

An excellent precaution is to have a tapered wooden plug tied to every through-hull fitting. When you find water pouring in through a hole where a fitting should have been, drive one of these tapered wood plugs into the hole. Because wood swells when wet, a dry plug driven into the opening will quickly form a tight seal.

A failed through-hull fitting is only one of several storm-related causes of flooding. Another cause is holing from collision. When tossed by waves with your attention on the seas and motion of the boat, you might not see a rocky reef or a submerged floating object.

A hole caused by collision is always a serious problem. You must work fast to stop water from pouring through a hole into the boat. A four-inch hole can allow as much as 200 gallons of water a minute to enter the vessel. Use anything handy, such as a blanket or a pillow (but not a life jacket) to plug the hole. Some boaters carry spare pieces of plywood and some self-tapping screws to patch a hole or crack.

You may be able to reduce the flow of water coming into the boat by placing a collision mat (if you have one) or a piece of canvas over the hole on the outside of the hull. However, positioning a collision mat in heavy seas will be very difficult. If you are not able to secure this patch quickly with ropes, and water pressure against the hull does not hold it in place, you should forget patching. This can be a waste of valuable time.

Your patch probably will only slow the flow, not stop the leak, because the pressure of water outside the hull is tremendous. This is a frightening situation, but don't panic. Don't abandon ship, because as the water rises inside the boat the difference in pressure between outside and inside is reduced. Just when it appears that all is lost, the water coming in may slow down.

It is possible that the vessel will settle into the water, but remain afloat. The vessel's natural buoyancy and positive floatation built into all small boats manufactured since 1971 may keep the boat from sinking.

Notice I said, *may* keep the boat from sinking. You must operate on the premise that the vessel is sinking. If you aren't already wearing a PFD put it on now. Call for help. Start the backup pumps.

This is when you need that auxiliary pump. It is also when you will be glad you kept the bilge free of debris, because trash in the bilge can clog or disable your pump. A boat pitching and rolling in heavy seas can really stir up the dirt in the bilge water. A clean bilge could be the difference between an operating pump and a clogged one.

The next time you check the bilge to see if it is clean, remember, it could save your boat and your life.

Heavy weather flooding

In most cases, flooding from breaking waves and spray can be managed by using a little common sense. However, common sense is not a universal trait.

I once worked a houseboat accident where the operator watched his boat slowly fill with water and did nothing about it. This inexperienced boat handler drove his vessel into a head sea too fast, allowing waves to break over the bow onto the deck.

During an interview after the accident, the operator told me he had watched a lake form on the bow. Confident a four-inch lip on the cabin door would prevent the water from going inside, he did not slow down or change course. When the water on the bow reached a depth of four inches, it formed a waterfall over the door coaming leading into the cabin.

What the operator had thought was no big deal quickly became a disaster he could not stop. As the boat settled deeper into the water under the additional weight, more water surged over the bow. By the time this boater slowed down and stopped it was too late. Water poured in and the vessel upended and sank within a few minutes.

The lesson here: If you discover water accumulating onboard, do something about it immediately. Start by turning on the electric bilge pumps (if they are not automatic). Next address the cause of the water on board.

When water surges over the bow and into the boat, the

problem may be too much speed. Slow down and let the vessel ride up and over the oncoming waves.

If this does not correct the problem, change course. Angle into the waves instead of plowing through them. Quartering into wind and sea minimizes the steepness of the waves. When operating in a following sea remember: if the boat slips sideways, steer quickly in that direction. Just as you would in a car, steer in the direction of the slip and increase power.

But don't stop. I've worked with several swamping accidents that resulted from the vessel coming to a dead stop and allowing a large wave or the boat's own wake to surge up over the transom.

Do whatever is necessary to keep the boat as dry as possible. Maybe something as simple as snapping canvas covers over the cockpit will deflect enough spray to make a difference. At the same time make sure the bilge pump is working. Since bilge pumps can fail when needed most, it is a good idea to have two pumps — an electric pump and a backup manual or battery-operated pump. A large vessel needs two and possibly three pumps.

The automatic bilge pump is usually either a submersible type or an electric diaphragm pump. Both of these depend on electricity for power.

The open bow runabout has an outboard motor mounted behind the transom. This helps protect this style of boat from being pooped by a wave over the stern.

Transport guests to a secluded cove for a day of fishing, swimming, skiing and picnicking in this handsome craft. With no protection for operator and crew, this is a wet boat even in moderate weather.

Since the electrical system could be damaged by flooding, the wise boat owner has a backup system that is either manual or battery powered. The batteries for the latter type need to be kept fully charged.

If the boat is taking on more water than can be expelled by the bilge pump, or the pump doesn't work, start bailing. Use a bailing bucket or anything you can find. Some say, only half jokingly, that the best bilge pump in an emergency is a bucket in the hands of a scared sailor.

If you operate a small open boat, it is a good idea to keep a bailing scoop tied to the boat, so that water surging on board will not wash away your bailing bucket. Begin bailing and don't quit. Don't abandon ship. Both you and the boat will last longer than you might think.

Now is the time to make a distress call. A vessel taking on water can capsize or sink with little or no warning, giving no time to send a mayday message.

Also head for the nearest shore. If you have a choice, the windward shore is best. You've probably heard the old saying: any port in a storm. The same advice applies to shores when the boat is taking on water and in danger of sinking. Although the leeward shore almost always means your vessel will be damaged or even destroyed, when you are sinking your number one priority is saving lives. You can get a new boat, but you cannot replace a lost life.

When water splashes into the boat faster than it can be removed by the bilge pump:

- Change speed.
- Change direction.
- Batten down the hatches.

If water continues to accumulate:

- Call for help.
- Start the auxiliary pump and/or start bailing.
- Run for shelter.

Remember, some water will always find its way on board. A little is natural, but a whole lot is TROUBLE. Even the biggest, most seaworthy vessels can swamp and sink — as evidenced by the unsinkable Titanic and the Edmund Fitzgerald.

Capsizing

Small boats

Small open-bow boats are especially susceptible to capsizing. In fact, most rollovers involve boats less than 18 feet long and often result in deaths. Small-boat capsizings are the number one cause of boating fatalities.

There are several reasons for these alarming statistics. First, small outboard boats were not made for use in heavy weather. While they are safe enough when used properly in the right boating conditions, they were never intended for heavy seas.

Small boats usually have planing hulls that depend on speed for stability. When speed must be reduced due to heavy weather, they are hard to control. Add to this the fact that outboards generally have low freeboards and cut-away transoms to accommodate the motor, and you have a craft that is susceptible to waves breaking on board.

A low stern combined with a motor (often too large for the boat) with gas cans carried aft give the boat a heavy, vulnerable stern. If the engine stalls, a wave following the craft, or even the vessel's own wake, can surge up over the transom and capsize it.

Second, small-boat accidents often involve operator error or poor judgment. Many of these operators are inexperienced and often have not had any training. Probably the biggest mistake they make is overloading. The weight-carrying capacity of a boat is determined by its length and width. A 10-foot boat has a carrying capacity of roughly 410 pounds; a 16-foot boat about 975 pounds. All monohull boats manufactured since 1972 of 20 feet or less are required to display capacity information.

However, the load a boat can carry safely is greatly reduced in heavy seas. You need more freeboard when there is imminent danger of waves crashing on board.

Inexperience boaters sometimes make the mistake of improperly loading the boat. Heavy objects should not be stored aft. A heavy stern may cause a small craft to be pooped. Also the weight should be balanced to avoid list.

In a storm, list — which reduces freeboard — can cause the boat to capsize or sink. Passengers and gear should be kept in the center of the vessel and as low as possible. Gas cans and other heavy objects should be secured to prevent shifting; people should not move about.

The operator of a small boat is often primarily a hunter or fisherman, not a boater.

Some common mistakes made by inexperienced operators:

- Not understanding the hazards of an overloaded boat.
- Not realizing the dangers inherent in a shifting load.
- Being unfamiliar with results of a vertical downward pull on the boat's bow created by a short anchor line.
- Mistakenly believing that because a vessel meets Coast Guard flotation requirements, it will not capsize.

Mistakes such as these — often compounded by heavy weather — resulted in 226 deaths and 743 injuries in 1996. With these appalling statistics in mind, here are some safety tips for small boat operators:

- Wear a PFD at all times.
- Avoid heavy weather.
- Do not overload the boat.
- Secure heavy objects near the center of the vessel.
- Do not move around, stay seated.

Photo courtesy of C. R. (Bud) Clealand, Marine Salvage

Air bags are used to right a capsized vessel

Larger boats

Cruisers and motor yachts are highly resistant to capsizing, but in extreme conditions even a large boat can be turned over. A general rule of thumb for recreational craft: In a beam sea, when the height of the wave equals the width of the boat, there is danger of capsizing. On most lakes this is rare, but not impossible.

At Lake Mead, where I operate, winds sometimes exceed 50 miles per hour, creating 5 to 6-foot waves. A large vessel that is flooding is also a candidate for capsizing. Swamped boats are very unstable. A little assistance from a beam sea will roll a swamped boat over.

An alert operator will see the warning signs (a swamped vessel or extreme beam sea) of an impending capsizing. However, the rollover usually happens very fast. Many survivors tell me it took them completely by surprise; they had no time to react.

I have never personally experienced capsizing. I have, however, worked many capsizing accidents and have had escape training from a submerged aircraft cabin. I make the following comments based on these experiences.

If you are caught in or under the vessel, you will in all probability be disoriented and panic-stricken. Your best chance of survival depends on your ability to overcome these feelings.

To combat disorientation grab onto something and hang on throughout the rollover. Hanging on, of course, helps to control your tumbling, but it also gives you a reference point. Chances are, especially if the accident occurs at night, that you will be in complete darkness when you are caught under the boat. Without a reference point, you might not be able to find your way to safety.

But by hanging on during the rollover, you will know where you are. You'll be able to orient yourself and know which way to move to escape.

Controlling panic is a different matter: there is no simple answer. Imagine yourself in a small wheelhouse when your boat capsizes. Suddenly you're in the dark, trying to hold your breath in icy water. You reach out blindly to where the hatch handle should be, and it isn't there. There is no doubt this would test anyone's discipline.

Remember: Knowledge breeds confidence and confidence overcomes panic. Therefore, know your boat inside out and upside down. Further, anyone who is not a good swimmer, who works regularly on boats, had better become one.

On larger vessels you might find yourself in a compartment that did not immediately flood. You could be trapped in an air pocket. This is good. And bad.

Good because you have a little more time to plan your escape. Bad because you probably have a more complicated exit.

Generally in life you have choices; this is one time you don't. Staying inside the boat is not an option. You must get out. If you don't, you will either drown, suffocate or succumb to hypothermia.

When trapped in an air pocket, stay calm. It may help to remind yourself that even though the boat will not right itself, it probably will float long enough for you to think about what you are going to do. You may need to take off your PFD to swim under water, but you will need it when you reach the surface.

It's a good idea to tie a line to your PFD and any other flotation equipment that you have available. With a line attached you can pull your PFD along behind you as you make your way out of the overturned vessel.

Next, test the water. Hold your breath, cover your mouth and nose with your hand and duck under water. The sudden cold may cause a tightness in your chest and cause you to take an involuntary reflex gasp — covering the mouth and nose prevents this.

Experiencing this feeling of cold water before you actually begin your escape may help you to control panic. Stay calm and think clearly; this is vital to your survival.

If there is more than one person trapped in the compartment, the poorest swimmer should exit first. The reason — a poor swimmer left behind might panic and stay in the boat.

Once you swim clear of the vessel and get a gulp of fresh air, your duty is to make certain everybody else gets out. Take a head count. If anybody is missing, dive back down and attempt to rescue them. You certainly would want them to try if you were still down there.

Finally, climb onto the upside-down hull. It is important to get out of the water; the body loses its heat twenty-five times faster in water than in air. Even when the air is cold, you will live longer out of the water. Also it is easier for rescuers to see you on top of the boat. As a general rule, you should stay with the boat, even when the shore appears to be close. It is usually farther away than you think.

Unless you are wearing a life jacket and the shore is very close, don't try to swim. Never attempt to swim against wind and waves or in cold water. The danger of trying to swim to shore, even when wearing a PFD, is hypothermia.

The average person swimming cools 35 percent faster than a person not swimming. A good swimmer wearing a PFD will succumb to hypothermia in less than a mile in 50 degree F water. In most instances your best chance of survival is to stay with the boat.

Sinking

Sinking is the ultimate heavy weather emergency. There are some people who falsely believe that modern boats cannot sink because of Coast Guard flotation requirements. However, their confidence is misguided because flotation requirements only apply to small recreational vessels built after 1971. Commercial boats and special purpose craft, such as are commonly used by government agencies, are not required to have flotation.

If you are losing the battle against flooding, and sinking is a possibility, what do you do? You won't have much time, but there are three tasks you need to accomplish if possible.

1. Make sure everybody is wearing a PFD and cold water survival clothing or suits if appropriate.

2. Call for help.

3. Prepare the equipment you will need when you abandon ship.

Dress for survival

My mother used to say, dress for the occasion. Good advice and for this occasion, it means dress for survival. The absolute minimum requirement for abandoning ship is a personal flotation device.

When entering cold water, bundle up. Wear warm clothing: sweaters, jackets, long pants, boots and caps. Keep all clothing fastened. By trapping a layer of water next to your skin, even wet clothing can help you preserve body heat.

If you have a float coat, put it on immediately, or better yet, an immersion suit or a wet suit. A wet suit made of foam neoprene has excellent flotation, but you should also wear a PFD. You will last much longer in cold water if you are wearing some type of immersion suit, and any vessel that is operated in cold water regularly should carry one for each person on board.

This equipment could be the difference between life and death.

Crew members should practice putting on immersion suits and PFDs. If you don't wear your PFD at all times when you are on the water, as I do, you should practice donning it in the water. Survival suits are to be donned on board, not in the water; putting them on can be difficult when the boat is pitching. Practice on fair weather days and in non-emergency conditions, because when you need an immersion suit, and need it in a hurry, you don't want to be trying to figure out how to get it on. (For detailed instructions on donning an immersion suit see Chapter 12.)

Call for help

As soon as it becomes apparent that the boat might sink, radio or call on your cellular telephone for assistance. Don't wait! Flooding may damage your electrical system and batteries that power your radio. Call for help as soon as you recognize that you have a serious problem. Better to cancel the call because help is not needed than not to have made the call when help is needed.

The most important part of the message is where you are. Give a precise and complete description of your position. If you don't have a radio or telephone or they are inoperable, fire a distress rocket, flare or smoke. Do not, however, use all your distress signals. Save some to use later when you may see or hear another boat or airplane. Nothing is worse than to watch helplessly, unable to attract their attention, as would-be rescuers pass you.

Prepare equipment

On the ocean, preparation is critical because you might have to survive at sea for days. But on lakes and reservoirs it is not as important. The longest I have ever personally known of a person being in the water was about twelve hours.

Nevertheless, even for short periods, I would rather do the time in a life raft than in the water. So if you have a raft, get it ready. (For directions on deploying a raft and equipping an abandon ship bag see Chapter 12.)

Lacking a raft, you can lash floatable objects such as ice chests together to give you something to hang onto. The survivor of a tragic accident at Lake Mead gave this account of his safety-wise actions prior to the sinking of the boat: "I jerked the two seats, just reached down and gave them a good jerk to break them — the screws — loose out of the floor....When the boat went down the seats floated up....I grabbed the seats, pulled them together and laced them together with a ski rope."

This victim did many things right. Unfortunately, they were not rescued before his two companions succumbed to hypothermia. (This terrible accident is detailed in Chapter 10.)

A survival kit could be a real life saver. There are commercial kits available, but you can easily make up your own using a waterproof fanny pack to hold these items:

- knife
- whistle
- mirror
- smoke signal
- aerial flares
- strobe light
- space blanket
- matches in a waterproof container.

The space blanket and matches can be used when you reach the shore. With the matches you can make a fire for both a signal and heat.

In addition to a survival kit, you should also have survival items in your PFD pockets for the unexpected fall overboard. These items can be fastened to your PFD or carried in the pockets of a wet suit:

- A whistle
- Mirror for signaling
- Flashlight and/or strobe light
- Distress rockets or flares

Abandoning ship

Only abandon ship when it is more dangerous to remain on board than to enter the water. Which usually means: let the ship abandon you. Even if the boat swamps or capsizes, stay with the hull — use it as a platform to get as much of your body out of the water as possible.

Abandon ship together and stay together in the water.

The skipper should make sure this happens. Your chances of surviving, especially if the water is cold or when you are in the water for a long time, increase if you are with someone. Individuals who are weak, either physically or mentally, can be given the will to hang on by stronger people.

Don't try to swim — save your energy

Abandoning ship in heavy weather is not the same as going for an afternoon swim. Breaking waves, driving spray, constantly being pummeled and beat by seas — all challenge survivors. The secret is: don't fight it; you will only exhaust yourself and lose body heat.

Unless the shore is very close or there is no chance for rescue, don't swim. Put your back to the waves and ride them out.

Remember to use cold water survival tactics

Use the HELP (Heat Escape Lessening Posture) and Huddle Heat Conserving Posture even in relatively warm water. Don't wait until your teeth are chattering to think of cold water survival.

COLD WATER SURVIVAL TACTICS

Heat escape lessening posture (HELP)

Press arms against the sides of chest, hold thighs together and raise legs to protect these high-heat-loss areas of the body. This position increases a person's survival time in the water about 50 percent.

Huddle heat conserving posture

If more than one person is in the water, huddle together. Sides of the chest should be held close together to prevent heat loss from these parts of the body.

Continue to signal for help

At night, turn on your PFD strobe light, if you have one, and stay alert for passing vessels or aircraft.

If you see somebody, signal them any way you can. Use the whistle you attached to your PFD for just such an emergency, send up a smoke signal or flare, use a mirror to reflect the sun's rays and wave your arms.

Keep a positive attitude

Don't give up. Never take a passive "my fate is in someone else's hands" approach.

It is important for your survival that you continue to do everything you can to solve your problem or improve your situation.

The will to live may be the one thing that will keep you alive.

Hypothermia

A PFD will reduce your chances of drowning. But what about hypothermia? Hypothermia is the leading cause of death for victims of capsizings or sinkings who survived the initial accident. In other words, if you don't drown in the accident, your next big concern is hypothermia.

Some years ago a husband, wife and two young sons were on a Memorial Day outing at Lake Mead with 10 other boats — part of a US Power Squadron. The family had recently purchased a 14-foot open motorboat, and this was their first excursion with the squadron. About noon, even though the wind was blowing and waves were choppy, the boaters decided to return to the Lake Mead Marina. Apprehensive about the weather, the wife telephoned the Marina, asked about water conditions and was told that the lake was rough, but safe.

Halfway back to the Marina, high waves forced the group to pull into a cove, but after a brief conference they set out again. The family in their small vessel were third in the line of 11 boats. However, when the water became rougher, the husband, thinking that following the others would make his ride smoother, pulled out of the line and let the other boats pass him. Soon after this, as he started around a point of land, the bow dipped into a swell and the boat filled with water. A second wave capsized the vessel.

Wearing life jackets, the man, woman and two young boys climbed onto the upside-down boat, certain they soon would be rescued. Ironically, the Power Squadron, an organization that promotes safe boating, rounded the point of land unaware that one of its boats was missing.

The small vessel drifted toward shore until the dangling anchor caught on a sand reef. The family tried unsuccessfully to signal passing boats. Twice the man tried to swim to a rock outcropping about 200 feet away; exhausted, he gave up both times and returned to the floating hull. In a last attempt, he tried to turn the boat over. He failed.

The accident happened at approximately 4:30 in the afternoon. Shortly after dark, the wife died of hypothermia. About 20 minutes later the younger boy died. The father tied himself and his other son to the motor mount.

Sometime after midnight a group of boaters making camp on a nearby island to escape the rough water heard faint cries for help. Searching the surface of the dark water, probing the night with flashlights, the rescuers discovered the father and son tied to the boat. The victims were barely alive.

A member of this rescue party reported that the boy (about 10 years old) was unconscious when they pulled him from the water. Neither father nor son could have survived more than a few minutes longer.

Even though this family all wore PFDs, they were unaware of the dangers of hypothermia.

Hypothermia: the silent killer

Hypothermia occurs when the body's core temperature falls below normal. Theoretically, prolonged exposure to water even slightly below normal body temperature (98.6 degrees F) will cause hypothermia. People have been known to die in 70 degree F water.

The colder the water, the shorter the victim's survival time. In 60 degree F water a person might live as long as six hours; in 40 to 50 degree F water the survival time is less than three hours. In temperatures close to freezing, survival time is as little as 15 to 20 minutes.

The first symptoms are severe shivering and hyperventilation. These are caused by the cooling of the skin and the body's attempt to conserve heat and keep internal organs warm.

Next, as the body's core temperature drops below 95 degrees the arms and legs feel heavy and numb. This is a stage of sluggishness and confusion. Shivering is diminished, and although still conscious, the victim is unable to think clearly.

The final stage when death is a real possibility occurs when body core temperature drops to below 90 degrees.

The person no longer shivers, muscles become rigid and he or she may be either conscious or unconscious. As body temperature falls, breathing rate is diminished and the victim becomes unconscious.

Body fat and size help protect internal organs from hypothermia.

Men survive longer than women. Adults survive longer than children.

Increasing survival time

Use the HELP technique. Infrared pictures show that most heat loss occurs from the head and neck, sides of the chest and groin region. With HELP these heat-loss areas are somewhat protected. If more than one person is in the water, they should huddle with the sides of their chests held close together. Both the HELP and the Huddle Heat Conserving Posture will increase survival time as much as 50 percent.

A PFD will help protect you, and some PFDs are better than others in this respect. Jacket or vest styles that protect the sides of the chest are better than loose-fitting PFDs.

All PFDs help prevent hypothermia by keeping the victim's head (a high heat-loss area) out of the water. Further, the PFD allows the victim to float with the waves, conserving energy and heat.

Tests show that a person swimming in a life jacket loses heat 35 percent faster than a person holding still. Those forced to tread water without a life jacket lost heat 34 percent faster than those wearing a PFD.

Drownproofing is a technique in which the victims fill their lungs with air and float near the surface of the water, raising their heads every 10 to 15 seconds to breathe. This practice may keep a person from drowning, but it also is known to dramatically reduce survival time in cold water.

Drownproofing will keep a non-swimmer from drowning, but because the head and body are underwater, this technique increases heat loss and increases deaths from hypothermia.

Treating victims of hypothermia

The following first aid practices are based on the latest information provided by the U.S. Coast Guard and the American Red Cross.

If the victim is not breathing and has no pulse, begin CPR (Cardiac Pulmonary Resuscitation). Don't stop CPR until medical assistance arrives or you are absolutely certain the victim cannot be revived. Cold brain tissue requires less oxygen than warm tissue, so it is possible that a victim is not dead even when he or she has been in the water as long as 40 minutes without breathing. Young victims who have been in very cold water have greater chances for resuscitation.

Place the unconscious or semiconscious victim in a level, face-up position. Hypothermia victims must be protected from further heat loss. If you have dry clothing or can wrap the person in a blanket, remove the wet clothing with minimum body movement. To avoid moving the person, it may be necessary to cut clothes away with scissors or a knife. Also use body contact (huddle with victim) to warm him or her. If the person is conscious, place hot packs or hot water bottles that have been wrapped in a towel to the groin, armpits and neck areas. Care should be taken to avoid burning sensitive skin.

Check the victim's breathing and pulse frequently. Be prepared to give CPR if breathing or heartbeat stops. If vomiting occurs, turn the person's head to one side.

There are some things you shouldn't do when treating hypothermia victims:

- Do not give food or drink.
- Do not rub or massage the skin. It is core temperature, not skin temperature, that must be raised.
- Do not allow the person to walk or move about. Do not jostle the victim. Move him or her gently, because a jolt may cause the heart to stop beating correctly and result in cardiac arrest.

Get the victim of severe hypothermia to a hospital as soon as possible.

Important facts to remember

The two main factors that cause boats to swamp, capsize or sink in heavy weather are high waves and poor judgment. As Mark Twain pointed out, no one seems able to do anything about the weather. But poor judgment can be improved with knowledge. Here are some facts to improve your judgment:

Small open boats with outboard motors are dangerous in heavy weather. Eight out of 10 boating accident fatalities involve boats less than 26 feet long.

The most important safety device in your boat is the PFD. In 1995 the Coast Guard reported more than 600 boaters drowned; 561 of these victims were not wearing a PFD.

Anytime the boat capsizes or sinks in water temperatures lower than 70 degrees F, the survivors are vulnerable to hypothermia.

Hunters and fishermen who use small boats are especially at risk, because many of them are unfamiliar with the dangers of heavy weather and they often go out in winter.

Your survival depends on your ability to make correct decisions. Reading this book, taking safe boating classes and practicing the skills you learn will improve your ability to make the right call.

But the final responsibility is yours.

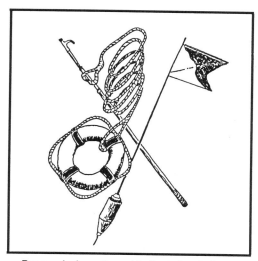

Rescue devices: throwable floatation device,
boat hook and marker with flag

Chapter 6:

MAN OVERBOARD

What to do when someone falls out of the boat

While working at Lake Meredith one wintry day in November, I decided to change the batteries in the lighted navigational buoys. The water was rough and a chilly 38 degrees F, but the job was easy — nothing I couldn't handle by myself — so I cast off alone.

A mile from shore I pulled in beside a buoy, left the helm, made my way on hands and knees to the bow deck and stretched out over the hand rails as far as I could to reach the light. Suddenly, an unexpected wave pitched the boat and sent me overboard.

As I fell, my foot caught on a deck fitting; this saved my life, but left me hanging upside down. Moments later, I struggled back aboard and told myself that I was extremely lucky.

I'm a pretty good swimmer, so I wouldn't have drowned if I had fallen into the water, but I most certainly would have died of hypothermia.

This frightening experience taught me that working on a

boat can be dangerous. Before I explain how to handle a man overboard accident, let me tell you what I have learned about working safely on rolling and pitching decks.

Prevention of man overboard

The first and most obvious lesson is: always wear a PFD. Nobody ever expects to fall overboard. In fact, most people who drown never intended to get in the water. When it gets rough, wear a safety harness tethered to an integral part of the boat.

For years, sailboaters have recognized the value of a safety harness, but only recently have recreational motorboat operators started using this equipment. I personally feel if your boating area exposes you to rough, cold water, buying a safety harness and a tether is a wise investment.

There are several different types of harnesses and tethers. Since the harness should be worn with a life jacket, you might want to purchase some type of combination harness and inflatable PFD or a foul-weather jacket with built-in harness. The disadvantage of this last type is if you need the safety harness when it isn't cold enough for the jacket, you will be uncomfortably warm.

Along with the harness you need a tether. This is a line about two yards long with a snap hook at each end. One end of the tether snaps to your safety harness and the other end fastens to a secure fitting on the boat, such as a U bolt, or a jack line.

Two tethers are better than one, because when moving from one part of the vessel to another, the lines can be successively hooked and unhooked so that at no time are you without protection. A Y-shaped tether also allows you to snap into a new location before unsnapping from the previous location.

When buying a tether, check the metal closures. The end that clips to the safety harness should be easy to unsnap, because you might need to unfasten it in a hurry. At the same time, you want a secure snap that won't come unfastened accidentally.

On larger boats that are not adequately protected with railings, a jack line is commonly used during heavy weather. A jack line is a rope, webbing or wire, usually running the length of the boat, into which safety harness tethers can be snapped. On some vessels, the jack line runs along the center of the boat.

Other vessels use two jack lines, one on each side of the deck. On boats designed in a way that forces the crew to walk the narrow gunwale around the wheelhouse to reach the bow, a jack line is a good safety precaution.

When the water is cold, each crew member should wear exposure coveralls and have immersion suits available. Additionally (I've said this before, but I will say it again and again because it could save your life), you should have in a pocket or fastened to your PFD: a whistle, strobe light or flashlight, knife, two or three mini-flares and a signal mirror. You cannot be rescued if you cannot be seen.

Advice for small boat operators

If you are a weekend boater, you may be saying to yourself, "This safety equipment is designed for the operator of a large vessel — a cruiser or motor yacht." You may feel that because you always check the weather forecast before going out, you do not need a safety harness and tether.

However, one day you might be caught in the middle of the lake when a thunderstorm develops or a front moves in. How will you avoid the dangers of a fall overboard when the boat is pitching and rolling?

What you should do if you don't have a safety harness and tether:

- Hang on.
- Wear a PFD.
- Don't go out onto the exposed foredeck unless absolutely necessary.

Hang on

The boater's rule is: one hand for the boat, one hand for yourself. Hold on, keep feet shoulder-width apart, knees slightly flexed and wear deck shoes. Do not walk barefoot on a wet, slippery deck.

Generally, you are better off standing than sitting. Unless you have air-ride seats or other similar shock-absorbing seats, sitting on the typical hard, minimally padded seat can be harmful to your back. The exception is small craft with low freeboard. In this type of boat, everyone should remain seated to give the vessel more stability.

In my experience, it is vessel roll, not pitch, that is most likely to cause a crew member to fall. Whenever you or a member of your crew has to let go of a support to perform a task, the vessel should be turned either into or with the seas.

Wear a PFD

When a person goes into the water, he or she experiences shock, disorientation and panic. A person without a PFD in heavy weather may not stay afloat very long.

Extra precautions must be taken with small children in an open boat. Children under ten years old should wear a PFD at all times. Toddlers should wear a safety harness in addition to a life jacket and be watched by an adult.

Don't go onto an exposed foredeck
unless you absolutely have to

Any place on board a small boat can be dangerous during a severe storm, but the bow and stern areas are the worst. The teeter-totter effect of pitching through the seas will be most pronounced on the ends of the boat.

These areas are also most likely to be swept over by towering waves. A crew member working in either place is at risk, but a crew member on the exposed bow of a small boat is in real danger. I make this observation based on my own close call and also having seen many a huge wave break over the bow.

Finally, don't do it alone. Had I gone into the water the day I was on the bow changing buoy lights, there would have been no one to rescue me and no one to call for help. I wouldn't now be writing about boating safety.

In heavy weather, the vessel operator cannot afford to leave the helm even for a moment. If something needs to be done, such as dropping an anchor, securing loose gear or rescuing someone from the water, the solo operator is in trouble.

Even when you've done everything feasible to make your boat safe, accidents can happen — someone may fall overboard. In heavy seas this is a true life-threatening emergency. Both the victim and the rescuer must know what to do.

Man overboard rescue

Making a rescue in heavy weather is probably the most demanding task you will ever be asked to perform. Everything must be done efficiently and quickly, and often you only have one chance to get it right.

In my first job as a boating officer my crew and I practiced rescues on a regular basis. We drilled over and over until we could make contact, immobilize and hoist an injured victim aboard in a matter of minutes. However, we always practiced on nice, calm, warm days.

Then came the day I was dispatched on my first real rescue. The lake wasn't nice. It wasn't calm. And it wasn't warm.

It was a nasty day; the wind was blowing a gale. Five- to six-foot waves had swept a young man on a surf board out into open water. A ranger on a high headland with binoculars spotted the surfer and saw his problem. Even though the surfer wore a wet suit, the cold water had sapped his strength.

Unlike other rescues I had practiced, I discovered it was difficult to find the victim. Although the ranger on the bluff directed us, we did not even get a brief glimpse of the surfer until we were less than a hundred yards away.

Immobilizing the young man, if he were injured, was not possible in such sea conditions. Fortunately he was not injured — only exhausted. With bow into the seas, I pulled to within 20 feet of him in textbook fashion. My deckhand threw a ring buoy and line, but the wind blew it away from the man's grasp. Not wanting to send out a rescue swimmer, I decided to move closer to within a boat hook's reach.

Imagine my horror as the side of the patrol boat pitched up and the man disappeared under the vessel's flaring side. I was certain he would be crushed when the boat fell back, or if he escaped being crushed, the twin screws would finish the job. I jerked the engine kill-switch lanyards and abandoned the useless helm to help my crew member.

Suspended over the side of the boat by his safety harness, the deckhand somehow had managed to grab the surfer. With engines shut down, the boat swung around until it was nearly beam to the seas. The deck rolled wildly.

With all our weight along the gunwale, and with the waves slamming into the boat, I thought we might capsize. Quickly, my deckhand and I decided to concentrate our efforts on the downward roll of the gunwale. On the next roll — with adrenaline-induced strength — we dragged the man aboard.

My point is: heavy weather rescues are difficult and dangerous.

To be truly effective, you need proper equipment. Federal regulations require all boats 16 feet long or longer to have one throwable flotation rescue device, in addition to a wearable PFD, for each person.

Equipment

The throwable flotation device is the minimum required by law, but to make a successful heavy weather rescue you will need more equipment.

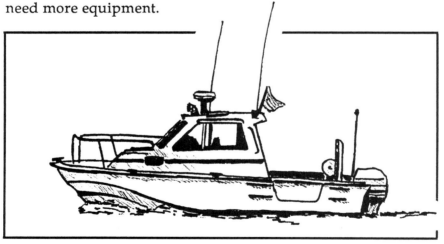

Patrol boat with tow bar and reel for towing. The radar receiving unit is mounted atop the cabin.

After responding to a man overboard rescue call, the crew of this vessel will find lifting the victim from the water to be relatively easy with a boarding door (a panel on the side of the hull that lifts out).

First of all, if the accident occurs at night, the victim will be lost from sight almost immediately. And believe me, this is when a fall overboard is most likely.

In fact, one retailer of boating safety equipment has suggested that the boater's corollary to Murphy's law should be: crew members tend to fall overboard when recovery is most difficult.

The safety-wise skipper will fasten a watertight strobe or battery-operated lantern to a Type IV flotation device and keep it near the helm. When it is needed, the boat operator can quickly turn on the light and toss it out.

A light attached to a flotation device can make the life-saving difference in the time it takes to locate a victim at night.

There are commercially available man overboard markers (a pole with a floating strobe light) that were designed for this purpose. You will also need a search light, or strong flashlight, on board to aid in locating the person in the water.

Next comes the problem of making contact with the victim. For this you will need, at a minimum, 50 feet of half-inch polypropylene line attached to a horseshoe or ring float.

In addition, it is a good idea to have a throw rope bag. This weighted bag contains approximately 70 feet of line.

The bag is tossed and the line pays out as it sails through the air. It is easy to throw, floats in the water and makes storage and deployment of a line simple.

The advantage of this device over a ring or cushion tied to a line is that it can be thrown further and generally with greater accuracy.

I firmly believe that no boat should be without a boat hook. It is good for everything from catching a mooring to making a rescue. This handy tool is a must when trying to rescue an injured or unconscious victim, who cannot grab a line or move about in the water.

Helping the victim out of the water and back on board is the next problem. To do this you will need some equipment for getting a person who may not be able to help himself or herself into the boat.

There are several ways of doing this and it is best to be prepared for more than one method of retrieval.

Some equipment options:

• A boarding ladder
• A swim step and/or boarding door
• A retrieval strap

A retrieval strap is a line with a padded loop which goes under the armpits of the victim and has a series of handhold loops for rescuers use in pulling the victim into the boat (See Figure 6.1).

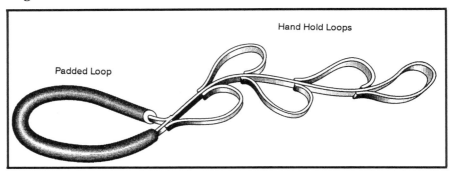

Fig. 6.1 Retrieval strap

Rescue steps

Since the skipper knows the vessel and what equipment is on board, this person is the logical one to direct the rescue operation. Remember, leadership is important. Talk to the crew. Tell them what to do and what to expect.

Three rescue steps:

1. Return to the victim.
2. Make contact with the victim.
3. Get the victim back on board.

Return to the victim

The first person to see someone fall overboard or discover someone missing shouts, man overboard! At the same time he or she should throw a life ring, PFD, or marker buoy overboard in the direction of the victim.

If a flotation device is not immediately available, throw anything that will float, such as an empty ice chest or water jug. At night a life ring fitted with a marker light is the device of choice.

The purpose of throwing an object immediately, whether you see the victim or not, is to provide the person in the water with a float if they are nearby and to mark the beginning of the search area if the victim can't be seen.

If anyone on the boat can see the victim, his or her sole job is to point toward the man overboard with fully extended arm and never take his or her eyes off the victim. This is of primary importance in heavy seas. It is very easy to lose sight of a person in the water as the victim and the rescue boat bob up and down in the waves.

The operator upon hearing the cry "man overboard!" must do several things immediately. First, shift to neutral just in case the victim is still close to the boat. Then record the vessel's heading. If the boat is equipped with GPS that has a man overboard function, the boat's position can be recorded with the touch of a button.

In heavy seas, knowing the vessel's heading at the time of the accident is vital. Many seamanship texts say, turn immediately. I say, check your heading, then turn.

Don't worry about kicking the stern away from the person. With most small boats, even at slow speeds you will have long since passed the victim before you can react. More important than kicking the stern away from the victim is knowing which way you should go if you should have to backtrack. It only takes a quick look at the compass to determine your heading.

Next, turn around. Make as tight a turn as possible and return on a reciprocal (180 degree opposite) of your original heading to the spot where the accident occurred. Don't back toward the victim, because of the danger of hitting him or her with a propeller.

If the victim is not in sight, immediately radio or call on the cellular phone for all the help you can get. With lookouts posted, start back along your reciprocal heading. Slowly go past the Type IV flotation device or the marker buoy that was deployed and continue to search.

Make contact with the victim

When the victim is located, the next task is to make contact. But how you may do this is somewhat controversial. Some texts recommend you approach from up-wind, citing advantages of creating a shelter for the victim and ease of throwing the rescue line.

But there is one real big disadvantage — you are likely to run or drift over the victim.

I recommend, and so does the Department of the Interior in their training, that you always approach from *downwind*. Even if you must go past the victim, go downwind, turn and come back facing into the seas.

By doing this you will have better control of your boat and if something should go wrong your tendency will be to slow and drift away from the victim, not over him or her (Figure 6.2 & 6.3).

An approach into the wind offers three advantages:

1. The operator will have the best control of the vessel.

2. The vessel is not likely to run or drift over the victim.

3. It establishes the most stable rescue platform.

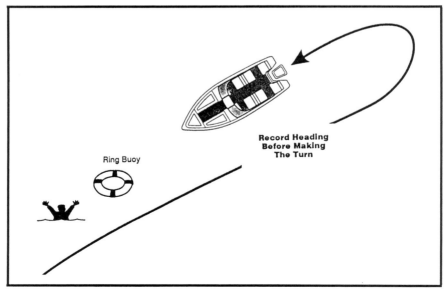

Fig. 6.2 Man overboard

When a rescue must be performed with the wind and seas from any direction other than on the bow, you should anticipate severe vessel control and drifting problems.

Sea conditions will determine how you make this approach. Tell your crew (whether it is one person or a dozen) which side of the boat the recovery will be made on and how it is to be done.

Communication is important. Your crew must know what to do and what to expect so they can be prepared for the next step, which is getting the victim back on board.

Also the crew must keep the operator advised of the victim's location, because when a person in the water is close to the boat, the operator probably won't be able to see him or her.

Maneuver to within 10 to 15 feet of the victim. Generally it is best to make the rescue on the side that gives the operator the best view of the victim.

If the victim is conscious, but not wearing a PFD, throw him or her a line attached to a Type IV flotation device.

A conscious victim in a life jacket only needs a line. A throw rope bag makes delivery of a line easier and more accurate. After fastening one end to the boat, toss the line to the victim.

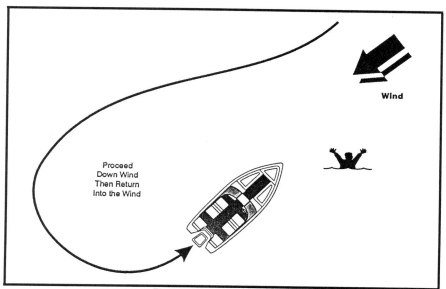

Fig. 6.3 Approach for rescue

Retrieval of man overboard without a boarding device

However, when you don't have time to secure the line, grip the bitter end firmly. Don't let the end of the line get away from you as you make the throw. If you miss, pull it in quickly, coil and get ready for a second try. Another technique, which works well in light to moderate seas, is towing the line into position. With this method the boat circles the victim, allowing the line to pay out, exactly the way you pass a ski rope to a water-skier.

If the victim is unconscious or badly injured, you will have to bring the boat in close enough to reach him or her with a boat hook. A crew member can then position the hook under the victim's armpit or snag a PFD strap. This is a very difficult maneuver in heavy seas and requires an operator capable of pulling close to a target and holding that position for a few seconds. There is always the danger of the person in the water being injured by the vessel's propeller(s). I use the kill zone concept — that is, any time the victim is aft of amidships I immediately shut down the engine.

Only as a last resort, and only if you have the equipment and a trained person on board, should you try a swimming rescue. This is very dangerous. Attempting it has caused many would-be rescuers to become victims.

The dangers are:

National Park Service boat patrol rangers practice man overboard retrieval. This is the chin-up bounce technique, which requires a little know-how and a lot of brute force.

- Panicky victim pulling the rescuer under water.
- Succumbing to hypothermia.
- Becoming separated from the boat.

To perform a swimming rescue, the swimmer should have formal life guard training, must wear a PFD and harness with a tether line back to the rescue vessel and should wear appropriate thermal protection. With this gear, the rescuer's safety is ensured and should a problem develop he or she can either be pulled back to the boat or can return to it hand-over-hand.

In heavy seas, even professional rescuers are limited in the level of emergency medical care they can provide for an injured victim in the water. About the only practical care they can give is to open an airway and maybe administer a few breaths in an attempt to resuscitate.

Rescuers should try to limit neck and spine movement. It is extremely difficult and not practical to attempt to backboard or apply a cervical collar in heavy seas. It is best to retrieve the victim as quickly and gently as possible.

Get the victim back aboard

How you get the victim out of the water depends on the size and type of your boat, the weather conditions and the equipment you have on board.

Small boats

Let's consider first the appropriate procedure for a small open boat in moderate seas with no equipment. With this type of boat, balance is important. You don't want your vessel to capsize — making a bad situation worse. To maintain balance, you will probably have to bring the victim aboard over the stern.

This is risky because:

1. You will have to shut down the engine. In heavy weather it is difficult to determine if in fact you are in neutral gear and there is a danger that someone will accidentally bump the gear shift, setting the propeller in motion. Therefore, don't simply stop the boat — shut down the engine. But no propulsion means no control of the boat.

2. Even with the motor turned off there are a lot of sharp edges on the outdrive that can cause cuts and bruises.

Make this rescue quickly because the boat will rapidly swing around to its drift angle. Have the person step upon the cavitation plate and climb up the motor. Your only advantage in this situation is the fact that the transom is low and it is relatively easy to lift or assist the victim. As soon as you've made the recovery, start the engine and regain control of the vessel.

Larger boats

With a well-equipped Class 1 or larger boat, the procedure will be a bit different. Now amidships (not the stern) is the best place to hoist the victim aboard. The boat is larger, more stable and less likely to capsize, and the side of the vessel is an accessible, easy place to work. It also is safer for the victim to be away from the stern. But more freeboard means you have farther to lift.

With a ladder, swim step or boarding door and an uninjured victim the process is simple. But without this equipment you will need a little know-how and a lot of brute force.

Three boarding techniques

1. Chin-up bounce — This works both as a method for pulling a victim from the water and for self rescue. This technique is simple. The victim reaches up, grabs the gunwale or rescuer's arms. Next he or she bounces up as if doing a chin-up. On the highest bounce, rescuers pull the victim into the boat.

2. Rope Ladder — For this method, you use a line to make a simple ladder. Tie a series of loops in the line roughly one to one-and-a-half feet apart. Secure it to a cleat and you have a ladder the victim can put his or her foot into and climb up.

3. Rope Sling — When the victim cannot assist in the rescue, make a loop in a line large enough to slip under the person's armpits. Knots or handholds tied in the line help the rescuers to lift the victim. The advantage is: this method takes the strain off the rescuer's back and puts it on his or her arms and shoulders. Rescuers can stand instead of bend over. The rope sling is a jury-rigged version of the commercially available retrieval strap.

Whatever boarding technique you use, it is best to shut down all engines while you make this rescue. However, in heavy seas it may not be possible to hold a position for more than 10 to 20 seconds without power.

If you feel the rescue cannot be made in this length of time, or if there are nearby hazards such as reefs or a leeward shore, then do not shut down the engines. In this case, you must take extreme caution to ensure the victim is not struck by the propeller. Wave action can quickly and unexpectedly draw a person toward and under the vessel. If the engines are left running, the operator must be able to panic-kill all engines instantly. The skipper must remain at the helm or have engine kill-switch lanyards in hand if he or she leaves the cockpit.

With an injured or unconscious victim, the recovery should be by the method least likely to aggravate injuries. If neck or back injury is suspected, lift the victim vertically out of the water keeping the spine as straight and immobile as possible. Victims of hypothermia should be treated as gently as victims of trauma. Rough handling can cause severe cases of hypothermia to go into cardiac arrest.

Once on board, an injured victim should be given appropriate emergency medical care. This should be provided by the crew member who has the highest level of medical training.

Surf rescue

The lee shore is dangerous. If the man overboard is not injured or suffering from hypothermia, your best choice of rescue in surf conditions would be simply to throw a ring buoy or Type IV floatation device to the victim and allow him or her to float into the shore.

I recommend this, because if you try to maneuver in surf conditions to make a pick-up, you will be in great danger of swamping, capsizing or going aground.

Practice man overboard rescue

When someone falls overboard the rescue must be quick and effective. The operator and crew must know exactly what to do — in fact, it should be an instant reflex action. There is only one way to ensure this — practice.

At Lake Mead, where I instruct Department of the Interior boat operators, we have found that man overboard drills result in dramatically faster, more efficient rescues. One reason performance improves is reduced panic. Practice gives confidence, which overcomes panic.

It is not enough for you, the operator, to be familiar with man overboard techniques; your spouse or any person you regularly boat with should also know what to do. To make certain your boating partner can rescue a victim without prompting, have him or her demonstrate the procedure without your help. On a windy day, throw out a PFD and practice recovering it.

Besides practicing actual approaches and pick-ups, make sure everyone knows how to operate the radio and how to send an emergency message (See Chapter 10). Show your passengers where the man-overboard gear is stowed and where to find a searchlight or flashlight. Teach crew members how to tie a bowline knot, in case it is needed to make a non-slip loop in a line to help a victim back on board.

One last word: make this practice fun, not frightening. If your family or friends enjoy competition, make a game out of practice by timing rescues.

Be a good coach. Don't criticize or make anyone feel stupid or inadequate. Praise everyone's efforts. And don't dwell on the terrible things that might happen if a rescue can't be made in time.

Which brings us to the very frightening subject of victim survival.

Victim survival

A man-overboard victim's chances of survival in heavy weather are not very good. Waves make it difficult for rescuers to locate a swimmer.

In fact, those searching for a victim usually will not spot him or her until they are very close and then will only catch a fleeting glimpse of the person when both the boat and the victim are on a wave crest.

At night, it is almost impossible to find a person in the water, unless he or she has a light or other signal. This is why many PFDs are made with reflective tape and have a whistle and strobe light attached and pockets for mini flares. You must be seen to be rescued.

If you are not wearing a PFD, your life is in danger. But if you find yourself in the water, don't give up. Survival often depends on the victim's will to live. Swim or tread water. Air trapped in your clothing may also help to keep you afloat.

If you are wearing long pants, take them off, tie a knot in each leg or tie the legs together. Holding the pants at the waist, swing them up over your head and whip them down into the water quickly. Hold the waist under the water to keep the air trapped inside. The Navy teaches this technique to all sailors and it has resulted in dramatic instances of survival.

If you are near land, swim slowly toward it. Conserve your energy and rest between large waves by treading water.

A final warning

In May 1994, a group of divers were on their way to Isle Royale in Lake Superior. When they were well out into the lake and about 21 miles from the island, the operator left the helm and went to the stern of the vessel to retrieve a dangling line.

In moderately rough water, the boat took a wave from the side, sending the skipper overboard. He was not wearing a PFD and he was the only person who knew how to operate the vessel.

Finally, one of the men on board was able to turn, return and stop the boat. However, no one knew where to find the man overboard equipment. Someone spotted an ice chest and decided it could be used as flotation, but the cooler was tangled up in lines.

Neither the lines nor the ice chest could be tossed overboard in time. The victim sank in about 600 feet of water and the body has never been recovered.

The obvious lessons:

- Always wear a PFD.
- Be sure someone on board besides the skipper can operate the boat.
- Keep Type IV and other man-overboard equipment where it is easily accessible.
- Show passengers where the Type IV PFD and other man-overboard equipment is stowed when they board the vessel.

In 1994, the Coast Guard reported 208 deaths as the direct result of falls overboard. The accident near Isle Royale was one of these fatalities.

Fatalities that could have been prevented.

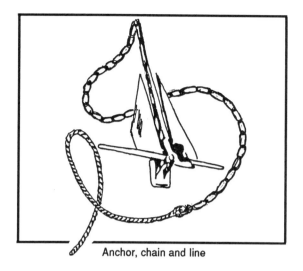

Anchor, chain and line

Chapter 7

ENGINE FAILURE
AND GROUNDING

What to do when the boat won't go

When driving a car, engine failure means the car won't go. When the same problem occurs on a boat, the boat does go — with the wind and waves.

The boat drifts, and in heavy weather it drifts amazingly fast. On small bodies of water, the vessel will usually drift onto the leeward shore and become grounded. This can result in significant damage, even total destruction, of the vessel. Then the boat really won't go.

The two problems — engine failure and grounding — although very different, are in many cases part of the same chain of events. In this chapter, these subjects will be discussed separately, starting with engine failure.

Engine failure

Two out of every three calls to the Coast Guard for assistance are for boats that are disabled and adrift. Unless you're in a sailboat, engine failure in heavy weather is a real emergency. Without power, the boat is at the mercy of wind and waves — and that can be very little mercy indeed.

As soon as power is lost, the boat swings around to its drift angle and begins moving leeward. With most small power boats, this usually means a stern quarter to the seas. In a vessel with a low freeboard, waves will begin breaking on board and once this starts, swamping, capsizing or sinking is almost inevitable.

I worked a fatal boat accident in which this was exactly what happened. Two fishermen in a small 14-foot boat were caught out in a thunderstorm. As they attempted to flee the storm, their motor stalled and would not restart. Without power, their boat turned and exposed its stern to the seas. Waves crashed over the transom.

The boat swamped, upended and partially sank. Only the point of the bow remained out of the water. The two men clung to the hull, but eventually the air bubble escaped from the bow and the boat sank. Shortly after that one of the fishermen drowned.

A large boat probably will not flood or sink immediately when it loses power. But on a big lake, it could drift outside the search area before it is reported missing or be blown onto a leeward shore before help can arrive. The pounding surf of a leeward shore is vicious.

As with every emergency problem the best solution is prevention.

Prevention

A well-built boat of appropriate size for the body of water with an experienced operator can handle most heavy weather if there is no equipment failure. Boat maintenance is very important (See Maintenance of Vessel and Equipment, Chapter 3).

Most engine failures start with a small problem that goes uncorrected. Each time you leave the dock, be especially aware of your engine's performance. If you detect some abnormality, fix it immediately, or at least determine that it is not something which will get worse.

One other important reminder — make sure you have plenty of fuel. It is a good idea to fill your fuel tank each time you take the boat out. Carry a spare fuel tank if necessary. The boater's rule is: allow one-third of the fuel to reach your destination, one-third for the return trip and one-third for reserve. Remember, in heavy weather you will use more fuel, a lot more fuel, than in fair weather.

Even a veteran operator can sometimes underestimate his fuel consumption. Bud Cleland, a local marine salvager, told me a story which illustrated this point. Bud began his tale by explaining, "Mostly I raise the big ones — 65-footers." One in particular that caused him trouble was a rental houseboat. Bud remembered that it was sunk in the stern under about 20 feet of water and the nose was still touching the beach.

He and his daughter worked most of the afternoon raising the boat and hooking up the tow. "It took us to about 5 o'clock in the evening," he said, "and we had a 30-mile tow to bring it back into the marina. It got dark on us."

Bud didn't like towing at night, but everything was going all right until the wind came up. As they rounded the point heading for Callville Marina on Lake Mead the seas began to kick up. They were within sight of the harbor when five- to six-foot waves began battering his 24-foot tow boat. And it got worse!

He said, "I considered, because it was so bad, maybe cutting our tow loose. But I couldn't do that because my daughter was on it. My boat was twisting and turning. It got so bad with rain and wind — I couldn't see the marina. But I knew I was headed in the right direction."

Approaching the harbor, he couldn't make out the breakwater, "but somehow or other I made it past the tires — I don't know how — I couldn't see them."

Once inside the breakwater, he was able to identify the lights of the marina. He radioed the houseboat rental company to have someone meet him at the dock. He concluded the story by saying, "They came out. They'd been waiting for us. We were right at the gas docks. We were right there and it (his tow boat) just stopped. My boat was out of gas."

Bud laughed. He'd been lucky.

Being disabled and adrift in heavy weather with a tow are

the ingredients for disaster. It had been a close call, but everything had turned out all right.

Related to the problem of running out of fuel are the problems caused by low fuel. Air sometimes gets into a fuel line or sediment in the bottom of the tank may clog the line. In either case, engine failure is the result.

The old saying that two are better than one is certainly true in the prevention of engine failure disasters. Two engines almost eliminate these emergencies, because it's unlikely that both engines will fail at the same time.

Also, two boats are better than one. Wherever possible, go out on the lake with other boaters. Besides being safer, it makes the outing more fun. But not everyone can afford a twin engine craft and there may be times when you will go boating alone.

Your best protection when boating by yourself is a well-maintained boat. However, even with the best of care the engine may, at some time — usually the worst time — quit.

What should you do when this happens?

Managing engine failure

1. Quickly deploy your anchor and/or your sea anchor.
2. Try to restart your engine.
3. Call for help.

Anchors and how to use them

I recommend that every boat carry at least one anchor. There are many times when anchors are needed and engine failure is just one of those times. When your boat is disabled, you must have an anchor to prevent your stern from being exposed to the seas and to slow or stop your drift.

The number and types of anchors you need depends upon your boat. Bigger boats require bigger and more anchors. Large boats should have three anchors. Two should be stowed on deck, where they can be deployed in 30 seconds or less, and a storm anchor should be stowed below.

Notice, I said stowed. Anchors should not be left lying loose on the deck, where they can shift when the boat rolls, creating a potential hazard or even going over the side.

Ranger Jeff Goad demonstrates the proper deployment of an anchor.

Deck chocks can be purchased to fit your anchor, making it accessible yet not underfoot. Also don't pile gear on top of the storm anchor stored below deck. When you need an anchor, you won't want to have to hunt for it.

Your local marine supply store can help you decide which anchor is best for your boat. Different lake bottom conditions require different types of anchors. Two good anchors are the Danforth and the kedge. The Danforth, developed by Richard Danforth in 1938, is light-weight with good holding power. There are several variations of this type of anchor and all work well in mud and sand. Another type is the kedge anchor. It looks like the anchors which decorate yachtsmen's caps and jackets. Its hook design makes it good for anchoring where there are weeds or rocks, and it makes a good storm anchor.

You will need anchor line, called rode. I recommend three-strand or double-braid nylon line no less than three-eighths of an inch in diameter — a half-inch is better. Bigger boats require stronger, thicker rode.

Nylon is a strong line with the ability to stretch — a definite advantage. Your anchor line should be at least seven times the vertical depth of the water you will be anchoring in. This 7:1

ratio is called scope. The long line allows a low angle of pull on the anchor and gives more holding power.

As with all gear, you should inspect your rode and anchors from time to time. Look for chafing, loose shackles or bent flukes. Your life can depend on your equipment, so replace worn lines and repair damaged anchors.

In hazardous conditions, you want to get the bow upwind and pointed into the seas, because that is the end of the boat designed to take big waves. The anchor or sea anchor should always be deployed from the bow.

A few dos and don'ts when you deploy an anchor:

- Do secure the bitter end of the line to a cleat or bitt before lowering.
- Don't stand on the line when lowering.
- Do lower the anchor. Don't throw it.

Anchors hold better when the pull of the rode is as near horizontal as possible. For this reason, the scope should be increased to as much as 10:1 in heavy weather.

One device to aid in making a horizontal pull is a sentinel. This is a weight on the line that will hold it down. A sentinel can be made by fastening a light anchor to the storm anchor's rode. Lower the light anchor on its own line, stopping it before it reaches the storm anchor. When the storm anchor gets a good grip on the bottom, it will hold your boat into the seas and off the lee shore until help arrives.

Sometimes, open water is too deep for an anchor. That's when you need to deploy a sea anchor (Figure 7.1). A sea anchor looks like an underwater parachute. It creates drag and if sized properly for the vessel, it can be very effective in slowing drift.

Manufacturers of sea anchors have size recommendations and usually give complete directions for deploying the anchor. Don't wait until you need the sea anchor to read the manufacturer's directions.

If you don't have a sea anchor, and need one in a hurry, you can improvise. Make up one using a strong bucket, loose gear, chains, or lower your anchor and hope it catches as you drift into shallower water.

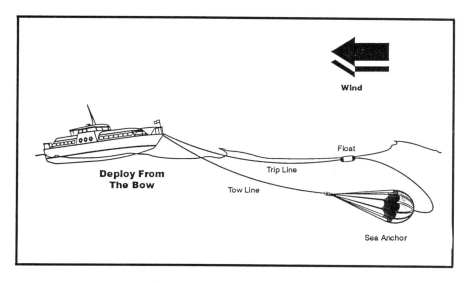

Fig. 7.1   Deploying a sea anchor

If you can't get your anchor out in time, your boat may wash up on a beach. This happened to a ranger friend of mine.

As he attempted to make a rescue from a leeward shoreline, his engine quit. Because he was close to the shore, he didn't have time to deploy his anchor. He was lucky because he only suffered wounded pride and embarrassment. But a rocky bank and bigger surf could have turned this embarrassing situation into a disaster.

After deploying an anchor or sea anchor, the next thing to do is try to restart the engine.

Troubleshooting

The first thing to remember is to keep calm. The problem may be easily fixed. Ask yourself:

- Is the fuel valve on?
- Is the fuel tank empty or low?
- Is the fuel filter dirty?
- Are fuel-line connections tight?
- Is a line wrapped around the propeller?
- Are the battery and battery cables clean and tight?
- Is the kill switch off?

If your problem is a leak in the fuel line, start the bilge blowers and don't try to restart the engine until the leak has been repaired and the fumes removed. Engine failure is bad, but an explosion and fire are worse.

If the engine is overheating, check the water cooling system. On a number of occasions I've seen garbage in the water wrap around the lower unit and plug the water intakes. Always check the intakes.

Small outboards take a beating in heavy weather. Sometimes they quit because their fuel line connection to the engine vibrates loose. This snap-type fitting usually can easily be reconnected.

Consult the engine manufacturer's operator's manual. You've got nothing to lose and everything to gain, so continue trying to find out why the motor won't start and make repairs as far as your mechanical ability will take you.

Steering failure can also leave you disabled and adrift.

Steering failure

Steering failure, often caused by broken cables or links, may be prevented by periodically inspecting the steering mechanism for wear or damage.

Managing steering failure

Although it is difficult in heavy weather, you might be able to:

- Steer with engines.
- Trail a warp of lines from one quarter or the other depending on which way you want to turn.
- Turn the outboard motor with lines which have been tied around it.
- Lash an oar or paddle to the outboard motor to turn the engine.

It would be almost impossible to repair or jury rig an inboard boat's rudder, because the rudder is located underneath the stern. With an inboard or inboard/outdrive engine your best option is to keep the rudder or outdrive straight and steer by creating friction. At slow speed drag something on one side, making the vessel turn.

With twin engines, steering failure is not as great a problem. Point the outboard motors or lower units straight back and turn with your power.

Most small boats only have one outboard engine. Since the boat steers by directional thrust of the motor, you can turn the boat if you can turn the engine. I've seen boaters get their outboards in a bear hug and turn them. Don't do this, because hanging out over the stern of your boat is risky.

A better way would be to tie a line to the motor, then wrap the line around the engine housing and bring the two ends back into the boat. With the lines you might be able to turn the motor a little bit.

Better yet, if you have a paddle or boat hook lash it to the motor and use it like a tiller to move the engine.

Whatever means you use to steer the boat — friction or turning the motor — it is important that you slow down. You should barely be making headway as you turn.

When attempts to restart the engine or rig a makeshift means of steering fail, call for help.

Call for help

Before you run down your batteries trying to start your engine, radio for help. National Park Rangers, Coast Guard employees and other rescue agencies are ready and willing to aid a boater who has a real emergency. Don't wait too long, thinking you might get going again. When you contact the rescue unit, clearly state your problem and position.

Remember: if you do get started, you can call off the cavalry, but if you don't get restarted you want help to arrive before your boat becomes surf splinters. And this is a definite possibility.

A final thought on engine failure: if it turns out it's just not your day and it looks like you are going to drift onto a lee shore, then you should think about how you can make it safely. In most cases it is best to stay with the boat and ride it all the way in.

Photo courtesy of Bill Jean

The operator of this cabin cruiser returning to Lake Mead Marina at night homed in on the lights of the marina but did not see the 10-foot-high breakwater until it was too late to stop or turn. The result: a grounding.

Abandon ship only as a last resort.

As the vessel enters the large breaker zone, capsizing is a very real possibility. Be prepared for this.

If you end up in the water, waves can smash you against the rocks, so protect your head with your arms. Go through the surf feet first so that your legs can absorb the shock if you slam into a rock.

Grounding

Several years ago I was called to rescue a large houseboat that had run aground on a steep, rocky leeward shore. When I arrived on the scene, the seas had pushed the heavy vessel onto the rocks. The boat was listing and the lower compartments were flooded. All the passengers had made it ashore.

The operator, an old man, asked me if I would recover his wallet and a few prize possessions. Being a rookie, and not yet wise to the power of the surf, I said yes.

I climbed up the high side of the hull, entered the dark, strangely tilted craft. The boat shook each time a wave slammed into it and rivers of water poured in through a broken window. I felt like I was on the *Titanic*, with an iceberg right outside knocking on the door.

As I raced to collect the operator's personal belongings, the rocking became more violent. Wood creaked and snapped.

Suddenly, I heard a loud crack. The entire seaward side of the cabin pitched toward me and daylight appeared in a widening gap between the bulkhead and the overhead.

I bolted from the cabin, bailed off the hull and raced up the beach. When I stopped and turned, I saw the boat break up. Within an hour, the vessel became a heap of splintered wood and fiberglass.

Could this accident have been prevented? Probably. If the operator had lowered an anchor off the bow — it might have required two or three anchors to hold it in the high seas — the vessel would not have drifted onto the lee shore. When disabled and adrift, an anchor is the only way to save a boat.

However, boats under power also run aground. To prevent this type of grounding the operator needs to:

- Know the waters and have a detailed chart.
- Check depth with a depth sounder or fishfinder.
- Act with caution, stop and proceed slowly.

In heavy weather, it is easier to avoid grounding than to deal with the problem after it occurs. It is wise to exaggerate your avoidance of any shallow water or shoals.

There may be a time when you strike an underwater object such as a rock, but do not become lodged upon it. Anytime you feel your boat strike something, immediately switch on the bilge pump and inspect for damage.

Getting free

A hard grounding in heavy weather is an emergency, but as with any crisis, you must stay calm and think clearly. First check for injuries to crew and passengers and for damage to the boat.

Before you make any attempt to free the vessel, be certain the hull is not holed and the propeller has not been damaged. If the boat is leaking and the seas are rough, getting off the bottom may be trading a bad problem for a worse problem.

What you need is not to get free, but to get help. Don't let pride keep you from making that call, because you will need the assistance of professional rescuers with proper equipment, such as a towline and a high-capacity pump.

By the way, the Rules of the Road state that you are supposed to make "some ... efficient sound signal" every two minutes. I take that to mean something other than swear words.

If you are not hard aground and there are no leaks or damage to your vessel, check the water depth under your propeller(s) then put the engine in reverse and try to ease off.

Next try turning from side to side and shifting weight in the boat to break the bottom's grip. Do not give a burst of power because you could damage your rudder or cause the raw water intakes of your engine to clog.

If turning and shifting weight fails to get the boat off the bottom, it is time to take action to keep the boat from being driven even harder aground. This means get out the anchors.

Secure the anchor rode to your stern cleats and set the anchors into the seas as far away from the boat as possible. This is one time when — if you are wearing a safety harness tethered to the vessel — you should throw the anchor.

With huge waves washing over the boat, this will be about all you can do. But in more moderate seas you might be able to use a dinghy to take the anchor out from the grounded vessel.

Another method of transporting the anchor away from the boat is to swim with it on buoyant cushions. Don't try this, even in light seas, without a safety harness with a line fastened to the boat.

And don't ever try this without wearing a PFD. This action is called kedging.

Kedging

If your propeller is a right hand, set the kedge (anchor) off the stern and slightly to the starboard. You can then alternately pull on the anchor line, which will rock the boat to starboard, then release the line and reverse the engine, which will rock the boat to port. This wiggle may be enough to free the vessel.

If you have two kedges, set one slightly to starboard and the other slightly to port. Pull first one line and then the other to rock the boat. This action, together with a little reverse power, may do the trick.

All the time you are grounded keep the kedge lines taut, because a wave may break the bottom suction and the taut line will ease you off. At any rate, a taut line will prevent the boat from going even harder aground.

In heavy weather, this is all you can do. Any action that involves leaving the vessel, such as trying to push the boat off the bottom or swimming for help, is too dangerous. All you can do now is wait for help.

Towing

It is best to wait for professional rescuers, if your boat is damaged. But if there is no apparent damage you might decide to accept help from another boater. Recreational boaters are usually friendly and helpful — and upon seeing your predicament, they may offer assistance. Before you accept this offer, consider the pros and cons.

Ask yourself:

- Is the other boater's vessel large enough to handle hostile seas and a tow?
- Does the other boater appear to be knowledgeable and competent?
- Would it be better to ask this boater to notify the Coast Guard or Rangers?

Towing a boat is not the same as towing a car (See Chapter 9). It's a job best left to professionals.

If you feel comfortable with the Good Samaritan's ability to help, fasten a floating messenger line, such as a ski rope, onto your towline, then throw the messenger line to the assisting vessel.

This does two things:

1. It keeps the assisting vessel at a safe distance. You don't want a collision.

2. It avoids the possibility of the towline fouling the boat's propeller.

When only the bow of your boat is grounded, attach the towline to the stern and pull straight back. Your boat should be towed off the bottom in the opposite direction to which it was going when it ran aground.

When a straight back pull does not free the boat, try alternating the pull from side to side in order to break the hull loose from the bottom.

After your boat is freed and the tow disengaged, the other boat should stand by to make certain you have no further problems. A leak or propeller damage may not be apparent until you attempt to make headway in deep water.

Last words

Engine failure and grounding in themselves are not life-threatening emergencies. Coast Guard statistics show that in 1996 less than 2 percent of all reported fatalities involved groundings and they list no statistics for fatalities due to engine failure.

In most instances, engine failure and grounding result in property damage rather than loss of life. However, in heavy weather either of these problems can rapidly escalate to flooding and sinking.

Your best protection is an anchor (or two anchors). Don't cast off without one.

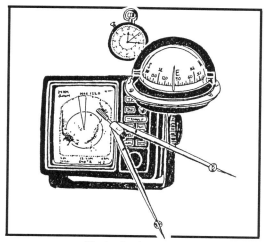

Navigation instruments

Chapter 8:

LOSS OF POSITION

What to do when you don't know where you are

The night I couldn't see where I was going was the most frightening experience of my boating career. New at this boating business and with my navigation skills as yet untested, my deckhand and I found ourselves in a narrow passage in a blinding downpour.

One minute I could make out a rocky island no more than a quarter mile to port, a cliff the same distance to starboard and a bend in the channel about a mile ahead. The next minute all I could see was a wall of rain. Visibility dropped to less than 15 feet. No land, no navigational lights, nothing but drumming rain.

In a panic, my deckhand switched on a searchlight and tried to locate the nearby rocks. The light only made things worse as the beam reflected off the rain.

If I continued on my present course, I would hit the bank in the bend ahead. If I stopped, the winds would drift the boat aground. The water was too deep to drop anchor.

I had no choice. I had to navigate blind through the channel, around the island and into open water. That night a problem that had only been an exercise drill before suddenly became a real crisis.

However, the boat was equipped with navigational instruments, charts and a log book that contained pre-canned courses, speeds and times. A situation that might have been an emergency for many boaters turned out to merely be a test of my ability to navigate by dead reckoning.

Piloting skills

Offshore boaters know they must be proficient navigators, but the inland boater also needs to have well-grounded skills in simple navigation and piloting.

At the very minimum, a boat operator has to know how to use a marine compass and how to read a chart. In addition to this limited knowledge, I believe every skipper should learn how to figure the boat's position, how to follow a course and how to perform dead reckoning navigation.

Since this is not a book on navigation, I will not attempt to teach you these skills. If you feel you lack competence in this area, I strongly recommend you either seek formal training or study a good piloting text. The US Coast Guard Auxiliary, US Power Squadron, or your local community college may offer a course in navigation or can tell you where the class is being taught. There are a number of good books on this subject, two of which are: *Chapman Piloting* and the USCG Auxiliary's *Boating Skills and Seamanship*.

You will also need some basic equipment.

Piloting Equipment

The two most important tools are a compass and a chart.

Compass

Every boat should have a steering compass mounted where the boat operator can easily see it. Even if you never intend to venture into unfamiliar water, you still will need a compass if you get caught out in fog or rain at night, or need to report your position in case of emergency.

A compass has a free-spinning magnetic pointer that, when adjusted for accuracy and mounted properly away from magnetic influences caused by metal or electrical currents, will always point to magnetic north. The pointer is placed within a ring calibrated into 360 degrees.

The compass allows you to determine your boat's heading quickly. When buying a compass, remember that a bigger compass will have better performance and is easier to read.

It is important to remember that your compass will not point to true north because of variation and deviation.

Variation is the difference between true north and the direction a magnetic compass points (magnetic north). Magnetic north is located in northern Canada, a considerable distance from true north. The amount of variation depends on your location. At Lake Mead, magnetic north is 14 degrees east of true north. You need to know the variation for your part of the country.

Deviation is caused by magnetic influences on the vessel. If deviation is less than 3 degrees a compass adjustment is probably not necessary. If deviation is greater than 3 degrees, you should have your compass adjusted, if it has calibration adjustments, or have a deviation table prepared for the compass.

Basic navigation techniques for developing courses from a chart or plotting bearings taken to create a position fix cannot be done simply by using your compass readings. You must make corrections for deviation and variation. Navigation texts and/or classes will teach you how to do this.

The accuracy of your compass should be checked. A simple way to check your compass for deviation is to position your vessel at a navigational marker, such as a buoy, and aim your bow directly at some distant object that can be identified on a chart. Take the bearing, correct it to true north and compare it to the bearing from the chart. If your compass is off more than a few degrees, you need to have it corrected. Navigation books or the manufacturer's manual for your compass describe how to calibrate the compass. In some localities there are compass adjusting services available.

A hand-bearing compass, in addition to your steering compass, is useful for plotting lines of position from land objects.

Taking a reading with a hand-bearing compass.

Since the same bearing can be found by sighting across your steering compass, the hand-bearing compass, while handy and easy to use, it is not an absolutely essential piece of equipment.

A final word of caution: When taking a reading with a hand-held compass, find a clear place to stand and brace yourself, because you will be looking at a distant object and not at the waves. You don't want a huge, unexpected wave to catch you unaware, sending you overboard.

Charts

Maps are drawings of land areas. Charts are drawings of water areas, and the wise boater always has an up-to-date chart. It provides a great deal of useful information in a compact, easy-to-read form.

For instance, charts show water depth, type of bottom, obstructions or hazards, shore details and location of buoys and other navigational aids. Charts are available for most navigable waterways. They cover such places as the Great Lakes, coastal areas and large rivers. However, for many smaller inland bodies of water, there are no true charts available. In these places some other type of map, such as a topographic map, will have to substitute. Next to the compass, charts are the most important navigation tool onboard.

Once you have learned some simple techniques of piloting, you will need more tools: parallel rulers, course protractor, divider and drafting compass.

Electronic equipment

The best solution to the problem of navigating in limited visibility is to have radar and GPS. These marine electronics can spoil you.

A good radar will paint the shoreline and detect large objects in the water. A GPS can pinpoint where you are to within 25 meters, in most cases. Electronic instruments can tell you where you are, which way to go, your speed and even how long it will take to reach your destination.

I realize these electronic spoilers are expensive and require a larger boat with space to accommodate them. However, the hand-held GPS is small enough to be used on any size boat and is becoming more affordable. You now can purchase a hand-held GPS for less than $100.

Radar is more expensive and takes up space. LORAN-C is a good system in areas where it can be used, but you have to do some computations to use it; you have to be more of a navigator, whereas the GPS gives you a direct reading. (For more information on marine electronics see Chapter 12.)

If you have these electronic tools, learn how to use them. Set your depth sounder to warn you if you are straying into shallow water. Use your radar to map the shoreline and help you avoid collisions with other boats. And use your GPS or equivalent system to track your position.

But don't rely solely on electronics. Like other machines, they have limitations and can fail. Heavy precipitation or large choppy seas, for example, can interfere with a radar's picture. Moisture can short out a depth sounder or GPS unit. Use your chart and compass, watch your instruments, but also watch where you are going.

Conditions which may cause loss of position

Loss of position almost always happens when there is limited visibility, such as at night or in heavy fog. A fatal accident which occurred on Lake Okeechobee, Florida, illustrates what can happen when the operator cannot see.

About 7 o'clock on the evening of December 10, 1995, a man and woman in an airboat set out with several other airboats from a point of land near Kissimmee River. The group planned to meet at Okee-Tantie and have dinner together.

However, it was dark, a front had moved in, winds were strong and waves were between 2 and 6 feet high. As they left the area near Kissimmee River, the operator of the doomed airboat lost sight of the other members of the group.

Attempting to locate the others he used a headlight hat. Then the headlight hat blew off, temporarily blinding him.

He tried to maintain course and speed while searching in the boat for the hat. When he finally recovered the light, he didn't realize he'd been blown off course.

Disoriented, the operator traveled out into the open lake. A large wave came over the bow; the vessel capsized and partially sank. The operator and a woman passenger put on PFDs and clung to the overturned boat.

Authorities were not notified of the missing craft until the next morning. Rescuers searched all day, but were unable to locate the boat and at sunset, December 11, the search was discontinued for the day.

A fisherman found the boat operator at about 7:00 the next morning. The woman had died during the night and the man, who had been exposed to the cold water for 35 hours, was suffering from hypothermia.

This story illustrates the dangers of improper night operation and brings us to the next subject.

Operating at night

When operating a boat at night you must:

- Use proper lighting.
- Protect your night vision.
- Proceed at a safe speed.

Use proper lighting

When you buy your boat, you should equip it with proper navigation lights (red, green and white) and be sure they are installed properly. I have heard of instances where the red and green side lights were on the wrong sides.

Your boat should have: a white masthead light with an arc of 225 degrees shining forward, a white stern light with an arc of 135 degrees shining aft, a green light on the starboard side and a red light on the port side. The side lights should each have an arc of 112.5 degrees shining from straight ahead to abaft the beam. Some vessels have a white all-around light instead of a masthead and stern light. The purpose of these lights is to let other boats see and identify you and for you to be able to see and identify others.

Lights should be shielded so they shine only in the prescribed direction and not into your boat. It is the masthead light that is the worst offender in this regard. A proper shield for a masthead light is an oblong plate underneath the light, so it cannot shine down onto the boat. Any scattered light that beams on the boat is damaging to your night vision.

Many people who are used to driving a car think that when you drive a boat at night you should turn on the headlights. Since a boat does not have headlights, they turn on a searchlight or the docking lights.

Several years ago on Lake Mead, a man was teaching his son what he thought was the proper way to operate at night. He instructed the boy to shine a spotlight on the beach to make sure he was maintaining a safe distance from the shore and then to shine the light ahead to see what was in front of the boat.

The boy followed his father's instructions, aiming the light toward the beach and then shining it on the water ahead, then back to the beach.

Suddenly, their 30-foot boat hit and ran over the bow of a 20-foot fishing boat anchored out in the lake. With their eyes blinded by the glare of their own beam, neither the boy nor his father saw the fishing boat, which incidentally was displaying its anchor lights. Fortunately the two people in the fishing vessel were not hurt.

When you turn on a spotlight you can see only what is in that beam of light. Every light has an effective range based on its brightness and local atmospheric conditions. Anything within this effective range can be seen, but anything outside the beam is obscured. You actually see less with a searchlight, not more.

The Rules of the Road state that a vessel can only display navigation lights when being operated at night. Running with docking lights or searchlight on is a violation of the law and it is dangerous. It prevents others from seeing your navigation lights and it prevents you from seeing others.

Protect your night vision

Light ruins your night vision. Have you ever, when sitting around a campfire at night, tried to see beyond the firelight? When you look away from the fire, all you can see is pitch black.

But if you walk away from the fire, your night vision begins to develop. It takes about 30 minutes or more for your eyes to adjust to optimum night vision; if you turn on a light, you destroy it. For this reason, instrument lights and cockpit cabin lights are usually red. Red light does not ruin your night vision.

If the airboat operator (during the accident detailed earlier in this chapter) had not turned on his spotlight, he might have been able to see the lights of the other boats in his group. He would also have been able to make out the reflective channel markers and the flashing beacon at the mouth of Kissimmee River.

Another word of advice: when operating at night, do not look directly at an object. The center of the retina in the eye sees color better than the outer area, which is better for seeing black and white. There is little or no color at night, so your peripheral vision is your best vision. Keep your eyes moving, scan the water and look off center. You will see more.

Proceed at safe speed

You should be able to stop in half the distance you can see. For example, if you can see 100 yards, you should be able to react and stop in 50 yards. Remember, a boat coming toward you will probably see you at the same time you see it and will need the same distance for stopping.

I worked an accident in which a cabin cruiser returning to the Lake Mead Marina one night at planing speed hit a 10-foot high breakwater. The operator could see the lights of the marina over the top of the breakwater. He homed in on the marina lights.

At the very last second he saw there was something between his boat and the lights. He turned hard and throttled back, but it was too late. The boat went up the breakwater and landed on top of it.

Fishermen on the breakwater scattered when they saw a speeding boat coming toward them, and then returned to see if anyone had been hurt after the accident. The people on board suffered minor cuts and bruises, but no one was significantly hurt.

The lesson is, when visibility is reduced, slow down. The people on board this cabin cruiser were very lucky.

Operating in fog

Thick fog can feel like being in a darkened room and even on a small boat, you may not be able to see the bow of your vessel.

As with other potential emergencies, avoidance is the best solution.

- Don't cast off in fog.
- Check the weather forecast before going out.
- Be aware of changing conditions.

When you are out on the water and you see a fog bank moving toward you, change course if possible. If you can't avoid the fog, record your position before the weather closes in and be ready to steer a dead reckoning course.

Marlin Bree in his book, *In the Teeth of the Northeaster*, describes the terror that will undoubtedly grip you if a fog bank catches you unawares. One moment Marlin was battling gale force wind and the next he was enveloped in fog.

He writes, "...my entire world turned white." He became completely disoriented. The sound of a harbor entryway foghorn seemed to come from the wrong direction. Using his compass he steered away from the land, which he could not see, toward the deeper water, saying as he did this, "So long as I have water under my keel, my boat is safe."

You should, as Marlin did, steer away from a shore you can't see and stay in deep water. Slow down and maintain a sharp lookout for other vessels and objects. If possible, get clear of the main channels and shipping lanes, drop your anchor and wait for the fog to lift.

The law requires you to give a sound signal every two minutes. If you don't have a horn, use any available means to make a noise: bang pot lids together, blow a whistle. This is to let others know where you are. Also turn on your running lights.

And listen. When you can't see, your ears become as important as your eyes. In fog, sounds can be deceptive. Sometimes sounds that are far away seem to be close, or nearby noises can skip over you and not be heard at all: it is difficult to determine the direction of the sound.

To avoid collision or running aground, stop the engine from time to time and listen for other boats and for the sounds of pounding surf.

Another trick is to lower some heavy object tied to a line from the bow. Since an anchor might grab the bottom and jerk out deck fittings, it is better to tie a couple of wrenches from your tool box on a line instead of using an anchor to determine depth. Drop the weight off the bow, run the line through a bow chock and bring it back to the helm. In this way you can hold the line as you steer. You will feel a vibration in the line when the weight hits bottom.

How far down should this weight hang? Use your own judgment. Every boat is different, every bottom is different and weather conditions vary.

Certainly the weight should hang down deeper than the draft of your boat. Remember your outdrive is also below the bottom of your boat, and even moving at a slow speed you will need to be alerted in time to react and stop. Give yourself a good margin for safety.

If you are equipped with a depth sounder or fish finder, you have another option. When the numbers on the depth sounder decrease, you are heading for a shore or some obstruction; head off.

By maintaining a safe position until the fog or heavy weather abates, you can remain relatively safe.

Your best protection is being prepared.

Preparation

You need to:

* Know your boating area.
* Know the meaning of the navigation aids in your area.
* Know how to take a position fix and navigate by dead reckoning.
* Practice navigation skills.

Know your boating area

You must know the location of landmarks, navigational aids and hazards. Talk to other boaters. Old-timers know the danger spots. People have been wrecking their boats on these shoals and reefs for years. Listen and learn from their bad experiences.

Also be certain you have an up-to-date chart.

Since most loss-of-position incidents occur at night, you should know your lake so well during the daytime that you won't have to worry at night.

Bob McKeever, president of the National Boating Safety Congress, says, "If you go out after dark and try to guess what's out there, you are in trouble."

Know the meaning of navigation aids

A navigation aid can be anything that assists the boater, such as buoys, day markers, lights and gongs. Color, shape and numbering all have significance. Some navigation aids provide regulatory information, some mark or warn of hazards, and some indicate a safe channel.

Ranger Nancy Bernard plots a course

There are several systems of navigation aids used in the United States. For example, one of these systems is the Uniform State Waterways System; another is the IALA-B (International Association of Lighthouse Authorities) system used in North America.

All of the systems are designed to aid boaters in navigating through safe waters and away from hazards. But since each system is different, it is important for you to know the one used in your locality.

In times of reduced visibility, you can navigate from one navigation aid or landmark to the next. Have someone look for the buoy lights and listen for sounds.

But keep in mind the fact that as water rises and falls in a lake, an anchored buoy can move away from its charted position. Also, buoys can be damaged or sunk, so don't rely entirely on them.

Know how to plot a course and take a position fix

Inland boaters do not need to worry about keeping a continuous plot going the way ocean-going sailors do. But when heavy weather is closing in, the wise freshwater skipper will begin minding his or her navigation.

You should learn how to take a position fix, read a chart and plot a course.

Practice navigation skills

You must practice piloting on fair weather days so you will be ready for bad weather. Plot a course and run it in the daytime before trying it at night.

Remember: dead reckoning is subject to mistakes. It is better to make those mistakes when you can see and correct them.

After you feel secure piloting the boat with a compass and chart during the day, try it at night. Navigating in darkness will build your confidence. Nothing beats back the veil of heavy weather at night like being able to trust your ability to chart a safe passage.

What you can do when lost

The one thing you definitely don't want to do is wander aimlessly. If you keep motoring along you will make it more difficult to figure out where you are and you will greatly increase your chances of running into something.

Four things you can do:
1. Get a position fix.
2. Turn to the windward.
3. Drop anchor.
4. Heave to.

Get a position fix

The very first thing you should do is try to get a position fix. Shoot at least two, more if possible, bearings to reference points. If you take two bearing lines of position at the same time, you can establish your vessel's position.

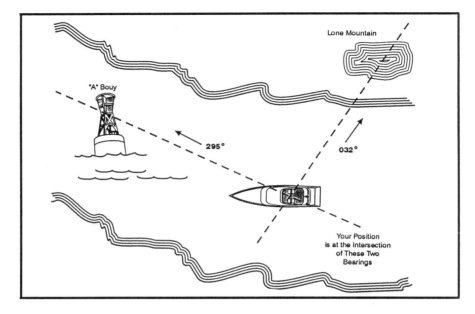

Fig. 8.1   Taking a position fix

The intersection of the two lines is where you are and is termed a FIX (See figure 8.1). Of course, you will need to do this before heavy weather, fog or darkness obscures all landmarks.

Once you know where you are, you can navigate by dead reckoning. To do this you need:

• a speedometer
• a compass
• a watch
• and a chart.

Start from where you are and plot a course on your chart to your destination.

Determine the course heading and distance for each leg of your route. Then steer the course and figure the distance traveled by time and speed. That is, figure the time it will take to arrive at your destination by dividing the distance by your speed (Miles on the Chart divided by Speed of Vessel = Travel Time).

Dead reckoning is simply calculating where you are going in relation to where you started using speed, time and direction. Reminder: to navigate by dead reckoning you must know the location of your starting point.

Here is a little trick I learned while working at Lake Meredith in Texas. Our compasses were not calibrated. Which means they were subject to error caused by deviation.

However, even though an uncalibrated compass may not measure direction correctly relative to magnetic north, it does indicate directions in a stable, repeatable way if local conditions on the vessel are unchanged. You can proceed from one point to another, read the compass when you are right on course and record that value.

For example, you can go from one channel marker to the next and record the compass heading. If you make the same run on another day, the reading will be the same provided you have not changed any magnetic influences near the compass.

In this way you will have a course heading you can use when it is foggy or during heavy weather at night. It is a good idea to record compass headings for all runs you regularly make, particularly a route you would follow during periods of reduced visibility.

Remember my story at the beginning of this chapter? This little trick is exactly how I managed to avoid a loss of position emergency. I simply looked in my log book, found the compass headings for that narrow channel and monitored my speed and time. I followed one compass heading until my watch indicated it was time to change headings.

A word of caution: you cannot add or subtract 180 degrees from the forward run to get the reverse heading because of residual deviation. Deviation, as I have explained, is caused by magnetic influence on the vessel.

An engine or electronic equipment on board produces a magnetic field with north and south poles, just as the earth has north and south poles. Since like poles have a tendency to repel and opposite poles tend to attract, a reciprocal heading may cause the magnetic influences on board to affect the compass in a different manner.

This deviation is called residual deviation and it is different for each direction.

Also, remember you can only use these previously established course headings if:

1. you know where you are before visibility becomes limited

2. you have previously established the heading and have it written down and

3. you are using the same boat and the same compass.

Turn to the windward

This only works on small inland bodies of water, but in those cases it works well. Don't try this on the Great Lakes.

When you realize you are completely disoriented in heavy weather, turn your boat into the seas. This course won't help you find where you are, but it will take you to safety.

By proceeding upwind you will eventually reach the windward (sheltered) shore. You'll know you are getting close to the windward shore even before you see land, because the waves will get smaller. From here you may be able to figure out where you are or you can shelter up and wait out the storm.

Drop anchor

If the seas are not too large or the water too deep, dropping anchor could be an option. However, you will need to guard against a dragging anchor. The theory here is: wait at anchor until conditions improve and you can safely get underway again.

Heave to

This is similar to dropping anchor, but it has the drawback that your location is not fixed. It is virtually impossible to hold a vessel in one place without an outside reference point.

Here, a GPS and a depth sounder will be invaluable. Without these navigational aids, I'd only use the heaving to technique when I was sure I had plenty of water around my boat.

Another technique for locating your position is to use a depth sounder, comparing the contours of the bottom to the contours on a chart. In this case you need to have some idea of where you are. Use this technique to pinpoint your location.

Also, in some cases, such as heavy fog, boaters have run the contours (using a depth sounder and chart) back to a safe harbor. Following the contours will only work if you are in a lake with a fairly uniform bottom.

If you are in an area with lots of little islands and shoals, this technique probably won't help you. You might find yourself going around an island. In any event, if you decide to try this, travel at a very cautious speed and be extra alert.

My best advice

The best way to deal with a loss-of-position emergency is not to lose your position in the first place.

Getting lost and becoming totally disoriented is a frightening experience, but with the tools and skills I have detailed in this chapter, you will not be without adequate resources to cope.

Heavy weather navigation is really nothing special. It only becomes a problem when you are untrained and unprepared. Every boat should have a compass and chart on board. Every operator should know how to use a compass and chart.

If you are on a large or unfamiliar lake, you probably should have electronic navigational aids.

Getting lost in a storm these days is a kind of self-inflicted wound.

A good set of binoculars: important for any boater

Chapter 9:

RESCUE

What to do (or not do) to aid another boater

One foul winter night, my supervisor and I were dispatched to search for two missing brothers. The wife of one of the men had reported that they were out on the lake and overdue. After a search of about an hour we spotted their signal fire.

Their boat had swamped and drifted ashore. The two men were not hurt, and after inspecting the vessel, my supervisor and I decided it had not suffered any damage from the accident, either. The boat appeared safe to tow.

We made a routine hook-up and following protocol had the two men put on their life jackets. The brothers elected to stay on board their boat and I stood on the aft deck of our vessel shining a searchlight, watching the tow, as we slowly pulled away from the shore.

All went well, until I suddenly noticed the vessel was towing strangely, with its bow extremely high. Speaking into my headset, I exclaimed, "She's towing funny!"

Immediately, my supervisor backed off the throttles. As we slowed and stopped, the boat behind us stood up on its end and sank stern first.

The tow line, instead of trailing astern, began rapidly angling downward. What was the water depth? I couldn't remember. I shouted, "How deep, how deep?"

The answer, "Eighty feet. Unhook."

I couldn't unhook. The tow line was already stretched tight under the weight of the sinking boat. We were trained professionals and we were in trouble.

I'd like to say I whipped out my knife — actually I fumbled for my knife and, after what seemed like an eternity, sawed through the line. The important point is: I had a knife and knew what to do.

Next we turned our attention to rescuing the two men who had been on the other boat. I panned the search light across white caps as we circled back.

Seconds ticked by without any sign of the brothers. Almost freezing water made quick rescue imperative. At last we spotted them — supported by their life jackets — too numb to swim.

After picking up the victims, we followed standard hypothermia treatment procedures — wrapped the two brothers in blankets and quickly transported them inside the boat's cabin to the marina.

Rescue, including towing, is dangerous. There are many things that can go wrong, so unless you are certain you can safely tow a disabled boat, don't attempt it. Often, it is better to stand by and wait for professionals who have the equipment and training to deal with emergencies.

If all you would ever have to do were stand by and wait, there would be no need for rescue training. But it has been estimated that 90 percent of all fatal and near fatal accidents occur where there is no professional help available.

Since in most cases there will not be an official rescuer standing by, many boaters have a marine radio — a tool for summoning the help of nearby boaters. If you have this equipment you should monitor Channel 16 at all times, especially during high seas, and be prepared to go to the aid of a fellow boater.

When you hear a mayday call, wait a few seconds, to give a professional rescue unit in the area the opportunity to respond. If no one answers, you should answer the call. If you can't render assistance, make every effort possible to notify the

Coast Guard, rangers or other patrol units in the area.

Sometimes simply standing by to give moral support will be of great importance to the operator and the crew of the distressed vessel. Even when you cannot offer direct assistance, do not leave a vessel that is disabled and adrift.

For most people, the desire to help someone who is in trouble is almost instinctive, but before you offer to help, think of your safety as well as the victims. Well-intentioned people have died trying to rescue someone when they did not have knowledge, training or the right equipment. You must make your decisions at the time of crisis based on your ability, your equipment, and the weather conditions you face.

You someday may need to perform one of these types of rescues:

1. Aiding a boat that is disabled and adrift — Towing.

2. Rescuing victims in the water —Water Rescue.

3. Rescuing persons or boats stranded on a shoreline — Shoreline Rescue.

Towing

Towing in fair weather is difficult, but towing in heavy weather can be dangerous. Before you offer to tow, consider the situation carefully and if possible obtain the latest weather report.

Then ask yourself these questions:

- Is the disabled boat in immediate jeopardy?
- Is the boat damaged or taking on water?
- And of course, the most important question — is a life in danger?

Also consider the alternatives to towing:

- Could you send a mayday message and stand by until professional help arrives?
- Would an anchor stabilize the situation?

If after weighing the pros and cons you decide to tow, be forewarned that you can damage your boat. You can also damage the vessel being towed. When you take on a tow, you become responsible and liable for the other vessel and its crew.

Cactus McHarg, volunteer rescuer at Lake Mead, says, "The most dangerous thing you can do with your boat — and that includes racing, skiing or whitewater boating — is tow another boat, because most boats are not built or rigged to tow."

Having made more than 4,000 tows and worn out five pairs of outboard engines during the past 40 years, Cactus is a qualified authority on the dangers of towing.

But Cactus has had to make this same judgment call that all boaters someday face — to tow or not to tow. He remembers being asked to make a rescue in March 1979. At that time his 22-foot aluminum boat was powered by two worn-out 45 h.p. engines. He'd been scrounging parts just to keep the motors operational. (Shortly after this incident a group of boaters at Lake Mead collected money and bought Cactus two new 70 h.p. outboards.)

But when called on to pick up three people and their boat stranded on a beach, he decided to gamble on his worn-out equipment in seas that were far from ideal for towing.

A member of the stranded group had suffered a heart attack. The victim and his daughter had been removed, but the other members of the party and the disabled boat were left for Cactus to help. Because there were 3- to 4-foot waves breaking on shore that day, he decided to do a touch and go rescue.

Thirty-one foot patrol boat used for heavy weather search and rescue.

Cactus remembers, "I put my bow on the beach just long enough to get them. And while we were picking them up, we had both engines in reverse to keep from going aground.....We hooked a towline on and started to back out when one engine quit. I reached over the side and cut the towline. About that time the other engine quit."

Two of the stranded boaters jumped into the water and held Cactus's boat off rocks the size of basketballs while he restarted one engine.

When he cleared the rocky beach, he backed around behind a point out of the wind and restarted the other engine. He had to leave the park visitors' grounded boat, but promised to return for it the next morning.

However, when he reached the marina, he discovered his boat was badly damaged. He said, "When we got in, we found we had cracked the hull along the keel, right under the bow about 18 inches on either side."

Even though Cactus couldn't remember hitting a rock on the shoreline where he'd made the rescue, he knew that is what had happened. Indeed, with this damage, he'd been lucky to make it back to the marina.

Cactus ended this story by saying, "Word got around that we had damn near lost the boat." He shook his head when he told me this as though he could not imagine how such a wild rumor ever got started.

Would he do it again? Yes, if a life were at risk.

If you are forced to tow in heavy weather, you must make a decision concerning how to care for the people on the disabled craft.

Generally, it is preferable to transfer everyone on board the disabled vessel to your boat. By bringing them aboard your vessel you have better control of their safety. But in heavy weather that may not be practical or even possible. When you come alongside to transfer people in high waves, you invite damage to both vessels and injury to people.

On the flip side, leaving people on the disabled vessel also puts them at risk. What if the tow sinks?

Remember my story at the beginning of this chapter? There is no right answer. You must be the judge of the best course of action for each case.

Transfer of people from one vessel to another

Only as a last resort, when it is absolutely necessary, should people be moved from one boat to another in high seas. The boats will slam together. You risk vessel damage.

But the big problem is that people can be seriously injured. Falls in the boats or overboard are likely and a hand or foot caught between the two vessels will be crushed.

If both vessels are capable of maneuvering you should rig plenty of fenders, turn both vessels into the seas and heave to. This will make as stable a platform as possible.

With both boats directed into the wind, the rescue craft eases alongside the other boat. A line should be tossed from one boat to the other and used to hold the boats together. Do not reach across with your hands.

However, if you are aiding a disabled boat, you cannot do this. You cannot turn both vessels into the oncoming waves to establish a more stable platform for the transfer.

The disabled boat is going to be at its drift angle and rolling significantly. This is why it is not a good idea to take people off a disabled boat in high seas. If you must make a transfer, the larger vessel should be on the windward side, because:

1. The larger vessel will provide some shelter for the smaller vessel.

2. A bigger boat will drift faster than a small one. This faster drift will hold the two vessels together while the transfer is made.

Come alongside with your fenders rigged and be as careful as possible. With a firm, forceful voice instruct the people on the disabled boat not to reach out or let any part of their bodies extend over the gunwales of their boat.

To prevent falls, tell the passengers not to jump or lunge, and when you are ready to make the transfer, extend a boat hook to assist the passengers in leaving the disabled boat.

Say, Hold on. Ready. Step now!

Make the transfer quickly. As soon as the transfer is completed the boats should separate.

After solving the problem of transferring people or electing to leave them on board the disabled vessel, you must face the difficulty of making the hookup.

Vessel prepares to come alongside: fenders are rigged and line is ready for use.

When the water is smooth, you can boat up next to the disabled craft, reach out and attach the towline. But in heavy seas this can be very tricky and potentially the most dangerous part of the operation.

For safety you should have the right equipment.

Towing equipment

Professionals — National Park Service Rangers, Coast Guard patrolmen, officers of various state boating safety agencies and members of volunteer rescue organizations — use towlines, bridles, deck fittings and hardware, fenders, fender boards, boat hooks, kicker hooks, heaving lines or throw bags, drogues and chafing gear. As a nonprofessional, you probably will not have all of these tools at your disposal, but the more you have the better off you will be when you need to tow.

Towline — This is your most important piece of equipment. At Lake Mead we use half-inch double braided nylon line. As a second choice I would suggest twisted nylon. Because this synthetic line stretches, it is better able to absorb the shock load it will be subjected to when towing. Polypropylene also is good in heavy weather because it floats. I avoid natural fiber lines because they deteriorate rapidly in our boating area. Search-and-rescue boats often carry as much as 300 feet of towline. I would recommend that the recreational boater have 100 feet of towline on board.

The snap on the end is as important as the towline. Use a stainless steel or galvanized metal marine snap hook. Don't use hooks of zamac metal or a mountain climber's carabineer.

A friend of mine made the mistake of using a carabineer and ended up in the hospital when the strain of the tow straightened it out. Released, the clip shot through the air like a bullet, hitting him in the leg with tremendous force.

Deck Fittings and Hardware — A word of warning — the cleats and deck fittings on your boat may not be stout enough to hold when you tow or are towed. Some of them are of poor quality pot metal.

Many cleats on recreational boats are simply screwed into the fiberglass. When a strain is put on them, they pop loose. Before attaching a towline to a fitting, make certain the hardware is secured to the deck with through-bolts and backing plates.

The bow eyebolt is usually a secure fitting. However, houseboats and other large non-trailerable boats often do not have eyebolts and their deck cleats may not hold.

This Park Service vessel is equipped for towing, but most recreational boats are not built or rigged to properly tow.

When a secure deck fitting cannot be found there are several possible options:

- Several cleats of uncertain holding strength can be bridled together to distribute the strain.
- On some sailboats, a line can be made fast around the base of the mast.
- On some cruisers and houseboats, a line can be wrapped completely around the superstructure.

A little creative ingenuity will usually produce a suitable attachment point.

Towing Bridle — These are devices that spread the strain of the tow over two or more attachment points. They can be relatively sophisticated with a pulley to constantly equalize the load on the attachment points (See Figure 9.1) or they can be simple fixed lines.

A towing bridle should be made of double-braided nylon. The breaking strength of the bridle should be equal to or greater than the strength of the towline. A bridle can be used on either the towing or towed vessel or both.

Messenger Line — A messenger is a light line that will float. It is attached to the towline and thrown or floated to the disabled boat. In rough weather a messenger line is often the only way to pass a towline to another vessel. There are several types of these lines and devices for delivering them on the market.

An excellent one is the throw rope bag, which can be used for a man overboard emergency as well as for passing a towline. The bag contains about 70 feet of polypropylene line and it is easy to toss accurately.

Drogue — This will reduce yawing when attached to the stern of the towed boat. It can also be used to slow and stabilize a towed boat in a following sea. The average recreational boater will have little or no need for this piece of equipment, but should the need arise a sturdy bucket with a hole in it can sometimes be used as a drogue.

Chafing Gear — This can be canvas, split rubber hose or anything that will protect your line at points of wear, such as the edge of a deck or around a chock.

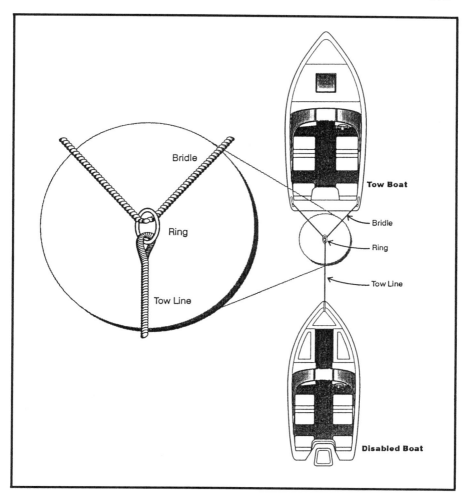

Fig. 9.1   Towing bridle

Almost as important as having the right equipment is caring for and storing it properly. Keep your lines free from tangles, easily accessible, and to prevent rot, you should store natural fiber line where it will stay dry. Inspect lines and hooks regularly for signs of wear, and always inspect equipment after a heavy tow when there has been severe stress and shock loading.

We have considered the alternatives to towing and looked at the proper equipment on board. The next topic is learning how to tow.

Approach and hook up

Step One. Hail the disabled boat and ask all aboard to put on their PFDs. Next find out what the problem is and decide on the appropriate action. If possible, make a complete circle around the vessel to check it from every direction. Tell your crew and the crew of the disabled boat what you plan to do and what, if anything, you want them to do.

It is at this point that you must decide if you are going to remove the boat's occupants. If you decide to transfer people, rig plenty of fenders and take every precaution to make sure no one falls overboard or gets an arm or leg between the vessels. In severe weather, getting people off the boat may not be possible. If you must leave people on the disabled vessel, you should establish some form of communication between the two boats — radio communication or even agreed-upon hand signals.

Step Two. Decide how you will approach the boat to make the hookup. In most cases, the disabled boat will be drifting with a stern quarter into the wind. The best approach is to proceed downwind far enough so you can turn and come back to the vessel heading directly into the wind. This is the approach the Coast Guard recommends for heavy seas and is called Crossing the T Approach.

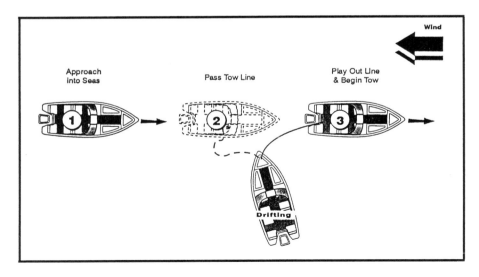

Fig. 9.2   Approach & hook up

When you reach a point in front of the disabled vessel's bow, pause for a few seconds and pass the towline (Figure 9.2). Attempts to approach from any other direction will be more difficult and risky.

Step Three. Pass the towline and make the hookup. This task requires considerable concentration and often helmsman and crew become so intent on passing the line that they forget to watch for underwater obstructions, floating debris or large, freak waves. If possible, assign someone to be a lookout.

There are several methods for passing the line and making the hookup. Generally, the best way is the one that requires the least assistance from the crew of the disabled boat. In moderate conditions, with a boat hook and a kicker hook, you and a deckhand can complete the hookup by yourselves. As you pass within reach, a trained deckhand can reach out and snap the towline directly into the disabled boat's bow eyebolt.

However, this method requires practice and coordination between the helmsman and the deckhand (Figure 9.3).

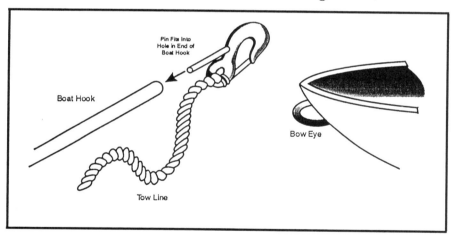

Fig. 9.3　　Boat hook method

When seas are rough, the boat hook method is not practical, because you must keep a greater distance between your vessel and the disabled vessel. Once, during a training exercise, I witnessed what can happen.

Two-foot waves completely frustrated the student at the helm. Over and over we circled past the bow of the mock disabled boat as the students unsuccessfully tried to snag the vessel's bow eyebolt with the boat hook and towline.

Finally, the students decided to try a much closer pass. All went well until we were directly in front of the much larger disabled craft, then the bigger boat suddenly raised out of the water with a wave and crashed down on our smaller boat. The bow eyebolt the students had been so intent upon knocked a two-inch-diameter hole in the thin fiberglass skin of our vessel.

When the boat hook method is not practical, you must rely on help from the crew of the other boat. If it were a perfect world we would all have line guns and could shoot a line over and be done with it.

But 99 percent of us don't have such a tool, so we have to manually throw a line across to the other vessel.

For short passes of less than 40 feet, it is usually easiest to coil and throw the end of the towline. Remember though, there is a steel missile called a hook on the end of the line which can harm a boat or a person if it hits them.

Yell, "Heads up!" before throwing and do not toss directly at the boat or the people on it. Aim over the disabled craft and try to make the hook land in the water on the far side.

For longer passes, you'll need a messenger line. The best heaving lines are lightweight lines stuffed into throw bags. By holding the free end of the line and winding up, you can throw a line bag a long distance — easily 60 to 75 feet.

Once the disabled boat's crew has the messenger line you can tie the towline onto it; they can haul the line across and complete the hookup. However, you should watch to make certain the line is secured in a safe and workable manner.

Getting underway with a tow

If you are doing it right, you are doing it slow. Motor up slowly to a position off the disabled boats bow, pause and pass the towline. After the line is hooked to the bow eyebolt, ease forward while paying out the line.

Here is where a costly mistake is often made. Do not throw the towline overboard as you pull away. Chances are you'll regret it if you do. Even a floating towline can foul your propeller if it is washed up and under your stern by a wave.

Bob McKeever (left) watches as student instructor Jeff Lewis demonstrates attaching a kicker hook to a boat hook. With this equipment, a trained deckhand can reach out and snap a towline directly into the disabled boat's eyebolt.

I knew a ranger who had this frustrating experience. As he attempted to rescue a vessel on a leeward shore, a loop of slack line got into his propeller. Instantly, his engine stalled and within a matter of seconds his patrol boat washed up on the rocks next to the boat he was trying to help. To avoid fouling your propeller, pay the line out slowly. Allow no slack to form. If slack develops, reel it aboard quickly.

There are risks at every stage of the towing operation. Crew members can fall, deck fittings can be pulled loose, towlines can part and propellers can get fouled by slack lines. A Coast Guard manual for its trained professional rescuers issues this warning, "Nearly everything you do when you take a boat in tow is potentially dangerous." In heavy weather it is even more dangerous.

Safety

To mitigate risks, the following precautions should be observed:

- Do not attempt a tow that is beyond your capabilities or the capabilities of your vessel.

- Be sure all crew members wear proper safety gear — PFDs, exposure coveralls (if appropriate), safety harness (if a fall overboard is possible), eye protection and leather gloves.
- Make sure all persons on the disabled craft are also wearing PFDs and/or survival suits.
- A knife should be immediately available in case a tow line needs to be cut.
- Use a towline that floats of not less than one-half inch in diameter with marine rated hooks that have a breaking strength greater than the line.
- Hand tend the towline until it is secured to the other vessel. Keep it clear of your propeller.
- Allow no one, on either vessel, to sit or stand in alignment with the towline.
- Assign a tow watch. This should be someone other than the operator to watch the tow at all times.
- When towing at night, display proper navigation lights and/or illuminate the towed vessel with a searchlight.
- If people are left aboard the disabled craft, be prepared to rescue them. Have lines and Type IV PFDs ready.

Underway with a tow

It is best to use a long towline in heavy weather. I use a 100-foot line because a long line acts as a shock absorber. The irregular forces caused by waves are called shock loads. Without the energy-absorbing stretch of a good towline, these shock loads can cause deck fittings or line to fail. Since a parted line can snap back with the force of a .30 caliber bullet, never stand where you might be hit.

Pay out as much towline as you need — in heavy weather this will probably be your entire 100-foot line — while slowly accelerating to your towing speed. In high seas, you will move very slowly.

The skipper should be able to give his full attention to the operation of his craft and should not have to constantly look back to check the tow. Assign one crew member to monitor the tow.

Your observer at the stern should have a sharp knife and be ready to cut the tow immediately if necessary.

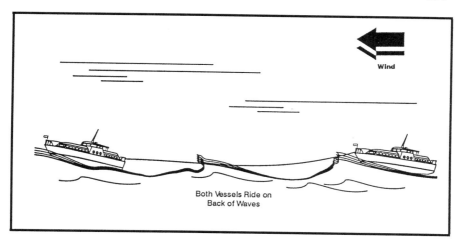

Fig. 9.4   Towing in step

If you are lucky, your destination will lie into a head sea and the tow will be relatively simple. But when you are forced to tow in a beam sea your best maneuver is to tack. Or if returning to the harbor puts you in a following sea, you will need to tow in step (Figure 9.4) to avoid constant slacking and jerking on the line. Towing in step means both boats reach the crest of a wave at the same time. To do this, you adjust your speed, length of towline or alter course so that you cross swells diagonally.

Some problems and special towing situations are: yawing, sinking and towing at night or in fog.

Yawing

Severe yawing, or swerving sideways, in heavy seas can cause the disabled vessel to capsize and/or sink. To prevent yawing:

- Slow down.
- Use a bridle on the towing vessel to distribute the strain.
- Shorten the towline.
- Make sure the towed boat is trim with no list and bow slightly higher than stern.
- Make certain that the towed vessel's helm, i.e. rudder or outdrive, is straight.
- Deploy a drogue from the stern of the towed boat.

Sinking

If your tow sinks in deep water, you have only one choice — cut the towline. Your number one concern in this event is the safety of any persons left on board the towed vessel. Prepare for water rescue.

In shallow water with nobody on the sinking vessel and a long towline, you could allow the line to pay out as the towed boat goes down.

However, there are dangers:

- A slack line could foul the propeller on the towing vessel.
- A crew person could become tangled in a slack line and be pulled overboard.
- An error in calculating either the depth of the water or the length of the towline could sink the towing vessel.

A safer course of action would be: stop the towing vessel, allow the line to go slack, unhook quickly and fasten a flotation device such as a life jacket to the line to mark the place so the vessel can be salvaged.

Night towing

When towing at night, turn on the towed boat's navigation lights or shine a searchlight on the disabled vessel.

Do not rely on the Rules of the Road configuration of lights which indicate towing to prevent collision. Many recreational boaters do not know what they mean, so watch for other boaters.

Towing in fog

In fog, the towing vessel sounds one long blast and two short blasts of the horn every two minutes.

The vessel being towed (if manned) should sound one long and three short blasts immediately after the towing vessel's signal.

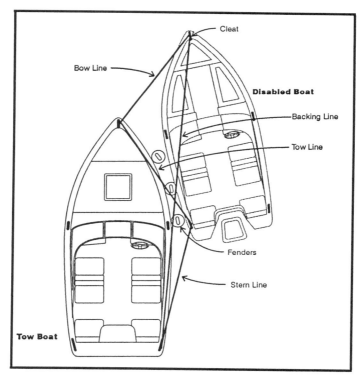

Fig. 9.5 Side tow

Ending the tow

The final problem is trying to get up to the dock with a tow. In heavy weather, this can be a real challenge. Upon entering the harbor, slow down and stop. Remember a boat being towed will not stop when your boat stops, so decelerate slowly, rig fenders and keep the line away from the propeller.

A side tow (see Figure 9.5). is good strategy in tight-congested areas. If you feel this can be accomplished safely, communicate your intention to your crew and the crew of the disabled boat. Tell them which side the tow will be taken on and then take in the slack line as the towed boat drifts toward your vessel. Rig plenty of fenders and/or fender boards.

Position the towed vessel alongside and slightly ahead of your vessel. It is important for your stern to be 3 to 4 feet behind the stern of the boat you going to tow, and the disabled vessel should be angled slightly toward the bow of your boat.

When you tow alongside, the towed boat becomes a drag on

that side. For example, if the tow is on the port side, both boats will tend to turn toward port. You can offset this tendency by placing the disabled vessel at an angle with its stern a few feet ahead of your stern. Water pressure against the hull of the angled vessel will tend to counteract the turning force of drag when the boat is moving.

Steps for rigging a tow alongside:

- Without unhooking the tow line from the disabled boat's bow, run the line to a stern cleat on your boat and secure it.
- Using the remainder of the towline, run it back across to the stern of the towed boat and secure it.
- Pass the line from the stern cleat to a cleat on your bow.
- Pass the line back to a cleat on the towed boat's bow

With this configuration you can boat to the dock and the towed vessel will not shift as you maneuver. Remember that your steerage will be greatly reduced by a side tow. Your boat will turn easily to the side that the towed boat is on, but it will turn sluggishly in the opposite direction. Plan your docking and try to make most of the turns toward the more responsive side.

A skilled operator can maneuver a side-towed boat with ease. However, during a severe storm, harbor conditions may not permit this. In this case, if you feel confident in your ability, shorten the towline to approximately 50 feet and move with the stern tow slowly toward the dock. When docking your vessel back up as little as possible and tend the towline carefully. Secure your boat first, then pull the towed boat into position by hand.

If the towed boat is too big to manipulate in this way or you are unsure of your ability, advise the disabled boat to drop anchor and wait for better weather or call for a professional tow. Towing is not simple. I suggest you practice in fair weather before attempting a tow in rough seas.

Water rescue

I believe every boater should know how to swim, have some first aid training and know how to do CPR (cardiopulmonary resuscitation). If you don't have these skills, I strongly advise you to acquire them because there is more to heavy weather water rescue than boat handling and learning the techniques for assisting a victim in the water.

However, swimming instruction and first aid are outside the scope of this book. My purpose is to provide information that will allow you to make a rescue with the skills you have should you be required to do so during heavy weather.

When called upon to save a life, you will need some basic equipment.

Rescue equipment

You should have:

- A Type IV PFD with a 75-foot floating line attached
- A 75-foot throw line in a throw bag
- A boat hook
- Some method of getting a person out of the water
- Several wool blankets
- A first aid kit.

Professional search-and-rescue boats will carry much more rescue equipment, but this list will provide you with most of the things you will need.

Responding to a water rescue

If you are called upon to rescue someone in heavy weather, you should treat it as a life-threatening emergency. You should go to the scene of the accident as rapidly as possible, and while en route crew members should get rescue equipment ready for use.

This all seems to be common sense, yet time and time again I have seen inappropriate responses to emergencies.

The worst example of an inappropriate response was by a professional rescuer. I overheard a radio call from our dispatch center to a fellow officer. The dispatcher relayed information reported by a boater that a vessel with two men on board had sunk about a mile out from the harbor.

After being in the water for a short time, one of the two men was picked up by a passing boat.

The other man, who was not wearing a PFD, was still missing. In a response that sounded annoyed, the officer said he would "make his way back and check it out," after he finished his present business. That business was writing a traffic ticket.

Making the rescue

Several years ago when I was stationed at Lake Meredith, Texas, my one-man crew and I were often called on to make water rescues in heavy weather. One typical rescue happened late on a stormy afternoon.

Wind howled, sideways rain hammered the windshield and spray lashed our bow, when suddenly the radio crackled, "Two forty-one, dispatch. We have a report of a vessel sinking off Fritch Fortress." Immediately I turned onto a new course heading.

With the seas now on our beam, the boat rolled wildly and my partner clipped on his lifeline before he began flaking out a rescue line to get it ready for use. In the fading light of evening, I scanned the water as I eased the throttles forward. I knew if we didn't make the rescue before dark, our job would be ten times harder.

Through rivulets of water washing down the windshield, we saw something bobbing on the crest of a distant wave. It was the point of a boat's bow with a man clinging to it. My deckhand moved to the after deck. He would have no more than 30 seconds after I pulled alongside the victim to make the rescue. Holding the boat steady any longer would be almost impossible, and in the rough seas I could not leave the controls to help him.

We closed the distance. Headed into the oncoming waves, the deck steadied. My partner stood poised with ring buoy and line in hand. Fifty feet, 30 feet, then a gust of wind pushed the bow off course. Quickly, I countered and eased the vessel back on track. At 15 feet I snapped the throttles into idle and yelled, "Okay! Do it!"

My deckhand swung the buoy over his head. Braced against the wind, he put every ounce of muscle into the pitch. The red-

and-white ring arched up...the yellow line snaked out...and the victim reached up to meet the throw.

This was a good rescue. The boat was well equipped and my deckhand and I were trained and ready. This was just one of the dozens of rescues I have made. It's one I like to remember because everything went well.

If you spend any time at all on the water, sooner or later you will have to make a rescue. When that moment comes, the pressure will be intense and you cannot fail. Your only defense is to prepare ahead of time. Practice the skills you will need.

Although you must hurry to the scene, once you arrive you need to slow down to make the rescue. Whenever possible, approach a victim from downwind, so that when heading directly toward the person you are also heading directly into the wind and waves. In some cases, this may require you to travel past the victim before turning around and heading back into the wind. (This procedure is detailed in Chapter 6, Man Overboard.)

Four Retrieval Options:

1. Approach close enough to throw a line or a ring buoy with a line attached to the victim. Using the line pull the person in the water up to the boat.

2. Approach close enough to reach the victim with a boat hook and pull him or her up to the boat.

3. Bring the boat close beside the victim. Reach out and lift him or her into the boat.

4. Deploy a rescue swimmer to help the victim.

Option one, throwing a line and pulling the swimmer in, is the preferred method of retrieval, the one you should consider first. Option four, sending out a rescuer, should be attempted only if you have a trained professional rescue swimmer on board and the victim is injured or unconscious.

One day a few years ago when I was working beach patrol in the patrol car and Cactus McHarg and his wife, Mary (now deceased) were operating the volunteer rescue boat, we had four water rescues in one afternoon. The first victim was reported to me by sail boarders on Wind Surfer Beach. One of the group had gone out and had not returned. I called Cactus and Mary. Cactus told me afterward that it took about 20 minutes to find the surfer. The young man without a life jacket was hanging onto his board. Exhausted and suffering from hypothermia, the surfer was unable to move. Cactus hooked him with a boat hook and pulled him alongside and with Mary on one side and Cactus on the other, they lifted him into the boat. About that time I took a report of a second overdue sail boarder. I relayed the information to Cactus and 10 minutes later they made that rescue.

I requested an ambulance and drove on to check the swimming beach, where I spotted a swimmer beyond the swim buoy. With a 35-mile-an-hour wind blowing off the beach, she was in real trouble. I got on the radio and called Cactus. He had just unloaded the two wind surfers into an ambulance.

Standing on top of the patrol car, I watched the struggling swimmer and waited. My responsibility was to keep my eyes on the girl (or the spot where she was last seen, if she went under) and direct the rescue boat. The wind blew the girl away from shore faster than she could swim, but Cactus didn't waste any time getting there.

As the rescue boat arrived, the exhausted swimmer stopped struggling. Mary threw a ring buoy on a line. It landed directly in front of the girl, but the victim did not reach for it. Quickly, Mary took over the helm and Cactus moved into position for the rescue. The boat swooped in close as the girl went under. Cactus reached over the side, and his arm went under the water to grab a handful of hair. While this was not a textbook rescue, it worked.

I suddenly spotted another girl in trouble. As Cactus checked the first victim and prepared to begin CPR, Mary drove toward the second victim. They picked up the second girl and brought them both in.

These last two victims were rescued close to shore. While the wind blowing off the beach had contributed to the problem, it also made a quick rescue possible. If the wind had been blowing onto the shore, it would have created dangerous surf conditions.

Shoreline rescue

Shoreline rescue almost always means leeward shoreline rescue because that's where a disabled vessel comes to rest during heavy weather. Based on personal experience, I know this to be true.

I did a tour of duty as a boating officer in the Midwest. In the summer, we got the most beautiful and powerful thunderstorms. After each storm, we circled the lake rescuing its victims. Very rarely would we come upon a vessel in trouble in open water and almost never on the windward shore. But we always found swamped boats along the lee shore.

Let me reemphasize, stay out of the surf zone. The shallow water will lessen your vessel's maneuverability. When a breaker moves through shallow water, it leaves a trail of aerated water which affects propellers and rudder.

Propellers will not give as much thrust and rudders will not direct propeller force as effectively. The surf is a trap, one that has sprung on the unwary and experienced alike.

The following story illustrates what can happen to even a professional rescuer.

One day when the winds were blowing 30 to 35 miles per hour and the waves were running three feet or more, a sailboat ran aground on a reef. A fellow ranger received the report and responded. Upon arriving at the scene, the ranger saw an elderly man standing on an island reef near his sailboat.

Although the old man was unhappy about this turn of events, he was safe and secure for the time being and not in need of immediate rescue.

The ranger, however, unwisely decided to attempt a rescue. As he approached the reef, he struck rocks, killing his engine and grounding his boat in the pounding surf. In an even more unwise move, he exited his boat in a futile attempt to push the vessel off the rocks. Realizing this wouldn't work, he tried to climb back aboard, but couldn't.

By the time the incident was over, the ranger's boat was damaged, his back was injured and he very nearly drowned. The old man standing on the island suffered no injuries.

Surf rescue

The following information is intended only to complete our discussion of rescue. Recreational boaters should never venture into heavy surf.

If you try to maneuver a boat to make a pickup in breaking waves, you will be in great danger of swamping, capsizing or going aground. Even qualified rescue crews are at great risk. For this reason, Coast Guard surf rescue boats are self righting, self bailing and watertight; the crews are strapped in, wear safety helmets and have specially designed PFDs and exposure suits. Because of the inherent danger, the rescue of a victim caught in the surf should generally be made from shore.

When professionals, such as Coast Guard rescuers, make a surf rescue they watch for a period of relative calm to make their approach. They try to move in on the last breaker in a series. If water depth allows, they go past the victim toward the beach, turn and approach into the waves. The crew will try to make a quick recovery as the operator holds the boat with minimal power to meet the surf.

This may sound easy, but it is not. Two National Park Service volunteers found out about the dangers of surf when they attempted to follow this procedure. With a park visitor on board, the volunteers were dispatched to rescue the visitor's stranded friend and his grounded boat from a leeward beach.

The volunteers approached the beach, quickly hooked around, got the bow pointed out into the waves and were about to float a line to shore, when the "helpful" visitor jumped off the back of the boat intending to swim ashore with the towline.

The boat operator immediately shut down the engine, because the visitor in the water was much too close to the propellers. Suddenly a wave swung the boat around and drove it onto the beach. In a few seconds the boat swamped. Batteries, radios, electrical equipment — everything went under water.

Late that night, the volunteer's wives called the Park Service to find out why their husbands had not come home. A search-and-rescue operation was begun and about one o'clock in the morning we found them cold and shivering on the shore.

My advice is: do not attempt a leeward shore rescue. One small mistake can put you and your craft in great jeopardy.

Making a shoreline rescue

Helping someone in trouble is one thing, but getting yourself in trouble for replaceable property is quite another thing. If you should ever find yourself looking at a person on shore frantically waving for help, stop and think.

- Look the situation over and try to determine if the problem is a life-threatening emergency.
- Ask yourself: Is anyone injured and needing immediate evacuation?
- Is anyone at risk of further harm?
- Is everyone on shore?

Are there other options to resolve the problem? Such as:

- Returning after the storm when it is safe to beach
- Rescuing the victims by land
- Sending for a helicopter to perform the rescue
- Beaching in a sheltered nearby cove and walking to the victims

Communicate with the victims. If you have a marine radio or a cellular telephone to make contact, that's great — but chances are that you won't. Over the roar of wind, breakers and your engine, it is doubtful you will be able to hear shouts from those on shore.

However, because of the wind direction they may be able to hear you. Communicate by having the victims raise one arm for yes and two for no as you ask a series of questions.

Good first questions:

- Is anybody missing?
- Is anybody hurt?
- Can you wait until conditions are better for rescue?

If waiting for better conditions is not an option and rescue by any other means is not possible, then you have to make the rescue.

This means you will probably have to beach your vessel.

Beaching

Beaching on a shoreline with surf of any size is to be avoided. There are vessels designed to do this, but recreational boats were not made for surf conditions.

The only realistic solution is to look for an area nearby where you can safely beach. The best place is a protected windward shoreline, such as the back side of an island, peninsula or cove. In light seas, you can beach on a shoreline where seas are running roughly parallel to the beach.

When evaluating a beach (Figure 9.6) look for:

- A sheltered area where the waves are smaller.
- A landing zone least likely to damage your hull. Choose a sandy beach over gravel, and gravel over rocks.
- Deep water. Choose deep water over shallow water and avoid areas with reefs and other underwater obstructions. The shoreline you see is a good indicator of what lies below. A gradual sloping beach probably means shallow water; a steep bank usually indicates deep water right up to the shoreline.

Contrary to what some people think, beaching is not simply pointing the bow toward land and motoring until you hit something solid.

Here is a five-step procedure:

1. Circle close to the beach to check the water depth and look for submerged hazards. If sea conditions permit, assign a crew member to maintain a lookout on the bow.

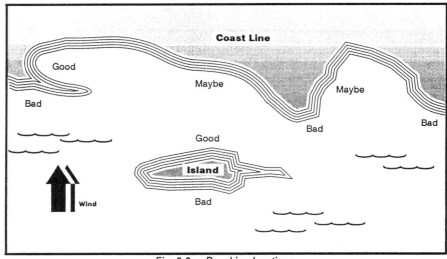

Fig. 9.6   Beaching locations

Ridged hull inflatable boat (RHIB). Size ranges from 10 feet to more than 30 feet in length. The Coast Guard Avon RHIB is 10 meters in length.

Government agencies use this safe and stable vessel for rescue work. Shallow draft and low freeboard make it very functional for going onto beaches or picking up victims in hostile seas.

Turn on your depth sounder, if you have one, and set the shallow water alarm to sound when you are in water 2 to 3 feet deeper than your draft.

2. After your survey pass, when you are fairly certain of underwater conditions, start your run to the beach. Move at the slowest speed possible while still maintaining control of the boat. Float in neutral as much as you can, because if you strike something when your propellers aren't turning there will probably be little or no damage.

3. Just before your bow touches the beach, check to make sure you have sufficient water around your propellers, then reverse engines. The bow will gently contact the land. There should be no noticeable collision.

4. When the bow touches the shore, shift back into forward and let the vessel's engines push and hold you on the beach. Remain in forward gear. New operators sometimes feel nervous about this maneuver and prematurely shift to neutral or reverse.

Do not go into reverse unless you intend to leave the beach. If there is a cross wind your vessel will begin to turn and broach on the beach. To counteract this simply turn the helm to move the vessel's stern into the wind. (Figure 9.7)

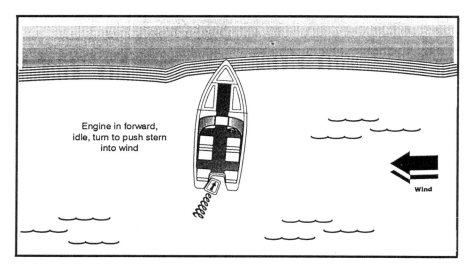

Engine in forward,
idle, turn to push stern
into wind

Wind

Fig. 9.7   Holding a position on a beach in a cross wind

5. Do not leave the helm while engines are in gear. Crew members can disembark while the operator remains on the boat. If all hands including the operator are needed on shore, turn the motor off and secure the boat with at least two lines. One line should run from the bow to a beach anchor point. A second line should run from the windward side of the stern at about a 45-degree angle to the shore.

There are times when the water conditions are too dangerous to beach your vessel without damage, but not too dangerous for a touch and go. Do not try a touch and go in surf conditions on a leeward shore. With this maneuver, you ease up to the shoreline, drop off or pick up a person and back away quickly.

Approach the beach bow first, just as you would for beaching, but make only brief contact with the land. Sometimes, you can pick up or drop off a person in the shallow water without touching the shore. Limiting your stay on the beach greatly reduces the chances of damaging your boat. A touch and go can be accomplished in seconds if crew members are pre-positioned on the bow.

Be careful. There are hazards. When the vessel is backing away from the beach the low stern is vulnerable to seas breaking on board.

Also make certain the crew member going ashore doesn't

literally get in over his head. Another ranger and I once found a group in need of help on a large, gently sloping beach.

The surf was high enough to make beaching unwise, so we decided to do a touch and go. My partner crouched on the bow waiting for my signal to jump off.

As we approached, I became concerned about the shallow water. At fifty yards the depth sounder showed only five feet under our keel. Then turbidity caused the depth sounder to lose its signal. In the blind I continued moving toward the shore another 10 to 15 yards. When I estimated the water to be about 3 or 4 feet under the keel, I stopped.

My partner stepped over the handrail and while holding to the lip of the deck lowered himself. Hanging by only his fingers he shouted, "I can't feel the bottom."

"It's there," I replied. "Let go."

Being a trusting fellow, he did. I heard a loud splash. Into the water he went — gunbelt, radio, pride and all.

Hmm...that's odd, I thought. Then I remembered that our keel was three feet below the surface. My 3 to 4 feet was more like 6 to 7 feet.

Use good judgment

Rescuing another boater can be very dangerous. Unfortunately, there are few specific guidelines as to when you should attempt to assist another boater and when you should stand by and call for professional help. If the situation is not life-threatening, you must think of the alternatives and make a best guess as to what will be the safest course of action for the circumstances.

There will be many times when you must make a choice based on the information I have given you and your circumstances. Use my advice, benefit from my mistakes, and always carefully consider how it applies to your unique problem.

Flare gun

Chapter 10:

MAYDAY! MAYDAY!

How and where to get help

One night, a friend's elderly, disabled mother fell out of her wheelchair. Unable to get up she pulled the telephone off the bedside table and yelled, Mayday! Mayday! An alert operator traced the call and sent rescuers.

Mayday or M'aidez is one French word everyone understands. The problem is not one of being understood, but of being heard. Electronics failure, distance and lack of time can prevent your distress call from being received. Which brings us to another issue knowing when to yell, Mayday!

Pride has kept many a boat operator from calling for help until it was too late. When seas are building and the boat won't start, that's the time to get on your radio and say, "I need help." Don't run the battery down trying to restart your engine and then find yourself faced with a real heavy weather emergency such as flooding and a dead radio.

Emergencies have a way of escalating. A small problem often expands into a bigger problem. Coast Guard statistics show that the majority of all reported fatal boating accidents in 1996 involved more than one event. It sometimes seems that when one thing goes wrong, everything goes wrong. And loss of radio power is only one of the links in this chain of events.

Calling for help and then discovering you don't need help is not the same as making false alarms or hoaxes which can result in stiff fines. When you believe you are in serious trouble, do not hesitate to call. If it turns out the situation was not life threatening, you will not be fined or criticized.

Not long ago, I was rousted out in the middle of the night to make a rescue. The message I received was to the effect that a houseboat had engine failure and was in danger of going aground in a storm and two people were missing overboard. The weather was bad and the call sounded serious.

My fellow rescuers and I sped across the lake hoping to get there in time. When we finally found the houseboat nosed into a niche in the rocky shore, the scene was as grim as something out of a movie: babies were crying, children huddled around their mothers' skirts, everyone ashen faced. It took a few minutes of questioning before I realized there was no serious emergency. These were simply inexperienced, panicky people.

This group with no background in camping or boating had rented a houseboat for a family adventure. While they were moored at a beach, a storm hit them. The wind blew crossways to the shore and pulled the houseboat loose from its beaching lines. The more experienced person in the group, the so-called captain, and a young woman left the boat to try to secure the lines. Two people, of course, could not hold a 65-foot houseboat and it drifted away leaving the two stranded. That's when the distress call was made.

After a few questions, I discovered there was nothing wrong with the boat. The problem, it seemed, was that nobody left on board knew how to operate the vessel. One of our patrol boats quickly found the missing people. By this time, the family did not want to be left alone. They had had all the adventure they could stand for one night, so we escorted them back to the marina where they tied up to the courtesy dock for their camp-out.

I lost a little sleep that night over a call that was essentially a false alarm, but I can understand the inexperienced boaters' panicky feeling. Water can be a hostile, unforgiving environment. When your car stalls, you get out and walk.

When your boat stalls (or you don't know how to operate it)...well, that's another matter. Fortunately for the boating public, there are a great many people who are trained and ready to help.

Rescue agencies

A host of organizations and agencies patrol our nation's waterways and answer calls for assistance. Depending on where you are, you might call on the National Park Service, the Coast Guard, the Army Corps of Engineers, state agencies such as the Department of Natural Resources or Fish and Game Department, the local sheriff or some other public safety agency.

Also there are two important volunteer organizations that aid boaters: the Coast Guard Auxiliary and the United States Power Squadrons.

National Park Service

On March 1, 1872, President Ulysses S. Grant signed a bill establishing Yellowstone as a natural reserve under federal jurisdiction and this date is generally considered the birthdate of the National Park Service. However, it was not until 1916 that the Park Service as an agency of the Department of the Interior was created.

From that date forward, the Park Service has implemented a policy of encouraging outdoor activities, including boating, as well as conserving park resources.

The agency's boating responsibilities were greatly increased when Boulder Dam National Recreation Area (Lake Mead National Recreation Area) was created in 1936.

This was the beginning of a trend and between 1952 and 1972, thirty-two recreational areas were added to the Park Service. More than half of these were boating areas. With this expansion, the Park Service became a major player in water recreation.

U.S. Coast Guard 41-foot motor utility boat

United States Coast Guard

The US Coast Guard was created by an act of Congress in January 1915. This act combined the Revenue Cutter Service, with a history dating back to 1790, and the Lifesaving Service, started in 1848. The Coast Guard is a military service. In peacetime, it is an agency of the Department of Transportation and in time of war it is transferred to the Navy. Among the Coast Guard's many responsibilities is the maintenance of navigation aids and search-and-rescue work. It is also charged with the duty of enforcing the provisions of the Boating Act of 1971.

Until the early 1980s, the Coast Guard rendered assistance to recreational boaters without questioning whether there were true emergencies. In recent years, under pressure from Congress and the administration, the policy has changed to one of emergency aid only. However, the Coast Guard still regards any call for help as an emergency until it is determined to be otherwise. According to the U.S. Coast Guard 1997 Annual Report, the Coast Guard undertakes more than 65,700 search-and-rescue missions a year. In a typical day it saves 14 lives and assist 328 people. These figures prove that this agency is still the boater's friend.

Army Corps of Engineers

The Army Corps of Engineers goes back to 1775, when the Continental Congress assigned the first Chief Engineer the duty of building fortifications at Bunker Hill. Since that time, the Corps has been active in diversified construction and conservation projects. When asked specifically about the organization's water-related projects, David W. Hewitt, a spokesperson for the Corps, said they are the people who build the lakes. He explained that they build dams, create lakes, maintain waterways and actively promote boating safety. At present, the Corps manages over 4,300 recreation areas at 463 lakes and patrols these lakes on an as-needed, or as-available, basis. Lake patrol is not a formal mission or primary function of the Army Corps of Engineers.

Other federal agencies

The Bureau of Reclamation, Bureau of Land Management, Forest Service and Fish & Wildlife Service all manage and/or patrol many lakes and reservoirs.

A popular style of boat is this type of runabout which ranges in length from 16 to 25 feet. It has a hard top and a center console, which is easy to walk around, and an open bow.

Often used by government agencies as a patrol boat, this style of craft is well built with plenty of floatation. Private citizens can purchase a similar model for fishing and pleasure boating. The open bow allows spray to come on board, sometimes making for a wet ride in heavy weather

Often regulation of recreational boating activities and search-and-rescue are not these agencies' primary functions. These duties are shared with or delegated to another federal or local agency.

State agencies

The Recreational Boating Safety Act passed by Congress in 1959 precipitated the organization of a boating law enforcement, safety and education office in each state. Some states had boating agencies prior to this date, but soon after 1959 all states created this office. In many states this agency is part of the Department of Natural Resources, and the name varies from state to state. In Arkansas, the boating office is part of the Game and Fish Commission. In Louisiana, for example, it is called the Fish and Wildlife Department. The state boating office in Utah is in the Parks and Recreation Department. Oklahoma, Missouri, New Jersey and some others have placed boating under the jurisdiction of the state police and call it the Lake Patrol agency. But no matter what it's called, these are the people who will help you on the various state lakes. Ask for the name of the agency in your state.

Coast Guard Auxiliary

The idea of a Coast Guard Auxiliary was conceived in 1939. It is a civilian organization created to assist the Coast Guard. The 35,000 members are volunteers who donate their time to promote safe boating.

This organization serves the boating public by:

- Teaching courses on seamanship and safe boating.
- Making safety checks on recreational boats. The examination is free and boats that pass are awarded the CME (Courtesy Marine Examination) sticker, which shows the vessel meets or exceeds minimum equipment and safety standards. An average of 290,000 courtesy examinations are conducted each year.
- Giving boaters information and assistance. It is estimated that the Coast Guard Auxiliary helps an average of 25,000 boaters each year and saves almost 500

lives. Although the organization participates in search and rescue operations, it has no law enforcement powers.

For more information or to find out about joining the Coast Guard Auxiliary, call 1-800-336-BOAT.

United States Power Squadrons

Power Squadrons grew from an original group of powerboat operators of the Boston Yacht Club into a national organization. In 1912, Vice Commodore Roger Upton of the Boston Yacht Club decided to provide drills and activities for powerboat operators, who up until that time had been largely left out of the yacht club's activities. Then in 1913, at the urging of Secretary of the Navy Franklin Delano Roosevelt, the organization was extended to other yacht clubs. At this time Charles F. Chapman, original author of Chapman Piloting, met with ten men from the yacht club and they formed the United States Power Squadron on February 2, 1914.

During World War I, members of the Power Squadrons participated in the war effort by teaching classes for the Navy. After the war, the Power Squadrons were reorganized without the drills. Now this organization offers boating instruction to the public as well as advanced instruction for its members.

To join a Power Squadron, the boater must meet certain qualifications, chief of which is a willingness to serve and foster safe boating.

Your call for help may be answered by one of the above agencies, depending on your location. Or help may come from a fellow boater (as detailed in Chapter 9). But before you can be rescued, your call for help must be heard.

Distress signals

Before Guglielmo Marconi invented the radio in 1895, semaphores and flags were used as signals. By 1899, ship-to-shore radio was used along the English coast to send distress messages. Now because radio makes possible fast, easily understood and accurate communication, it is used by boaters all over the world. As Ray Eicher, a boating safety columnist, says, "Communication is one of the most important areas of boat safety. If you have a marine radio, you have solved many problems ahead of time."

Radios

Although not required for recreational boaters, a VHF FM radio is your best means of obtaining help when you need it. All rescue agencies and your fellow boaters regularly monitor Channel 16, the channel for originating calls or for emergency transmissions. If you should need help, someone will undoubtedly hear you. Often this is someone nearby.

A marine radio can have a maximum output of 25 watts, but you must be able to reduce the output to one watt or less. Generally speaking, it is not the power of the radio, but the height of the antenna that determines how far the radio transmits. The usual range is from 10 to 15 miles. Mount the radio near the helm and as high as possible. In the event of sinking, you will want the radio to be one of the last pieces of equipment to be submerged.

Marine radios are simple to operate with only four basic controls: a channel selector, volume control, squelch control and a high power-low power switch. One important reminder: you cannot transmit and receive at the same time. There is a button on the microphone which you must push to talk.

The person who sells you a radio may also install it and show you how to use it.

After launching your boat, you will want to keep your radio turned on and tuned to Channel 16. If you hear a mayday call you should write down all the information and you must assist if possible. If you cannot assist and no one else responds, you should relay the distress call. Because of the large number of marine radios in use, the FCC (Federal Communications Commission) has imposed restrictions on their use. Channel 16 can be used only for distress, urgency, and safety messages and to initiate calls to other boaters. You can get information from the FCC (ask for Wireless Telecommunications Bureau Fact Sheet, No. 14, November 1996) which explains the rules and regulations.

Before making a call, listen to be certain the channel is not being used, then push the talk button on the microphone.

Speak clearly, hold the microphone 1 or 2 inches from your mouth and shield the microphone as much as possible from engine and wind noise. Say the name of the vessel you are calling, then give your boat's name and your FCC assigned call sign (if you have one.) Your time on Channel 16 should not exceed 30 seconds. If contact is not made, you may wait two minutes and try again.

After three failed attempts you should wait 15 minutes before trying once more. Once contact is made, switch to another channel, usually Channel 6. This procedure keeps Channel 16 clear for emergencies and for the use of other boaters originating calls.

The VHF radio is a serious safety device, not to be confused with the CB (Citizen Band) radio which is often used for chit-chat. Use procedure words when making a call on your marine radio, avoid CB slang such as, "got your ears on?" or "breaker, breaker," which are unnecessary chatter. Do not say "over and out." Instead, end messages with one word: "over", meaning you are waiting for an answer; or "out" to end transmission.

Your radio provides you with the means of calling for help in the event of an emergency. Check to see if it is operating properly before leaving the harbor and make sure everyone on board knows how to use the radio and how to make a distress call. Because a distress message can be misinterpreted, it is important to use the standard mayday format.

Remember my story about being called out in the middle of the night to rescue two people missing overboard? This is an example of the way a message can become distorted. The people on the houseboat knew what they were saying. The dispatcher thought she knew what they were saying. But because proper procedures were not observed, I received what I thought was a mayday (a life-threatening emergency) but which was in fact an urgency (a problem, but no immediate danger) message.

If you should ever have to make a distress call, you will be excited and you may have very little time. Even so, it is important to speak slowly and clearly. The most important part of the message is the type of emergency and your location.

MAYDAY FORMAT

Make sure that your VHF radio is on and tuned to Channel 16.
Speak in a normal voice.

1. Press the microphone talk button and say: *Mayday - Mayday - Mayday*

2. Say: This is (your boat name and call sign.) Repeat boat name 3 times

3. Say: Mayday (your boat name).

4. Say: Position is (give two lines of position if possible or state distance and magnetic or true bearing from a well-known landmark or navigational aid.)

5. Say: We (state nature of emergency.)

6. Say: We require (state type of assistance required.)

7. State the number of persons on board and the conditons of any injured persons.

8. Describe your boat: Length, type, color of hull, color of trim.

9. Say: I will be listening on Channel 16.

10. Say: This is (your boat name and call sign.)

11. Say: Over

Some radios have an emergency alarm button, and if your radio has this feature begin the transmission by pressing this alarm button. The alarm consists of two tones transmitted alternately for 30 seconds to a minute. It sounds like a siren and alerts listeners to your mayday call. Then make the call using standard mayday format.

I suggest you make a machine copy of the format given here, and tape it to your radio. As with all emergency equipment when you need it, you won't have time to hunt for it.

If you do not get a response after sending a mayday signal

several times on Channel 16, switch to another channel. Scan the channels until you hear radio traffic, then break in.

When you have a problem which is not a life-threatening emergency, send an urgency message. Use the mayday format, substituting the words Pan Pan (pronounced pahn pahn) for mayday. If you wish to warn other boaters of a potential danger the proper word is Securite, (pronounced Say-curiTAY).

Silence (pronounced see-lonss) repeated three times is a notice to all boaters to refrain from using the channel during an emergency. Silence Fini (pronounced see-lonss fee nee) signals an end to the emergency and a return to normal transmission.

Any message preceded by the words Mayday, Pan Pan or Securite has priority over any other radio transmission. If after alerting other boaters and rescue units you discover you can solve your problem, don't forget to cancel the distress or urgency message.

Troubleshooting

Your radio must be turned on and working. This may seem obvious, but under stress you may not think of the obvious. If the radio isn't working:

- Check the on-off switch.
- Make sure the squelch isn't set too high. To set the squelch, turn the knob until noise is heard, then turn the knob back slightly to block noise but not block out weak signals.
- Be sure to release the microphone button after your message. You cannot receive messages while the talk button is held down.
- Check the battery.
- Make sure the radio is connected to an antenna.

Other types of radios

Some boaters have amateur (ham) and CB (Citizens Band) radios on board. These are good backup equipment, but are not a substitute for a marine radio. One major disadvantage of ham and CBs: they are not routinely monitored by rescue organizations and other boaters. And with the amateur radio, you are apt to reach someone halfway around the world instead of a boater in the next cove. When you need help, you want someone close by to come to your aid.

A marine radio costs more than some other types of radios, but it's worth more.

A marine radio is:

- Easy to operate.
- Almost foolproof.
- A quality piece of equipment —it should not fail when you need it.
- Effective at a greater range. It has a range of 10 to 15 miles compared to the 4 to 5 mile range of most CBs.

Cellular telephones

Cellular telephones have some definite advantages:

- No license required.
- Access to all land-based telephones.
- Can be used almost anywhere. No installation required.

The main disadvantage is the fact that boaters in your vicinity will not hear your distress call and respond. Further, your cellular telephone will not provide a signal from which Coast Guard direction finders can take a bearing to locate you. Another disadvantage is the fact that in remote regions, such as on a large lake away from metropolitan areas with cell sites, there are dead spots where you cannot use your telephone.

However, the newest innovation in cellular phones is a link-up with a low-earth orbiting satellite, which gives the caller worldwide range. With the new cellular phone you will be able to call the Coast Guard, or other rescue agency, direct. As cellular telephones with greater range become affordable, more people will be using them. Remember: whether you call 911 or someone at your home, be sure to give your location.

The EPIRB (Emergency Position Indicating Radio Beacon) is the ultimate detection aid. At present the EPIRB is expensive and used mainly at sea and on the Great Lakes (See Chapter 12).

The ski or racing "muscle" boat has a powerful inboard or inboard/outdrive engine. Its fiberglass hull is light but strong.

Made for speed, this type of boat's planing hull skims across the water and is a fun craft for many boating conditions. However, the design usually incorporates a low freeboard — which sometimes can result in problems if the boat is caught out in heavy weather.

Visual distress signals

I cannot overemphasize the importance of distress signals. Next to a PFD, they are your most important piece of safety equipment.

A number of years ago a terrible tragedy occurred at Lake Mead — a tragedy which could have been avoided if the victims had only had visual distress signals. On May 23, 1980, at about 10:30 a.m. three young people — a man and two teenage girls — left the boat ramp at Echo Bay on Lake Mead headed for Stewarts Point. The young man told his wife to send someone to look for them if they didn't arrive at Stewarts Point in 20 minutes.

The water was choppy when they cast off and soon got worse. Waves began breaking on board and one wave washed over the transom, killing the motor. When the operator realized the boat was sinking, he broke the seats loose and pulled everything he could find that would float out of the bow compartment, so searchers would see floating debris. The operator made sure the two girls had their PFDs on properly and then lashed the boat seats together with a ski rope.

When the boat went down, the seats floated and the three of them held on, certain they would soon be rescued because they knew they would soon be missed.

When the boaters didn't arrive on schedule, the wife reported them overdue and in less than four hours a full-scale search was launched.

Wind and waves carried the three victims out into the lake. At one point, they could see people and campers on shore. They yelled, waved and fired a fire extinguisher the operator had saved to use as a distress signal. However, the white puff of a fire extinguisher could not be seen in whitecapping waves. Next, they saw the search plane fly over. The plane made two passes over them and they were sure they'd been seen. But they were never spotted by the aerial searchers.

All day they were tossed by angry waves. At about 6 p.m., a big wave swept the young man away from the floating seats and the girls. He began swimming for the shore. Again he saw a search plane and again he thought they'd soon be rescued. But that did not happened. The man swam to shore. Both girls died, probably of hypothermia, sometime during the night.

These people did many right things: they told someone where they were going and when they expected to arrive. They wore PFDs. They pulled anything that would float out of the boat before it went down. They even thought to grab a fire extinguisher to use as a distress signal. They stayed together. But they did not have anything that would make them easy to spot — no real distress signals.

This is why your life jacket should have pockets for signaling devices. My personal life jacket is orange with reflective tape and an attached whistle. In the pockets I carry three aerial meteors, a pen-type rocket launcher with seven .38 caliber aerial meteors, a knife, flashlight, floating smoke signal, chemical light stick, pocket strobe light and a signal mirror. If I end up in the water, I will definitely be able to signal my distress.

The Coast Guard requires boats 16 feet and longer used on coastal waters, at the mouth of a river more than two miles wide or on the Great Lakes, to carry three daytime signals and three nighttime signals. There are several combinations of pyrotechnic and non-pyrotechnic day and night devices that meet the Coast Guard requirement. For example: three combination flare and smoke signals satisfy this requirement.

Even though distress signals are not required on most lakes, I strongly urge every boater to have them. And where distress signals are concerned, I say more are better.

Pyrotechnics

There are several different types of pyrotechnic devices. They include guns, rockets, rocket parachutes, flares and orange smoke. These are excellent visual signals, but can cause injury or property damage if not handled properly. The Coast Guard suggests they be stored in a watertight container painted red or orange and marked DISTRESS SIGNALS.

Flare Guns These are most effective as nighttime signals. The gun or rocket should be fired into the air vertically. Or, if a strong wind is blowing, it should be fired at an angle into the wind, so it will be carried to a position directly overhead. There are four safety precautions you should observe when using a pyrotechnic pistol:

1. Hold the weapon at arm's reach overhead.
2. Do not fire or aim into an overhead obstruction.

The pyrotechnic pistol is an effective night-time signal.
For safety, the gun should be held high with head turned away when fired.

3. Turn your head and look away when you pull the trigger.

4. If the pyrotechnic pistol doesn't fire when you pull the trigger keep it pointed away from yourself and wait 10 to 15 seconds before reloading. These things have been known to misfire or explode.

The meteor produces red, green or white illumination, reaches a height between 200 and 500 feet (depending on the type used) and lasts 5 to 7 seconds. Since these signals last only a few seconds they should be fired in pairs a few seconds apart. The first flare attracts attention and the second allows rescuers to home in on you. Don't use all your flares at one time. Save some to use when you see or hear a boat or airplane.

Handheld Flares Used primarily as night signaling devices, they last up to 15 minutes — long enough to give rescuers time to see and home in on your location. When using a handheld flare hold it away from your body and over the leeward side of your vessel. These devices drip hot slag. Don't point them at anyone.

Handheld flares are best used when another vessel is within sight because:

- You will have a limited number.
- They last only a short time.
- They are low altitude signals and cannot be seen from a distance.

Parachute signals The parachute flare produces a white star suspended by a parachute. It reaches an altitude of 650 to 1,000 feet and will last approximately 30 seconds, sometimes longer. Both aerial meteors and parachute flares are good nighttime signaling devices.

As a small-boat operator you will probably never see the light of a parachute or meteor flare. But if you do, respond immediately. The need for help may be acute.

Smoke Signals These are for daytime use and are useful to attract the attention of aerial searchers. The orange smoke lasts for about 50 seconds.

Read the directions on all pyrotechnic signals when you buy them and store them in a dry place close to the helm, where they will be accessible. Upon boarding, direct passengers and crew members to the location of these signaling devices and make sure they understand how to use them. The directions are usually easily understood, but in an emergency everyone should know where the visual signals are and how to use them without having to hunt or stop to read directions.

To be Coast Guard approved, flares must be less than three years old. But don't get rid of your old flares, because they may still be good. The useful life of many flares, if stored in a dry place, is greater than six years. In an emergency try old flares first.

Non-pyrotechnics

Lights A strobe light or waterproof halogen flashlight are both good visual distress signals. A strobe light sends out a flashing high-intensity light, making it easier for searchers to locate you at night. To be a Coast Guard approved signal, the strobe must automatically flash the S.O.S. (a universal distress signal) when activated. Another good signaling device is a three- or four-battery halogen flashlight. Using a flashlight you can spell S.O.S. with three short flashes, three long flashes, three short flashes.

The appearance of two red lights, one above the other, also signals that the vessel is disabled.

Signaling Mirror Reflected light can be seen up to 5 miles away. Any mirror will do for signaling, but the one specially designed for this has a hole in the center for sighting.

How to use a signaling mirror:

1. Face the sun and the object you wish to signal.

2. Reflect a spot of light on a nearby surface, such as your hand.

3. With the spot of light on your hand move your hand in front of the object you want to signal, then move your hand away so it isn't blocking the light.

4. Move the mirror slowly, causing the bright spot to move. Aim the spot at your target.

Even when you can't see a boat or a rescuer, you can still use the signal mirror. Aim it at the horizon and sweep the spot of light back and forth. It can be seen for many miles. In fact, the Coast Guard considers the signal mirror to be one of the most effective daytime signals.

Plastic Streamer This is a long sheet of bright orange plastic on a roller. It fits into a small tube and when unrolled floats on the surface of the water. I think of it as a permanent dye marker, because it makes an orange streak on the water which is easy to spot from the air. The manufacturer states that the plastic streamer can be reused, but I've found it is very hard to roll up and get back into the tube. I suggest that you should not try it out to see how it works. If you are curious, ask your marine supply store for a demonstration. They may have a video which shows how to use the plastic streamer.

Whistle A plastic police-type whistle can be heard at a distance of more than a half mile. You will be able to blow a whistle longer than you can shout for help.

Flags Few recreational boats carry flags for signaling and even fewer boaters understand their meaning. A flag with a black ball and a black square on it is a distress signal. However, any flag being waved, such as an orange ski flag, is usually recognized as a distress signal.

If you have an emergency and you don't have any of the usual signaling devices, use anything at hand to summon help.

- Fire a gun at one-minute intervals.
- Sound a horn continuously.
- Fly the national flag upside-down.
- Repeatedly raise and lower outstretched arms.
- Wave a bright shirt or life jacket.
- Hold an oar in an upright position and wave it back and forth.
- Do anything that will attract attention.

Unfortunately, without obvious distress signals, the things you have at hand may not attract attention. On April 10, 1994, at sunset a boat near the entrance to Black Canyon on Lake Mead developed engine trouble. On board were three adults and one 15-month-old child. The engine died and the operator was unable to restart it. Winds increased and the water, which in this area is more than 400 feet deep, became choppy. The boaters apparently did not realize the seriousness of their situation, because although they had four adult life jackets on board, only one was used. The mother tied one of the PFDs onto her child.

The father tried to signal two boats that passed. Neither of the boats responded. Then the boat began to take on water over the stern and sank rapidly.

The baby came out of the adult life jacket and drowned before he could be rescued. The mother and a friend grabbed an ice chest and were carried by the wind away from the scene of the accident.

The father swam circles around the overturned boat in a desperate attempt to find the child. When the father became exhausted, he returned to the vessel, where he found a life jacket and a buoyant cushion.

Approximately four hours later, he was picked up by a passing boater who had spotted the bow of the overturned vessel sticking up out of the water. The bodies of the mother and friend were never recovered.

This accident happened in a narrow, well-traveled section of the lake. Several boats passed before and after the capsizing. A passenger cruise vessel, Desert Princess, passed within 300 yards of the accident, both going to Hoover Dam and returning, yet neither captain nor any of the many passengers saw the victims.

As I've said before, you have to be seen to be rescued.

The search

When I was a boat officer, a lot of what I did was search-and-rescue. It's called this because before a rescue can be made the victim has to be located.

Since many boaters having problems do not know where they are, we often began the mission as detectives fitting clues together.

Several years ago my partner and I were called out one night to assist a couple of inexperienced boaters, who were unfamiliar with the lake and had been cruising too fast for nighttime conditions. They had run aground on a spit of land. With a cellular telephone, the boaters contacted our dispatch center.

But they had no idea where they were. They said they had been to Hoover Dam, were returning to the Lake Mead Marina and were on an island.

Based on these clues, we decided they must be on Boulder Island.

When we couldn't find them, we called the dispatcher and asked for more information. She called the boaters asking questions. Next we tried turning on a blue light.

The dispatcher asked them if they could see it. First the couple said they thought they could see it, then they said they couldn't.

Each time the dispatcher talked to them, it became more difficult to communicate because their cellular telephone battery was getting weaker. Finally in desperation we had the dispatcher ask them if they had flares. They did, and the dispatched told them to light one.

We watched in the direction where we thought we might see their flare. Nothing.

Then I turned around. Way off in the distance, across the lake, I saw a little red dot.

If these people had not had distress signals on board, I think we might still be looking for them.

You can make a rescuer's job easier and shorten the time you must wait for help to arrive by knowing your position.

There are several other things you can do to facilitate your rescue. Always tell someone where you are going, when you expect to return and what agency to notify if you are overdue. Of course, the person you file your float plan with can always call the local police department and find out the name and number of the agency patrolling your boating area. But why not do it for him or her?

Looking for an agency's number in the telephone directory is time-consuming and frustrating. Anything that delays the receipt of a rescue call can result in tragedy.

As soon as a rescue agency receives a report of an overdue vessel it goes into action. Typically, the dock area and marina parking lots are searched first.

Many an overdue boat is found tied up at the dock or on a trailer in the parking lot. At the same time, all patrol boats in the area are notified.

If the vessel cannot be quickly located, a large search is launched. This search is carefully and scientifically planned. Coordinators analyze known facts and study environmental data: wind and seas. Rate and directions of drift are estimated to develop search areas and tactics.

Contrary to what most people think, it is not easy to spot a person in the water. Searchers pass by people and do not see them.

This is why the victims must do something to make their position known. You must appear bigger, brighter or different than your surroundings. The plastic streamer described earlier, mirrors or smoke signals are excellent devices for signaling during the day.

Pyrotechnics and strobes should be used at night. When you see an airplane or boat and it is as close to you as it will ever get, fire that rocket. This is when a distress signal can save your life.

In summary

Your survival depends to a large extent on you.

- Know when and how to get help in an emergency.
- Have on board and use the two most important pieces of survival equipment— a PFD and distress signaling devices.
- Know your position.
- Leave a float plan with someone.
- Watch for searchers.
- Have distress signals available and ready for use.

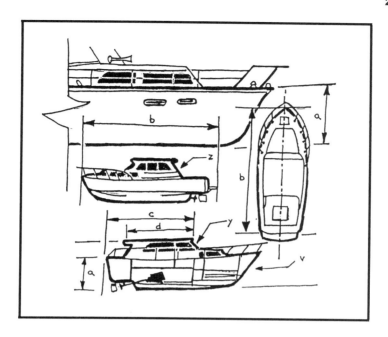

Chapter 11

VESSEL SEAWORTHINESS

What you should know about different types of boats

If you wanted to buy the ultimate seaworthy vessel, what would you get? Answer: the Coast Guard 47-foot Motor Lifeboat. This vessel's hull is made of marine aluminum with stainless steel fittings and it is powered by a 450 h.p. Detroit Diesel engine. It can travel 200 nautical miles at a cruising speed of 20 knots without refueling.

The Coast Guard, in a news release, states that, "The self-righting and self-bailing 47-foot motor lifeboat is designed to weather 80-mile-an-hour winds, tow a boat 2 1/2 times its length, navigate 30-foot seas and ride 20-foot waves in surf." This vessel is virtually unsinkable and when capsized will right itself in about 8 seconds. It was specially designed for Coast Guard rescue work. Would a boat like this ever be popular with recreational boaters?

No. First, it is not available to the public and, even if it were available, with a price tag of $1 million, it is not generally affordable. Further, for most people, seaworthiness is not a primary concern when it comes to buying a boat.

People buy vessels for a specific activity, such as fishing, skiing or camping, and for a type of boating area river, lake or ocean. Most boats, when used for the activity and boating area they were designed for, are seaworthy.

This is especially true for newer boats covered under the provisions of the Federal Boat Safety Act of 1971. Boats less than 20 feet built since 1973 are required to have built-in floatation and this greatly increases their seaworthiness. However, built-in floatation does not mean that the boat will not capsize.

Hunters and fishermen often use small utility boats powered by outboard motors. These boats are designed to be operated close to shore and are safe enough when used properly. The problem is many of these sportsmen are not experienced boat operators and are unaware of the dangers of heavy weather on open bodies of water.

An accident caused by using a small boat in heavy weather occurred on Mark Twain Lake in Missouri on November 16, 1996. Early in the morning, three men went deer hunting using a 14-foot aluminum utility boat as transportation to the hunting area.

The small Jon boat, with outboard engine, is a lightweight, inexpensive utility vessel.

Well suited as basic transportation on a small reservoir to an inaccessible hunting area or to a favorite fishing cove, this design is not intended for large lakes or heavy weather. The design usually has low freeboard. Care should be taken not to overload this type of vessel or put too much weight on the stern. Never equip this boat with a large, heavy motor.

They left the boat in a cove, hunted the nearby area and at about noon returned to their vessel, intending to cross the lake.

The water, which at 5:30 a.m. had been calm, was now rough. Wind blew across the lake and waves crashed on board. Without bailing equipment, the hunters used cups in a futile attempt to dewater the boat. As they struggled to keep the vessel from sinking, two of the men moved to the same side. The boat, already unstable from accumulated water, listed wildly.

Thinking they were about to capsize, all three jumped overboard. Two were wearing PFDs and the third man had a PFD on his arm, but the PFD came off when he entered the water. This man's first mistake was not wearing a lifejacket, and his efforts to stay afloat were undoubtedly further hampered by his deer rifle, stuck inside his pants to keep dry.

The two hunters wearing PFDs were rescued about 20 minutes later. The body of the third man has not been found.

More hunters die of drowning and hypothermia than of gunshot wounds. One reason for this statistic is the fact that hunting season usually comes in late fall and winter when water and air are cold. But the main cause of these accidents is overloading and improper use of a boat that was not designed for heavy weather on an open lake.

The first consideration when judging a boat's seaworthiness is its intended purpose and boating area. Don't take an open utility outboard out in the middle of a big lake during a storm. Remember, what is a pleasurable cruise for one boat may be heavy weather for another.

When you are being tossed about by angry waves is not the time to start thinking about the seaworthiness of your boat. In fact, the time to think about seaworthiness is when you purchase the boat. Even though sea keeping will probably not be your primary consideration, it should be a major influence on your choice.

There are many things which affect the boat's ability to survive in rough seas. I have divided vessel seaworthiness into three categories:

1. Sea keeping ability: Characteristics of size, shape and propulsion which influence the boat's handling in heavy seas.

2. Craft survivability: The vessel's ability to survive a heavy weather emergency.

3. Crew Comfort: Items that protect operator and crew.

Sea keeping

This first category includes hull shape, surface windage, vessel size, weight distribution and propulsion. All of these affect boat handling, but hull shape probably affects it the most.

Hull design

There are three basic hull types: displacement, planing and semi-displacement. The displacement hull settles into the water, displacing it. Planing hulls appear to fly on top of the water. These boats are held up more by forward motion than by water displacement. Most recreational boats have a combination of the displacement and planing hull and are properly referred to as semi-displacement hull.

Displacement Hull This is a low-speed boat, usually with either a round or flat bottom. In the world of recreational boating, sailboats, houseboats and yachts are usually this type of vessel. These boats give a comfortable ride and can handle rough water.

A commercial work boat, with enclosed cockpit, usually has a deep draft. Bigger boats of this type are displacement vessels.

Stout construction, aluminum or steel hulls, big engines, pumps and marine electronics on most of these boats make them dependable and relatively seaworthy.

The vessel forces its bow through the water and since it must push water aside, there is a limit to the speed it can achieve. If speed were not important, the displacement hull would be a good choice.

Planing Hull The direct opposite of the displacement hull, the planing boat must be operated at a speed great enough to lift it onto the surface of the water. The force which pushes the boat upward at the point where water surface meets hull is called dynamic lift. When not in motion or at low speeds, the planing hull, like the displacement hull, displaces the water around it.

The advantage of the planing hull is speed. Once the vessel has achieved planing speed, a small increase in power will result in a large increase in speed.

The disadvantages of the planing hull:

- Easier to capsize
- When stopped suddenly, can be pooped by a following wave
- Tends to porpoise or spank the tops of waves when operated at high speeds

The dangers from this type of vessel when operated improperly in rough water can best be illustrated by an accident that occurred at Lake Jackson, Florida, which took the life of both the operator and passenger.

The vessel involved was what we at Lake Mead call a "potato chip" boat. That is, it was a light, flat-bottomed, low-freeboard, high-speed powerboat. The length of the vessel was 15 feet, it had a beam 5 feet 4 inches and a depth of 1 foot 4 inches. It was powered by an 85 h.p. outboard motor. This boat had a lot of power and very little freeboard — a dangerous combination.

On February 21, 1995, the day of the accident, there was a 20-mile-an-hour wind, with waves reaching a height of three feet. The investigating officers found the trim button for the motor in the up position and theorized that as the boat was being driven into the wind it began to rise dangerously out of the water.

The inexperienced operator may have pushed the trim button to the up position, or it may have been accidentally bumped. At any rate the bow, already rising off the water, rose even higher.

Probably, in a panicky effort to correct this hazard, the operator pulled the throttle into neutral. This caused the stern to sink into the water, the bow to rise even more and the vessel to capsize bow over stern.

Semi-Displacement Hull Most recreational boats are a combination of displacement and planing hull. They are designed with a sharp V at the bow that gradually widens to a relatively wide, shallow V aft.

This shape allows the stern to dig in and the bow to rise as the boat accelerates to a planing position.

At slow speeds the boat performs as a displacement hull, but as power is increased the vessel begins planing. The boat should not be operated at the transitional speed because it is unstable with the bow high and fuel consumption is greater at this speed.

The semi-displacement hull is a good compromise between speed and seaworthiness. It gives the vessel the best of both displacement and planing hulls.

The deep V up front gives good turning performance and the flat V at the stern gives good planing performance.

Bow Shape Boats intended for use in heavy weather have flared bows. This increases the buoyancy of the forward part of the vessel and deflects water and spray.

Another bow consideration is the choice between open and decked over.

There are some seaworthy open-bow boats; the rigid hull inflatable boat, for example, is extremely seaworthy. But in most cases, a decked-over bow is better because the deck makes a shield to deflect water back off the boat in heavy seas.

Stern Design and Freeboard If seaworthiness were your only consideration, you would want a rounded stern, such as the Coast Guard's 44-foot motor lifeboat. This stern is buoyant, divides a following sea so waves do not splash on board and in heavy weather reduces yawing tendencies in following seas.

However, space is usually a greater concern on small recreational vessels. The wide, flat transom creates more deck space.

A ridged hull inflatable boat (RHIB) is a seaworthy vessel used for boat patrols and for search and rescue work.

Freeboard is the distance from the waterline to the top of the gunwale. Obviously, the more freeboard the boat has, the less likely it is that waves will wash on board. For most boats, the lowest freeboard is the stern. It is common for outboard motors to be mounted in a cut-down area on the transom. This also reduces freeboard.

Many outboard boats have a motor well or bulkhead in front of the engine to protect the boat from swamping. However, this wall is often compromised with holes for motor control cables. Some newer outboard crafts have a motor mount, a platform that is bolted on the back of a regular transom. Because it does not cut down transom height, the motor mount helps protect the boat from stern swamping.

Generally a cut-down transom is not good, but there is one exception: boats that are self-bailing. I have worked on a patrol boat with a cut-down transom that was very seaworthy. Because the deck and hatches were watertight, a big wave could crash on board and then run back out again. The deck would be awash and I'd be standing in 6 to 8 inches of water, but the forward movement of the vessel and the angle of the deck would allow the water to run off.

Windage When you have a boat with a high superstructure, such as a cabin above deck, a tower, a canvas top or a metal deck roof, and you also have a shallow draft, you should be concerned about the amount of surface presented to the wind in relation to the vessel's total weight. Excessive windage for the boat's weight will cause it to flip over in a strong wind. This is exactly what happened to a deck boat on the Missouri River on August 4, 1996. (This accident is described in Chapter 2.) A thunderstorm causing high winds and waves overturned this pontoon boat, trapping three people inside a closet-like bathroom.

Houseboats have tremendous windage, and although personally I have never known one to capsize, they are very hard to maneuver in wind. Which brings us to the next topic.

Size and Weight Distribution Where size is concerned, bigger is generally better. One also needs to consider length to beam ratio. This affects the vessel's lateral stability or ability to resist roll. For instance a 12-foot utility boat with a 5-foot beam is much less likely to roll than a 12-foot canoe with a 2-foot beam. A vessel should be wide enough to prevent capsizing.

Another consideration: to prevent roll, a boat should have a hard chine. That is, the intersection between sides and bottom of the boat should make a well-defined angle, because a vessel with a rounded bottom will heel easily, in heavy weather too easily.

Weight distribution is as important as size and shape. Weight distribution establishes the vessel's center of gravity, which for stability should be as low as possible amidships. A center of gravity that is too high makes the vessel top-heavy, a candidate for capsizing. Too much weight forward will cause the boat to plunge into waves. Too much weight aft, such as an oversized engine, and the boat could be pooped.

Propulsion

The type of propulsion affects both the vessel's handling and its survivability. As a general rule, twin engine, twin-screw propulsion is the most seaworthy. It also costs the most. However, there are advantages and disadvantages for each type of engine: outboard, inboard, inboard/outboard, single engine, twin engine and jet.

Outboard This is the most common marine engine. Its

popularity is partly due to its comparatively low cost; it also provides good maneuverability. The entire engine, shaft and propeller turns and tilts, giving the operator direct thrust turning. Also, trim can be adjusted by raising and lowering the unit.

Additionally, these small marine engines are quite reliable. Hugo Vihlen, author of *The Stormy Voyage of Father's Day*, who crossed the North Atlantic in a sailboat with a 4 h.p. engine, had nothing but praise for his tiny outboard motor. Another sailor, Marlin Bree, says, "These little marine engines are fantastic!" Marlin, however, did note that the snap coupling between the fuel line and the engine sometimes vibrates loose. He found this was not a big problem, because the coupling can easily be snapped back on.

The disadvantages are weight on the stern, which, coupled with some boats' cut-away transom, lowers freeboard. Some newer boats have eliminated the cut-away transoms with a platform for the motor mounted aft of the stern.

Inboard With the engine inboard and connected by a shaft to the propeller, the only way to redirect trust is by rudder. The propeller forces a powerful stream of water backward against the face of the rudder, which deflects it.

This redirected thrust turns the boat. Since the vessel does not pivot about either bow or stern, but at some point between, the operator must learn the turning characteristics of the vessel. Also, the inboard single-screw engine delivers a small side thrust called propwalk. A left-hand propeller moves the vessel slightly to port and a right hand propeller has the opposite effect. When maneuvering in close quarters or backing, the problems of propwalk become more pronounced.

The advantage of the inboard is a larger, more powerful engine. Also, the inboard engine's location tends to make the boat more stable in the water and more seaworthy. The disadvantage is poor maneuverability at slow speed.

Inboard/Outboard The inboard/outboard combines the advantages of an outboard maneuverability and inboard power. Most medium sized powerboats have this type of engine. It gives the steering control and propeller angle advantages of the outboard together with a more powerful inboard engine.

Twin Engine This type of power almost eliminates the problem of engine failure. Unless you have fuel problems, it is highly unlikely that both engines will fail at the same time. But the major advantage of twin screws is maneuverability. With forward power to one propeller and reverse power to the other, the boat can be turned completely around in a space not much longer than the boat's length. A skilled operator can even move the boat sideways — a real advantage in crowded dock areas.

Also, twin screws virtually eliminate the problem of prop-walk. Nowadays, these boats are usually equipped with a right-hand and left-hand propeller. The tendency of a right-hand propeller to push the vessel to starboard is offset by the left-hand propeller. If you try to dock a single-engine inboard in close quarters you will discover that the boat's stern moves to port. It is almost impossible to back a vessel with single screw in a straight line. With twin screws, this is not a problem.

One disadvantage of twin engines is higher fuel consumption. Unless the vessel has large fuel tanks, you will not be able to battle wind and waves for as long as a single engine craft before running out of fuel. On the other hand, with the added power and maneuverability of twin engines, you can probably make it to a sheltered area. You won't have to hang in there over a long period of time.

Jet Engine The engine of a jet boat draws water in through the bottom of the boat and pumps it out through a nozzle in the transom. The boat turns when the stream of water ejected is turned to one side or the other. This type of vessel doesn't have a propeller hanging down below the hull and is ideal for rivers and shallow water areas. It is also popular with skiers, since there is no sharp propeller that might injure someone in the water.

Disadvantages of the jet boat are:

• Poor maneuverability at slow speeds.
• Relatively flat bottom gives a rough ride.
• Large, inefficient engine results in high fuel consumption.

The jet is not a good choice for heavy weather. The wind and waves will bounce the jet boat around at slow speeds and if you try to go fast, you will get a pounding ride. The jet does not have the fuel endurance of a propeller driven craft.

The type of propulsion a boat has contributes almost equally to its sea keeping capacity and its survivability. Other qualities such as bilge pumps, adequate floatation, watertightness, and hull strength definitely belong in the category of vessel survivability as they increase the craft's ability to withstand the ravages of a heavy weather emergency.

Vessel survivability

Bilge Pumps A bilge pump is not a required item and on small utility vessels a bailing bucket is all that may be needed. But every boat, large or small, should have some means of eliminating excess water. Don't end up like the deer hunters mentioned earlier, who had to bail out water with a cup.

A plastic gallon bleach bottle with the end cut out makes an excellent and inexpensive bailing bucket. By fastening a string or wire through the handle, you can fasten the bottle to the boat so it won't be washed overboard.

The advantage of an electric bilge pump is that it eliminates water while you turn your attention to other aspects of the emergency. Often when you are bailing, that is all you can do and in most cases, you had better not stop.

A bilge pump needs to be of adequate size for the vessel. Does this mean a small boat should have a small pump? Not necessarily. Actually a small open boat with low freeboard needs a larger pump than a bigger boat with watertight hatches. Some pumps put out as little as 200 gallons an hour. When you consider that one big wave over the transom can put that much water on board, you see that a 200-gallon-an-hour pump is almost worthless. I recommend the largest pump you can afford that will fit your space.

Larger compartmentalized vessels need more than one pump and a backup system. Most bilge pumps are powered off the engine battery. If you have an accumulation of water on board, it could short out the vessel's electrical system. The backup system should be powered by a portable battery or manually operated.

I tend to favor the manual pump. Unless you are good about maintaining your equipment, you are apt to have a pump with a dead battery when you need it most. You can move a lot of water (between 30 to 48 gallon a minute) with a good manual pump and you never have to worry about dead batteries.

Floatation In 1973, the Federal Safe Boating Act became law and the Coast Guard was charged with the task of reducing boating accidents and fatalities. In response to this mandate, the Coast Guard requires boats less than 20 feet long built since 1973 to have built-in floatation. This is usually provided by polyurethane foam added to voids in decks, bulkheads and hull framework. In 1978, this regulation was upgraded to require horizontal floatation for powerboats under 20 feet in length. Many manufacturers of larger vessels offer floatation as an option, and I believe this is an option worth the cost.

Watertight Integrity and Compartmentalization A larger boat can sustain significant damage and still remain afloat if it is watertight and/or compartmentalized. For instance, if you have a hull divided into five watertight compartments, one section could be holed and the vessel would still remain afloat. When purchasing a large boat, look for a hull divided into watertight compartments. Although many recreational boats are not watertight, check doors, windows and hatches for a close fit.

Several years ago, a new patrol boat was delivered to the Park Service. Along with other rangers, I met the manufacturer's representative at the launch ramp to check out the new boat. The factory rep showed us a plastic bag of plugs which were to be put into various places in the hull. There were six plugs and there appeared to be only five places to insert them. We concluded that the manufacturer had sent an extra plug.

Next, we put the boat in the water and slowly made our way to the gas dock for fuel. While the boat was being fueled, I began opening compartments and looking at all the neat, new features. I opened the forward hatch and there was a pool of water. I was certain we hadn't ordered a boat with an onboard pool; something was wrong! Of course, we soon found out where the sixth plug went. We put the plug where it belonged, turned on the pump and pumped the compartment (a forward chain locker) dry.

But the important point is: the boat was in no danger of sinking. The water had poured into the forward compartment until it reached the water level outside the boat. With the flood contained, the vessel remained stable. In fact, the flooded chain locker didn't even change the trim of the boat when it was operated at slow speed. Because the vessel was compartmentalized and watertight, we didn't know the boat had taken on water.

Hull Strength It takes a well designed and constructed boat to stand up to the punishment of heavy seas. An important consideration in determining hull strength is the building material. Recreational boats are made of wood, metal or fiberglass.

Wood for centuries has been the building material of choice, and a heavily framed, planked boat that is well put together is a seaworthy craft. But because wood is no longer plentiful and requires a great deal of maintenance, these boats are becoming the exception rather than the norm.

Metal boats are strong, but generally metal is too heavy for small craft construction. However, aluminum is light and easy to repair. Utility boats in the 13- to 17-foot range are often constructed of this material. These boats, while durable, are too light for heavy weather. Even in moderate seas, the aluminum boat generally gives a rough, uncomfortable ride.

More and more, the building material of choice is fiberglass. It is strong, relatively inexpensive and requires little maintenance. One heavy-weather advantage, in addition to great strength, is the fact that fiberglass can be molded to provide such safety features as toe rails and non-skid deck surfaces.

Fuel Capacity In November 1913, Lake Superior experienced what has since been referred to as the Great Storm. During this terrible weather, a coal-burning grain ship, *William Nottingham*, bucked notorious seas for 48 hours before running out of coal. Without power, the ship was about to smash on the rocks of Coppermine Point on Canada's northern shore. There was little chance any of the crew would survive. That's when the captain ordered the cargo of grain shoveled down the coal chutes to be used for fuel. With this added fuel, the steamship headed toward Sault Ste. Marie and almost made it, but unfortunately struck a shoal. Three sailors drowned, but the rest of the crew were rescued by the Coast Guard.

Like the captain of the *Nottingham*, you will be in serious trouble if you run out of fuel in heavy weather. And unlike the captain of the *Nottingham*, you will not be able to turn to an alternative fuel. There is no readily available substitute for gasoline or diesel.

Fuel tank capacity is an important consideration when buying a boat. True, you can carry extra fuel, but this could add dangerous weight to a small vessel. In fact, a large motor and extra gas cans undoubtedly contributed to the sinking of the fishing boat described in Chapter One.

It is best to have a boat with adequate fuel tanks as an integral part of its design because you won't want to refuel when the boat is pitching and rolling in a storm.

Another advantage of large built-in gas tanks instead of carry-on cans is the fact that these tanks are usually positioned low near the vessel's center of gravity and have been figured into the vessel's load capacity.

Crew comfort

Whether the boat is a runabout designed mainly to provide transportation or a luxurious yacht, crew comfort is important because a powerboat in heavy seas is apt to have more endurance than the operator.

Heavy weather is cold, wet weather and anything that will keep the operator and crew drier and warmer is better not only for comfort but for safety.

A sturdy roof and windshield give this operator some protection from heavy weather.

When riding out a storm, the skipper must remain mentally alert. A cold, exhausted operator is apt to make unwise decisions.

When buying a boat, look for cockpit shelter. This can be windshields, heavy weather curtains or something sturdy overhead. I say sturdy because a flimsy canvas sunshade may come crashing down in a hard blow.

Small daycruisers usually provide shelter with enclosed cockpits and cuddy cabins. Even large cruisers with a flybridge for sighting fish or just allowing the operator to feel the breeze also come with an enclosed main bridge for comfort in bad weather.

The problem of which boat is best becomes not which boat is most seaworthy, but which one you can afford, which one accommodates your water activities, and which one is best suited to your boating area. At the same time, it is important to look for those things which also make the vessel seaworthy.

Different types of boats

Utility Boats These are small, usually open boats, powered by outboard motors. Popular with fishermen and hunters, this craft was designed for use in streams, on small bodies of water or near shore.

A canvas top makes a good sun shade, but it offers no protection from heavy weather.

Unfortunately, these boats are often overloaded, used on large open bodies of water and in unsafe heavy weather conditions. This was the case on November 14, 1997, when two deer hunters died at Burntside Lake, Minnesota.

The men were operating a 16-foot aluminum boat with a 25 h.p. motor in rough water at night, when according to a newspaper report they were thrown from an icy wooden boat seat. The victims had been contacted by cellular phone and were returning to a boat landing to help transport family members and equipment to a remote cabin site. Authorities theorize that after threading their way among eight wooded islands, the boaters came out into rough, unprotected water and were swept overboard by icy waves.

The victims' sons and a brother became aware of the accident when they heard the clinking sound of their father's boat, which had come to rest with propeller still turning on a beach near the launch area. Quickly searching the lake, they found one of the men floating unconscious.

However, the victim, apparently suffering from hypothermia caused by the near-freezing water, could not be revived. The body of the other man was located the next day.

A word of warning: Operating a small utility boat in rough open water is dangerous; operating under the same conditions at night is doubly dangerous.

Further, operating in near-freezing temperatures also adds risk. Kim Elverum of the Minnesota Department of Natural Resources says one-third of that state's boating fatalities in 1997 occurred in the months of October and November. The accident at Burntside Lake is typical of these tragedies, in which hypothermia was either the cause of death or a contributing factor.

Coast Guard figures for 1996 show 386 fatalities occurred in open motorboats. Further accident data shows that 25 percent of all boating deaths occurred while the person was engaged in fishing or going to or returning from fishing or hunting.

All of which points up the fact that the small, open utility boat is a very dangerous vessel when not operated properly in its intended environment.

Runabouts and Cruisers Runabouts are generally larger than utility vessels. They are used for many recreational purposes such as skiing, camping and fishing. The cruiser type has overnight accommodations. Both of these boats, because of their size, are fairly safe in open water and moderate seas. However, some large cruisers with above-water cabins and tuna towers for sighting fish are difficult to maneuver in high winds.

Houseboats, which are both house and boat, have some seakeeping problems. They are generally not too watertight, have a lot of windage and have large windows which can break during a storm.

I once worked a houseboat accident where broken windows caused the boat to swamp. However, glass breakage can be prevented. This advice comes from Captain Bowell, a Mississippi riverboat operator: a screen often will deflect enough water to prevent broken windows.

A houseboat is somewhat difficult to operate; with the helm inside the house, and a cabin, you generally have to walk through to get from the bow deck to the afterdeck. You can't see objects close at hand and docking is difficult.

Rental houseboats, which are very popular, are usually underpowered and often carry undersized anchors with too-short anchor lines. You can't outrun a storm and you can't set the anchor and ride it out. All you can do is move to a sheltered area. All the rentals at Lake Mead have marine radios. When people have serious problems they can call for help.

In spite of all its drawbacks and poor seakeeping abilities, a houseboat is by virtue of its size a generally seaworthy craft when used on most sheltered inland waters.

Rafts There are several types of rafts: inflatables, rigid hull inflatable boats and pontoon boats. All can carry a great deal of weight and have more floatation and stability than other types of watercraft of the same size. Because of this inherent seaworthiness, the quick inflatable raft is the best choice for a life boat.

The rigid hull inflatable boat has a rigid planing hull bottom with an inflatable tube along the sides. The RHIB combines the seakeeping ability of an inflatable raft with the speed of a conventional powerboat and is often used for rescue work. In fact, this is the fast, easy-to-handle 19-foot Avon rescue boat often used by the Coast Guard.

A pontoon raft is generally a stable, seaworthy craft in sheltered waters, although it lacks maneuverability. The exceptions to this generalization are rafts with high sides, sunshades (either fiberglass or canvas) and small closet-like structures for portable toilets. These superstructures give the vessels excessive windage in relation to their weight.

Personal Watercraft The small jet-powered boat for one or two people has become very popular because it gives high performance at a low cost. It is not a good choice for open water or heavy weather. These boats should be operated close to shore.

Some older models have a circle-back feature. The idea is that if you fall off, the craft will circle back to you. In heavy weather, don't bet on it! Newer models have a kill switch. When you fall off, the engine automatically shuts down. However, in a strong wind, the personal watercraft can blow away faster than you can swim to it.

Safety tips for personal watercraft:

- Always wear a PFD.
- In cold water, wear a wetsuit.
- Stay close to your launch site.
- Watch out for other boats, skiers and other hazards.

And remember: a personal watercraft is a boat, subject to all the rules and regulations that govern the operation of larger powerboats.

Which boat?

Boats come in all sizes and shapes and with various means of propulsion. What represents heavy weather for one type of craft may be a pleasurable cruise for another.

When it comes time to purchase that new boat, you will need to be the best judge of the most suitable craft for your purposes. By pointing out the seakeeping and survivability characteristics of various vessels, I hope to influence your decision in favor of a safer vessel.

However, it is important to remember that almost every boat can be relatively seaworthy when used in its intended environment, skillfully operated and not overloaded.

The dangers arise when heavy weather sets in.

Chapter 12

THE GREAT LAKES AND THE MISSISSIPPI RIVER

What you need to know about two different boating areas

On October 30, 1996, a 95-foot scenic cruiser broke free from its moorings and went adrift on Lake Superior near Grand Marais, Minnesota. This boat, the *Grandpa Woo*, described as "a little Love Boat," had been moored in a protected harbor with its propeller removed to undergo repairs when it was hit by an unexpected northwest wind. The wind rapidly became a gale that overpowered substantial moorings and pushed the boat with two crewmen aboard out into the main lake.

A large lake freighter, the *Walter J. McCarthy*, trying to weather the storm in the lee of an island, heard the *Grandpa Woo's* distress signal. The freighter responded, took the smaller vessel in tow and began making its way toward Thunder Bay, Canada. Waves became more violent, the towline snapped and once again the *Grandpa Woo* was adrift.

Next a Thunder Bay tug, *Glenada*, and a Canadian Coast Guard rescue boat, *Westfort*, arrived to render assistance. But winds of more than 45 miles per hour, 17-foot seas and heavy snowfall thwarted attempts to reestablish a tow. The Coast Guard cutter soon found itself in trouble as breaking waves froze on its windward side. The ice buildup caused the cutter to list and it had to turn back. The *Glenada* pulled alongside the *Grandpa Woo* and the two crew members made a daring leap to the safety of the tug.

Left to the mercy of the storm, the *Grandpa Woo* drifted to Passage Island at the north end of Isle Royale, where it went aground and sank.

This was no ordinary storm, but then this is no ordinary lake. It was a nor'wester on Lake Superior, the biggest, coldest and most dangerous of the Great Lakes. These lakes, known for their severe weather, cannot be compared to any other fresh water in the United States.

Most inland bodies of water have similar heavy weather characteristics, and because of these similarities, a life-threatening emergency on Lake Mead, Nevada, is not much different than the same emergency on Lake Okeechobee, Florida. There are, however, two exceptions: the Great Lakes and big rivers, such as the Mississippi River.

The Great Lakes

Lakes Superior, Michigan, Huron, Erie and Ontario have the largest surface concentration of fresh water in the world: 95,000 square miles. The lakes are accessible to ocean-going vessels via the St. Lawrence Seaway and to small craft traffic from the Atlantic Ocean via the Barge Canal System (Erie Canal) and Hudson River. Also, the lakes can be accessed via the Mississippi River and Illinois Waterway. This makes for a great deal of mixed traffic, both large freighters and small pleasure boats.

Geographically united, the lakes present the boater with similar problems, yet each has its own personality.

Lake Superior is the largest. It covers an area of approximately 31,500 square miles and has a maximum depth of 1,333 feet. It is known for quick storms and different wave patterns. Bob Whaley, a ranger at Isle Royale, tells me the lake can go from relative calm to 20-foot waves in a matter of three or four hours.

Writer Marlin Bree recounts the story of an old captain, Stan Sivertson, in his book, *Call of the North Wind*, which illustrates the capricious nature of Lake Superior. One night in June 1964, Captain Sivertson recalled that he went to sleep on board his boat on a beautiful, calm evening, only to be awakened at about 2 a.m. by pounding waves. The old captain went on to describe a freak wave — an unusual but not unheard-of occurrence on this big lake. From the pilothouse, he saw the wave two miles away, coming toward him. There was no escaping this monster and when it hit, he said, it was "...as though I had jumped off a cliff. We had gone down into this hole in the water, and suddenly, the wave just filled her up again, burying the bow. Finally she came up, shaking the water off."

Superior is also the coldest of the lakes. The water temperature in mid-May, 1997, was 36 degrees, and it never gets much above 50 degrees. Divers report the water is clear and extremely cold with few plants or fish in the deeper open areas. Additionally, the icy water prevents the bodies of drowned seamen from resurfacing. There is a saying that Superior "never gives up her dead." Ships and crews have disappeared, sailing out onto the stormy water never to be seen again.

The most famous of these disappearances was the *Edmund Fitzgerald*, a 729-foot ore freighter that sank during a terrible storm on November 10, 1975. Immortalized in a song by Gordon Lightfoot, the giant ship loaded with 26,013 tons of taconite simply disappeared from the radar of the *Arthur M. Anderson*, a freighter nine miles away. The *Fitzgerald*, considered as unsinkable as the *Titanic*, now lies 530 feet below the surface 17 miles from the safety of Whitefish Bay.

Lake Michigan is the third largest of the lakes. Its length (307 miles) gives winds a sweep that can create some very heavy seas. It has a maximum depth of 923 feet and is warmer than Superior. But according to Bill King, who has fished on the lakes all his life, "there's not a great deal of difference" in the temperatures of these two lakes. There is a scarcity of natural harbors on Lake Michigan and it has a reputation of being one of the most difficult of the lakes to navigate.

On November 18, 1958, it was the scene of one of the worst of the Great Lakes' heavy weather shipping disasters — the sinking of the *Carl D. Bradley*.

Lake Huron, the second largest of the lakes, is located in an area of wild scenic beauty. Beautiful and deadly, it was the site of the worst of the Great Lakes' storms — the Lake Huron storm of November 1913. During this storm, eight ships went down with a loss of 178 lives. Ships that sank in this terrible storm were the 524-foot carrier *Charles S. Price,* the 270-foot *Wexford,* a new 550-foot grain carrier *James C. Carruthers,* the 440-foot *Argus,* the 440-foot freighter *Hydrus,* the 269-foot Canadian freighter *Regina,* the 452-foot *John A. McGean,* and the 524-foot *Isaac M. Scott.* These eight ships — all large freighters — were lost in the worst three-day storm in the history of the lake.

Lake Erie is 241 miles long and 57 miles wide, with an average depth of 100 feet. The shallowest of the lakes, it is the quickest to kick up in a storm. Because the lake lies in an east-west orientation in line with prevailing winds, it is subject to changes in water level (seiches) caused by shifts in wind direction and relative barometric pressure. These changes can be as much as 6 feet and can occur in a matter of a few hours as major weather systems move across the lake. When the water rises, normally visible shoals become submerged, and when the water falls, rocks that had been too deep to be a danger become new unexpected hazards.

Like the other lakes, Erie also has had its share of storms. Black Friday of November 1916, is remembered as the worst storm: four ships went down and 55 sailors lost their lives.

Lake Ontario is the smallest lake. It is 180 miles long, 53 miles wide, has a maximum depth of 738 feet and has many natural harbors. Since the opening of the St. Lawrence Seaway, this lake has become increasingly important as the gateway for ocean-going traffic.

After taking into account their individual differences, we can still draw these conclusions: The Great Lakes are bigger, colder and have more severe storms than other inland bodies of water. In fact, the lakes are more dangerous than the ocean. In one 20-year period between 1879 and 1899, six thousand ships were wrecked on the Great Lakes. There is no section of ocean where an area this small has accounted for this much destruction.The Great Lakes boater faces three problems:

- **Size** The lakes hold the largest concentration of fresh water in the world.
- **Temperature** The water is always cold.
- **Weather** It is often severe and quick-rising.

The problem of size

How do you keep from getting lost on a lake the size of Superior?

Any boater who ventures out into open water must have a chart, a compass and at least some basic knowledge of navigation. Ruth Johnson, former harbor master at Cornucopia, Wisconsin, says she always had to lecture boaters about the need for a current lake chart. She says, "I tell people if you are going out you should let someone know you are going. You should have a chart. You should know where the shoals are." Good advice. Ruth undoubtedly saved some lives.

In addition to a local chart, you really need Chart No. 1. The cost is minimal and this chart is the key to understanding the symbols and abbreviations used. Charts can be purchased at a marine supply store, your local marina or ordered from a catalog published by the NOAA (National Oceanic and Atmospheric Administration).

If you plan to be out at night, you will also need the Light List. Published by the Coast Guard in seven volumes, it contains a list of lights, sound signals, buoys, daybeacons, radiobeacons and LORAN stations. Volume VII is for the Great Lakes region. Light Lists can be ordered from:

Superintendent of Documents

U.S. Government Printing Office

Washington, D.C. 20402

The serious boater will also want the *Coast Pilot,* which has information that cannot be shown with symbols and abbreviations on a chart. *Coast Pilot 6* is for the Great Lakes and is published yearly by NOAA.

To keep up with changing conditions in your boating area, you might ask to be put on the mailing list of *Local Notice to Mariners.* This is a free weekly Coast Guard publication that updates the information contained in the Coast Pilot.

If you plan to boat on the main body of water in any of the Great Lakes, you should have some electronic aids to navigation. Bill King, a retired fisherman still active in the fishing industry as an access site developer for the Chippewa, Ottawa Treaties Fishery Management Authority, knows what it takes to survive on the big lakes. His fishing vessel, now operated by his sons on Lake Michigan, is 52 feet long, 16 feet wide and weighs 50 tons. He says, "It's all steel, cabin, hull, very well built and fully equipped: radar, LORAN-C, automatic pilot, direction finders, fathometers, all of the electronics that you can think of."

Bill and his sons are conscious of risks in bad weather but they are prepared with electronic aids.

Electronics

Radar This device sends out a super-high frequency radio wave which, when it hits an object, is reflected (or echoed) back. The time it takes the radio wave to travel to and from an object is converted into a measure of distance. In principle, it works very much like a depth sounder. The radar pulses are sent out in every direction and not only show the operator the distance to an object, but also the direction.

A small craft radar is usually installed in two units:

The antenna, transmitter, modulator and part of the receiver are in one unit installed as high on the boat as possible. The antenna rotates at the rate of one complete revolution in four seconds. This may seem fast, but the radar pulses are much faster. The pulses are sent out at a rate of from 600 to 4,000 per second. In the time it takes a radar pulse to hit an object and bounce back the revolving antenna has scarcely moved.

The indicator and part of the receiver is installed near the helm, where the skipper can monitor it. The indicator is a round screen which displays the sweep of the radar beam. The center of the screen is the radar's position and reflected objects show up as patches of light in the outer areas of the circle. Direction is shown in relation to the radar with the twelve o'clock position being straight ahead. Distance is indicated by a range scale of circles on the screen and/or a moveable cursor.

Since radar pulses bend slightly the radar can "see" objects just beyond the horizon. This is maximum range. There is also a minimum range. Radar cannot be used to locate objects closer than 20 to 50 yards.

Radar helps the operator avoid collisions and assists in piloting. Its greatest usefulness is at night or on the Great Lakes, when dense fog banks limit visibility.

The liquid-crystal display featured on some newer radars makes installation of a radar possible even where space is limited on a small vessel. This liquid-crystal display is only 7 inches wide, and it is reported to be as good as the larger cathode-ray tube display.

If you cannot afford a radar unit, an inexpensive safeguard for small vessels is a passive radar reflector. This is a lightweight screen which will ensure your boat's detection by radars on nearby ships.

Still another safeguard is the search-and-rescue transponder (SART.) This unit when activated detects radar pulses and responds with a strong signal. A small vessel which ordinarily could not be seen on a radar screen becomes visible. There are occasions, for instance, if you are disabled and adrift or blinded by fog when you will want to let other ships in the area know where you are.

Large vessels on the open water of the lakes should have LORAN-C or GPS, as well as radar for navigation.

LORAN-C (Long Range Navigation) is an electronic aid to navigation.

A signal, much like the super-high frequency radio waves of a radar, is sent from three to five transmitting stations in your boating area.

The on-board LORAN-C receives these signals and measures the differences in lengths of time (time differences) it takes for the signals to travel to the boat. The operator then reads the time differences and plots his or her position on a chart that has been overprinted with LORAN-C lines of position. More expensive receivers have microprocessors that give latitude and longitude, tell which way to steer to stay on course and sound an alarm when you draw near a preset location.

LORAN-C is not a worldwide system, but coverage is very good on the Great Lakes. GPS (Global Positioning System), which can be used anywhere, is becoming more popular and is beginning to replace LORAN-C.

GPS Designed for the Department of Defense for military applications, GPS is now used by many boaters. Its advantages are:

- Accuracy
- Worldwide system
- Easy to use
- Rapidly becoming affordable

GPS is a system based on satellites which orbit the earth twice each day in six orbital planes and transmit data. The GPS receiver collects signals from three or more of these satellites, processes the information and presents it in a navigational display that gives your position to within 25 meters or less. A receiver in continuous operation updates your position approximately every second.

The receiver must be in direct view of the satellite from which it is collecting data. When it is installed in the cabin of a boat, it has to have an outside antenna. I have an inexpensive portable GPS which shows position and how to stay on course, stores waypoints and route information, and displays date, time, and speed. It also has a man overboard function, which records my position at the touch of a specially marked Man Overboard button and gives a reciprocal course for backtracking.

More expensive chartplotter units show your position on a chart of your area. The accuracy of your unit can be enhanced with a GBR Differential GPS Beacon Receiver, which decodes correction signals broadcast by the Coast Guard and the International Association of Lighthouse Authorities. The information collected by a GBR Differential GPS Beacon Receiver is transferred to your GPS unit to give you pinpoint accuracy.

Some units display navigation information in wide choice of formats and have display screens that interface with your other on-board electronics to show GPS data along with LORAN-C, radar, water depth and temperature and may even operate in conjunction with an automatic pilot system.

Based on personal experience, I highly recommend the GPS.

Depth Sounder Sometimes called a fathometer, it can be both a navigational aid and a warning device for shallow water. Comparing depth displayed by your depth sounder to depths given on a chart is another way to check your location. An alarm can be set to go off when water is only a few feet deeper than the draft of the boat. This will warn you of an impending grounding.

Depth is determined by an ultrasonic wave, which travels from the bottom of the boat, strikes an underwater object and is reflected back. The lapse time between the transmitted sound and the received echo is translated by the depth sounder into feet, meters or fathoms. Depth is usually shown on a digital display.

Fish finders, another type of fathometer, generally have video screen displays and show not only bottoms and depth, but what's in between — hopefully fish. A depth sounder with digital display used only to determine water depth is usually easier to read and better for navigation than a fish finder.

Make sure the transducer (the device for sending and receiving sound waves) is properly mounted on the bottom of your boat. It should be level so it won't give a false reading and away from the propeller and other hull obstructions that could cause loss of signal. Remember that the depth sounder shows the distance from the transducer to the bottom. Add the distance from the transducer to the waterline on your boat to get accurate water depth. Don't make the mistake I made once and let a crew member step into water over his or her head because the depth sounder showed water less than four feet deep.

When you are in trouble on a big lake you need the ultimate distress signal EPIRB (Emergency Position Indicating Radio Beacon).

EPIRB This is a small transmitter that broadcasts a distress signal to aircraft and/or satellites.

The 406 EPIRBs operate on frequency 406.025 MHz to communicate with satellites. This improved system can rapidly calculate your position to within about two miles and relay this information to rescue agencies such as the Coast Guard. The sophisticated 406 MHz EPIRB system broadcasts a signal which contains a code with the vessel's type, size, owner and identification number. The receiving satellite stores the signal, quickly computes position, then relays this information when it is over the nearest ground station. The latest 406 EPIRB gives fast, global coverage. Additionally these units transmit a low powered signal on 121.5 MHz which can be used by rescuers as a homing signal, and they come equipped with a strobe light.

The 406 EPIRBs are either Category 1 EPIRBs automatically transmitting the radio beacon when submerged, or Category 2 EPIRBs turned on manually. Category 1 units should be installed in a high, open place so they can float to the surface when hydrostatically released. Category 2 EPIRBs should be kept in a dry convenient location, such as in your abandon ship kit.

Advantages of the 406 EPIRB:

- It is small enough to take with you when you abandon ship.
- A class 1 EPIRB will activate automatically when submerged.
- The signal will be heard. A satellite will hear, store and relay your location.
- A rescue agency will respond.

Less expensive, and less reliable, are the 121.5 EPIRBs. These units are Class A automatically activated or Class B manually activated. They broadcast a signal on radio frequency 121.5 MHz and 243 MHz which alerts aircraft and satellites. The disadvantages of 121.5 EPIRBs are:

1. The satellite receiving the 121.5 EPIRB's signal does not store it. The satellite has to be in contact with the 121.5 EPIRB and a rescue station at the same time to relay the distress signal.

2. The signal is not as powerful as the 406 EPIRB.

3. Ninety to ninety-five percent of the 121.5 EPIRB's distress signals turned out to be false alarms caused by improper testing or handling of the unit.

A boater cannot depend on a quick response to an 121.5 EPIRB alert, because the Coast Guard must first determine if there is a real emergency before starting a search-and-rescue operation.

4. The 121.5 EPIRB's signal does not contain information that will identify you or your vessel.

Because it is much more reliable, I suggest that you purchase the 406 EPIRB. Even though it costs more, it is probably worth the extra money.

Whichever system you have, remember to check, test and log results once a month. To do this turn the unit on during the first five minutes of an hour for less than three seconds. The 406 system has a self-testing circuit. Be sure to turn the EPIRB off after testing. Since all EPIRBs are battery operated, remember to check the expiration date on the battery, and when you buy the 406 EPIRB register it. It is estimated that only 70 percent of the EPIRBs are properly registered. Proper registration ensures a quicker response to your emergency.

Now you can rent an EPIRB. If you only need an EPIRB occasionally, say for a few weeks vacation on the Great Lakes, then renting is probably the best way to solve your safety equipment problem. BOAT/U.S. has a mail-order EPIRB rental system, as well as marine centers that rent a safety kit containing: 406 EPIRB, handheld GPS, handheld VHF radio and two solar flares. Addresses for the two marine centers located near the Great Lakes:

2212 E. Fourteen Mile Rd.

Warren, MI 48092

Telephone: 810-939-5050

and

63 W. Rand Rd.

Arlington Heights, IL 60004

Telephone: 847-398-0606

The rental cost for this safety kit is minimal; the value, in the event of an emergency, is priceless.

In the event of a mayday emergency you should if you have time broadcast a call for help on your marine radio as well as activate your EPIRB.

Modern electronics have reduced the danger of not being found on the Great Lakes in the event of an emergency, and size has become a manageable problem. In fact, size is of little consequence if you know where you are and can let others know where you are.

The second problem is cold water.

The problem of temperature

The main body of water in Lake Superior never gets warmer than the low to mid 50s F. Even the so-called warmer lakes are always cold. This means anyone in the water is in grave danger of suffering hypothermia.

Bill King, of William King and Sons Fisheries Inc., remembers that sometime after 1981, when he and his three sons went into business for themselves, one of his boys fell overboard. The accident happened on a summer day when, according to Bill there was "pretty good weather" (high seas). His middle son, who was working with nets, lost his footing and fell overboard. He was not wearing a life jacket, but managed to hold on to the net. The other two boys backed the boat up, pulled in the net and lifted their brother back into the boat. Even though Bill's son was probably in the water less than four minutes, the extremely cold water numbed and exhausted him.

Bill says, "If he would have had to get aboard by himself, he couldn't have. He needed a lot of help." If one of his other sons had gone into the water in an attempt to save his brother, it would only have compounded the problem. Bill could easily have lost all his boys that day. He says, "And for no one else to jump overboard to try to help him was amazing. To get him back aboard was, I would say, a near miracle with that kind of weather and the drifting and the inexperience and all." Bill sums up the experience, "The good Lord was with them."

To survive in cold water, you must wear a survival or cold water exposure suit. For instance, during the week of Fourth of July, 1997, the water temperature on Lake Superior was 43 degrees. Life expectancy for an adult in this temperature is less than two hours.

Immersion suit

The great number of deaths due to hypothermia in the Great Lakes caused the Coast Guard in the '70s to initiate research on personal floatation devices that offered cold water protection. The result of this research is a neoprene immersion suit. This suit is loose fitting, goes on over shoes and boots, has a watertight zipper and can be put on quickly. It has 55 pounds of floatation with an inflatable pillow behind the head, which gives an additional 15 pounds of buoyancy. Since the suit does not require the wearer to remove shoes before donning, it is Coast Guard approved as a PFD when worn. Called a ship abandonment suit, or a Gumby suit by Coast Guarders, it comes in three sizes: child, adult and oversize adult (Figure 12.1).

Fig. 12.1   Gumby immersion suit

There are other types of immersion suits available, including a nylon-covered neoprene suit that looks like a snowmobile outfit. Popular on the North Sea, this suit offers hypothermia protection on deck as well as in the water, when worn over other clothing. Some suits have removable gloves and detachable boots. You should choose the best one for your activity. Write the name of your vessel and/or your name on the suit.

Before donning the suit, you should be wearing plenty of warm clothing. Even though the ship abandonment suit is an approved PFD, it can be worn over a vest type PFD. In an emergency, I certainly wouldn't take time to remove my Type III PFD before pulling on an immersion suit. A fully clothed adult in this neoprene suit will lose much less than 1 degree of heat per hour and people have been known to survive for several days without serious heat loss.

Every boater operating in open water on the Great Lakes should carry ship abandonment suits of some type for all passengers and crew members. Bill King's sons have immersion suits on their new 52-foot fishing boat and all National Park Service boats in Lake Superior are equipped with this survival gear.

Not only will the responsible Great Lakes boater have ship abandonment suits on board, but he or she will also store them properly for easy access and check them periodically for signs of wear. After using your immersion suit, make sure it is completely dry, check the inside of the glove fingers for mildew and rot, and oil the zipper with a paraffin-based lubricant. When you are certain the suit is clean and dry, roll it from the feet up with arms folded across the bundle before putting it in its bag for storage.

When you need to don an immersion suit, you will probably be in bad weather with the deck pitching and rolling. You also will be in a hurry. One manufacturer of these suits states that they are to be donned while on board, never in the water. It's a good idea to practice putting one on. Time yourself. You should be able to put the suit on in less than a minute.

Directions for donning an immersion suit:

1. Sit down on deck.
2. Put feet in first like putting on pajamas.
3. Put weak arm into sleeve. (If you are right handed, put left arm in sleeve.)
4. Pull hood over your head.
5. Put strong arm in sleeve last.
6. Arch your back and zip up.

The neoprene immersion suit is bright orange with retro-reflective tape on hood, shoulders and legs, making it easier to spot in the water.

A fully clothed person in a neoprene suit can survive in cold water for up to several days.

Because the suit is bulky and restricts movement, you might want to put on the lower half and tie the sleeves around your waist. This will enable you to quickly finish donning the suit just before entering the water.

If you have to abandon ship, you will be more comfortable, as well as easier to spot from the air, if you are in a life raft. Life rafts are the vessels of last resort. In general, Great Lakes sailors, for obvious reasons, prefer to stay with their boats as long as their boats stay with them.

Survival raft

The Coast Guard requires survival rafts on commercial vessels carrying passengers and fishing boats with more than six crewmen. Life rafts are not required on recreational boats and most boats under 30 feet do not carry them. Bob Whaley at Isle Royale estimates that about 25 percent of the powerboats over 30 feet do carry an inflatable raft of some kind. Many of these boats have dive platforms on the stern and the raft is fastened to this platform, where it is out of the water yet accessible. These inflatables are usually not a true survival raft but could be used in an abandon ship emergency.

Bill King's fishing vessel does not have a survival raft.

Space is the problem. He says the canister containing the survival raft would have to be fastened to the top of the boat and he notes, "The boats aren't that big. In a good breeze (hard blow) they thrash around considerably. It would be difficult to keep something up there that could be freed up if there was a problem."

Most boaters do not have a true survival raft because it is an expensive piece of equipment. On many vessels, especially sailboats, an inflatable raft or rigid dinghy is used when the boat is anchored out as transportation to and from the shore. If these rigid dinghies have built-in floatation, they can be used as life rafts. But neither the rigid dinghy nor the inflatable raft boat-tender are as seaworthy as a true self inflating survival raft.

They are, however, much better than finding yourself in the water, or as Bob Whaley says, "better than whistling the Gilligan's Island song." A word of warning: a personal watercraft (often carried on larger boats) is not and should not be used as a life raft.

The self-inflating life raft, the choice of yachtsmen, is:

- Easily stowed.
- Easy to deploy.
- Inflatable with a jerk of a lanyard.
- Comparatively stable in heavy seas.

This type of raft comes in a canister or valise and should be secured somewhere topside on the vessel. If it is stored below deck, you should be able to launch it in 15 seconds or less. The raft will contain many of the items you need for survival and when mounted topside will usually have a hydrostatic release if the boat sinks the raft will float to the surface. The inflation lanyard tethered to your boat will inflate the raft before a weak link in the lanyard breaks, setting the raft free.

One hopes, of course, that the raft would not be launched by the sinking of your vessel but would be launched manually before the boat sinks. The manufacturer of the raft will undoubtedly pack, install and demonstrate proper launching of the raft.

Life raft safety tips:

An inflatable raft is economical and relatively seaworthy. It is often used as a life raft.

- Make sure at least one crew member is trained in proper deployment of the life raft.
- Be sure the raft's tether line is fastened to the vessel before it is launched.
- Launch raft to the leeward, amidships.
- Step directly into the raft, not into the water.
- Fire one distress flare as soon as you abandon your vessel. Save your other flares to be used when rescuers are within seeing or hearing distance.
- Keep the raft tethered to the abandoned vessel as long as the disabled boat remains afloat. This makes it easier for rescue aircraft to spot you. Also, there have been cases where the abandoned ship survived, but the life raft did not.

Even though the survival raft has some gear packed in it, you will want to supplement these minimum supplies with an abandon ship bag. Certainly, if you are depending on an inflated raft or rigid dinghy, you will want to have a well stocked kit stored where you can grab it quickly.

Abandon ship bag supplies:

- 50-foot floating line
- Hand-held, battery-operated VHF radio and/or EPIRB
- Flares, signaling devices and a flashlight
- A knife

- Warm clothing, shoes, gloves, caps, blankets
- Food
- Medications (including seasick pills) and glasses

One important item which cannot be packed in the abandon ship bag, but which is essential for your survival, is the will to live.

A book first published in the 1960s, *Great Lakes Shipwrecks & Survivals* by William Ratigan, contains many stories of bravery on the lakes and victims' will to survive. Perhaps the most dramatic of these tales is the survival of Dennis Hale, a twenty-six-year-old burly wheelhouse watchman who lived 36 hours on an open pontoon raft in freezing water.

On November 29, 1966, the freighter *Morrell* with 29 crewmen aboard broke in two during a violent storm. Unable to find his pants or shoes, Hale escaped the wreckage wearing only a heavy pea coat and a life jacket.

He was picked up by other crewmen crowded on a pontoon raft, but a short time later the raft was rammed by the aft section of the *Morrell*. Everyone washed overboard and only four men made it back onto the raft. Two of Hale's shipmates died about six hours later; the third, a 42-year-old wheelsman, died the next day. Using the dead men as protection from the cold, Hale survived 36 hours.

A helicopter rescue crew found the raft aground at the water's edge. Too weak to wade ashore, Hale managed to wave to his rescuers. Later, when asked why he alone survived, he said, "I did want to get home. I wanted to be with my wife and four children for Christmas."

If you ever find yourself adrift in a life raft, think about Dennis Hale. He made it; you can, too. It is your duty to have a positive attitude and to help keep up morale on board.

Of the three big problems (size, temperature and weather) you face on the Great Lakes the biggest is severe weather.

The problem of weather

The location of the Great Lakes along the polar front is largely responsible for the severe weather. In spring and fall, there is a great contrast between cold arctic air and warmer tropical air masses. This often generates numerous, intense rapidly moving low pressure systems — wind.

So what should you do if you are caught out on a large lake in a small boat during a big storm?

Cornie Paauwe of Grand Rapids, Michigan, answered that question. After reading in *Lakeland Boating* magazine that I was writing a book about heavy weather, he wrote to tell me about his experience. He began his letter by saying, "My story goes back to October, 1968. It was during the first year of the salmon spawning run on Lake Michigan and people were in a frenzy over Coho Fever."

Cornie and his friend, Tom Glass, launched their 16-foot boat at Frankfort, Michigan, and headed for Platte Bay anticipating an exciting day of fishing. What they got was plenty of excitement, but no fish.

When they cast off early in the morning, they didn't see any small craft warnings and many small boats were on the water. Soon after they reached Platte Bay, the wind began to blow. Cornie wasn't too concerned because the wind was coming from the east. Since they were on the east side of the lake, he thought they would be on the windward shore, the safest place to be in a storm as they returned to the harbor. Nevertheless, they decided to head back to Frankfort.

When they left the bay, they discovered they had not been getting a true wind direction. The storm was coming from the southwest. They were, in fact, on the leeward shore. Out in open water near Point Betsi, the seas became six feet high. Cornie decided to turn farther away from shore where the waves would be easier to ride and they could avoid the white water and breaking surf. Suddenly, they encountered 20- to 25-foot waves. Cornie remembers that as they moved at slow speed, meeting the waves head on, they "would motor up the wave (to) the top...and then would almost fall and slam hard onto the water again."

Their next big problem was how to turn to enter the Frankfort harbor. Cornie says, "I didn't want to get caught sideways and neither did I want to travel into the harbor in the trough of the waves. So I went well past the harbor, picked a wave to make a quick turn on, and then we rode a wave right into the harbor."

"After loading the boat onto the trailer, we turned on the radio and were shocked to hear how many others were having a disaster....Most boats that tried to beach ended up overturned...That day five people drowned and hundreds had to be rescued."

Obviously, Cornie had a seaworthy craft with plenty of power (75 h.p.) and made wise choices. He summed up the experience by saying, "We made the right decisions that day. In the past 29 years, and well over a thousand hours fishing and cruising Lake Michigan, I have not experienced a storm like that one."

Cornie Paauwe was indeed lucky. Even larger vessels try to avoid storms of this magnitude. But when caught in high seas, your only defense is slow down and avoid the dangerous surf.

In addition to the winds produced by rapid moving low pressure systems, there are the problems of fog, rain, snow and extreme cold weather. These are caused by polar fronts.

In spring and fall, this cold air moves over the warmer lakes picking up both heat and humidity and becoming increasingly unstable. This produces clouds and rain or snow.

In winter, polar air often causes the lakes to freeze over. Coast Guard ice breakers keep the shipping channels open within the lakes. But the locks between the lakes and the St. Lawrence Seaway freeze solid.

Except for traffic within each lake, large freighters usually operate only from April to December. For recreational boaters, the season is even shorter.

Thunderstorms can develop any time, but are more likely during the boating season (May through October). The Coast Guard reports there are about five days each month with significant thunderstorm activity in the summer.

Another problem is fog, which forms when the water is coldest in relation to the air. As the water warms up in the spring and again as it cools in the fall, fog is prevalent.

Bob Whaley, a ranger at Isle Royale, says, "I pilot a 31-foot cruiser and there are times when you can't see the bow when you are in the pilot house." He describes it as being "like walking into a dark room."

Since boaters cannot change the weather, they avoid the storms when they can.

People on the Great Lakes take weather seriously.

National Weather Service

Bob Whaley says, "We don't get that many sinkings. And the reason is because the marine forecast is listened to. Life operates around the marine forecast at the Great Lakes. It is one of the first things a lot of people listen to when they get up in the morning. And their day is based on what the marine forecast says."

The National Weather Service broadcasts a continuous, updated forecast on VHF-FM frequencies ranging from 162.4 to 162.55 MHz. When there is severe weather, regular transmission is interrupted by a ten-second high-pitched tone followed by emergency information.

The NWS also issues weather warnings, which are displayed with flags or lights at most marinas.

Small Craft Warning A red flag, or at night, one red light over a white light indicates winds up to 38 miles per hour are forecast.

A fishing boat has protected cockpit and plenty of deck space aft.

The serious fisherman will enjoy this vessel, with room for fishing gear and nets on the after deck. Most boats of this type have built-in floatation and are relatively stable.

Gale Warning Two red flags, or at night, a white light over a red light means winds between 39 and 54 miles per hour are forecast.

A word of advice to boat operators: do not depend solely on these warning signals. Flags and lights are supplementary warnings. Your primary source of weather information is the NWS broadcast.

As Bill King says, "If it gets up in those kind of conditions (20 to 30 foot waves) we normally stay home. And if they (his sons) get caught out there, they run slow and take their time."

Fetch

Heavy weather conditions on the Great Lakes are different from conditions on other lakes. The storms are worse, the water is colder. But the biggest difference is big waves, caused in part by fetch.

As detailed in Chapter 4, waves are created when three elements are present: wind speed, wind duration and fetch. Due to huge size, the Great Lakes offer the winds plenty of fetch. On Lake Superior, gales can scour the waters over hundreds of miles, causing a sea with wave heights of 25 to 30 feet.

Generally, rivers do not have enough fetch to create waves and consequently do not have large waves. The exception to this is large rivers, such as the Mississippi.

Mississippi River

On both the upper Mississippi (above Cairo, Illinois) and the lower Mississippi (below Cairo) there are wide, long stretches of open water. As an Army Corps of Engineers spokesperson in St. Paul pointed out, "Any time you have a long reach of water that's exposed to wind that is blowing down the length of the lake, you can generate some pretty good sized waves."

One of these places is below the Chippewa River's confluence with the Mississippi. A natural constriction of the channel, augmented by a Corps lock and dam, makes a large body of water called Lake Pepin where on June 30, 1993, 70-mile-an-hour winds and 10-foot waves were recorded. An Army Corps of Engineers report of wave damage to the bank and breakwater states: "The winds were steady out of the southwest at probably 65 m.p.h. with gusts as high as 75 m.p.h. and lasted about 1.5 hours. A southwest wind has approximately an eight-mile fetch of open water, which is the longest possible at Lake City. The waves were estimated by eyewitnesses to be about 10 to 11 feet high."

There are also wide, long stretches of water on the lower Mississippi, where four- and five-foot waves are not unusual. Don Williams, who was a surveyor for the Army Corps of Engineers several years ago, recalled some very rough water at Cracraft about 50 miles above Vicksburg, Mississippi. On this straight stretch of river, wind-generated waves were a real challenge for his 26-foot survey boat. And Bob Rentschler, also with the Army Corps of Engineers at Vicksburg, remembers that Hurricane Andrew produced waves large enough to sink a barge at St. Francisville, on the Mississippi above Baton Rouge.

Both Williams and Rentschler mentioned the hazards of wind blowing against current. The combination can produce sizable waves. Also a danger on the lower Mississippi is the prevalence of hurricane and tornado-type winds, which can cause unexpectedly large seas.

Don Williams vividly remembers battling these waves on a day when the winds were blowing so hard the tow boats had to tie up. He says, "I was young and foolish then... Anyway, I said, 'Let's just go out there and see how big they (the waves) are.'" Don remembers that he and his expert boat operator soon found out how big the waves were. Fear may have made the waves seem larger than they actually were, but Don says, "They were at least 20 feet that day." He ends the story by saying, "So we just maintained between the two (waves) and eased back to the bank."

The Mississippi River does indeed have heavy weather, but as Captain Bill Bowell, a river boat captain with more than 40 years' experience on the upper Mississippi, states: "The most important thing is not to panic. Just realize no matter what the hell happens you can stop your engine and let the wind blow you to shore." And that is exactly what he did when 100-mile-an-hour winds at the edge of a tornado hit his 313-passenger paddle wheeler. He says, "I didn't even have time to close the windows in the pilot house when the damn thing hit. I just let it rain on the wheel and let the wind take me into shore."

He adds that boaters should watch weather reports and tie up along the bank before a storm hits. "Anticipate the problem. And resolve it before you're hit with high winds."

Because rivers are always changing, it's important to know your boating area. Talk to those who do know it. Have a current *River Chart and a Light List Volume V: Mississippi River System.* Also the Mississippi River boater will benefit greatly by purchasing *Quimby's Cruising Guide.* This publication was started by a little old lady who made a hobby of keeping track of all the places on the river that serviced boats. When she died, *Waterways Journal* took over the publication and professionalized it. It is available from:

Waterways Journal
319 N. 4th, Suite 650
St. Louis, MO 63102

One final word of advice for both lakes and rivers: Slow down in high waters. Captain Bill Bowell said, "Lower your cruising speed. Point the bow into the wind and ride it out."

A large, open utility boat, which is an oversized Jon boat. It has a fiberglass or aluminum flat-bottom hull and an outboard engine.

Transport supplies and tools to the job on the open deck space, and at the work site, this boat also becomes a base of operations. Divers carry tanks and diving gear. Anchored, this vessel becomes a good dive platform.

Life savers

The agency that enforces laws and protects life and property on the Great Lakes and the Mississippi River is the United States Coast Guard. This organization was created by Congress in 1915 by merging the Revenue Cutter Service and the Life-Saving Service into one unit. The Life-Saving Service branch of this merger included four Life-Saving stations opened in 1876 on Lake Superior. From the beginning the Life-Saving Service, now the Coast Guard, can proudly point to a long and distinguished tradition of service on the Great Lakes.

The Life Savers were brave, strong men between the ages of 18 and 45 who rowed wooden boats out into storms to rescue shipwrecked sailors. They had an unofficial motto: "You have to go out. You don't have to come back." For more information about the heroism of these men see Marlin Bree's *Call of the North Wind*.

In 1905, the Coast Guard began using motorized surf boats and it was one of these vessels that responded to the *Carl D. Bradley's* distress call in November, 1958. Viewers at the Charlevoix Coast Guard station watched in amazement as a 36-foot lifeboat with three men aboard battled waves that had sunk a 640-foot freighter. However, it was the 180-foot Coast Guard cutter *Sundew* that rescued the two survivors 14 hours after the disaster.

Today, as in the past, these heroic men are as devoted as ever to the protection of life and property. Recently, Peter W. Hocking, Chief Quartermaster of the Coast Guard Cleveland Rescue Coordination Center sent me a memorandum titled *The Great Summer Storm 1995*, which I have summarized:

Early on the morning of July 13, 1995, a severe thunderstorm began making its way across the Great Lakes. The first calls for help came to the Bayfield Station in Wisconsin, where the storm overtook several pleasure boats near the Apostle Islands. With winds in excess of 60 miles per hour, golf-ball-size hail and torrential rains, the storm moved across Michigan's Upper Peninsula and into northern Lake Michigan. Within 90 minutes, stations in Charlevoix, St. Ignace and Alpena responded to eleven maydays.

Moving at 40 miles per hour, the storm rolled through the

Straits of Mackinac and turned south into Lake Huron. During the next four hours stations Tawas, Saginaw River and Port Huron responded to 32 distress calls.

The Cleveland, Ohio, Rescue Coordination Center easily tracked the storm every hour the next small boat station in the storm's path was flooded with maydays.

Shortly after six o'clock, the storm hit Lake Erie, where it inflicted havoc on evening sailing and racing events. Even though the National Weather Service had issued a severe weather broadcast, the yacht clubs had not heeded the warning and were conducting exercises as usual.

The storm was moving so rapidly that even the fastest powerboats could not get away from it. Units of Coast Guard Group Detroit covering southern Lake Huron and western Lake Erie responded to a total of 152 distress calls.

Over a period of 14 hours, this storm directly caused more than 200 cases of flooding, capsizing, sinking, loss of position, disabled and adrift, grounding and man overboard.

All Coast Guard boats and flight crews were recalled for duty. Helicopters used in the search-and-rescue operations reported winds exceeding 45 knots with lightning, hail and severe turbulence.

One of the most dramatic cases was a powerboat reported overdue on a trip from the islands in western Lake Erie to Lorain, Ohio. A helicopter from Air Station Detroit was diverted to conduct a track-line search for the missing boat.

In late evening darkness, the pilot spotted a small red light. He turned the helicopter around and saw a small green light. A closer look revealed the bow of a small boat sticking out of the water with two people tied to it.

The helicopter deployed a rescue swimmer, who found a husband and wife clinging to the hull with mooring lines wrapped around them. The couple had been in the water eight hours with only one life jacket between them. They were bruised and suffering from mild hypothermia. If not for the vigilance of the Coast Guard pilot, it is unlikely that these people would have survived.

Nobody knows how many acts of individual heroism there were that night.

But after the storm front passed and fatigued boat and air

crews got their well-deserved rest, it became clear to them that a miracle had taken place.

Ninth District units responded to more than 200 search-and-rescue cases. More than 250 people were saved.

And not one life was lost!

Chapter 13:

THE CAPTAIN'S JOB

What the boat operator should know and do

During my years of boat patrol duty, I have observed many accidents and fatalities that resulted from operator error — poor judgment. And the biggest judgment error of all was casting off in foul weather. This is clearly asking for trouble.

An incident of this type happened here on November 11, 1955. Two men — ages 29 and 62 years — traveled with their families from California to Lake Mead for a weekend of fishing. When they arrived, they found a strong wind blowing. However, they had come a great distance to fish and they were not going to let the weather spoil their weekend's pleasure. Against the better judgment of family members and the advice of park rangers, they launched a 14-foot boat at Las Vegas Bay.

The two fishermen were last seen headed out of the bay into unprotected open water. The next day, the boat was found overturned in Callville Bay, but the bodies were never recovered.

If these boaters could have seen the consequences of their action, they would have canceled their plans — maybe had a bummer of a day — but would have been able to go fishing on another day when the weather was better. Being disappointed isn't the worst thing that can happen to you.

This accident resulted from boating in bad weather. With weather forecasts much more accurate than they were in the past, many fatalities are preventable. Except for quick-rising thunderstorms, the boater usually has ample warning.

However, most fatalities do not happen solely because of the weather. One of my supervisors at Lake Meredith studied all of our fatal boating accidents, breaking down the causes. He concluded that nearly every death resulted from a series of events and poor choices.

For example: A small boat goes out on a stormy day or when bad weather is forecast — bad choice number one.

Then the boat breaks down and nobody puts on a life jacket — bad choice number two.

Finally, the boat capsizes and those aboard try to swim, instead of staying with the boat — bad choice number three.

My supervisor believed, if you could break this chain of events at any one of the links, you could prevent a fatality. That is the purpose of this book: to give you information to help you formulate a plan to break a link in the chain of events leading to a death.

Additionally, someone has to be a leader, make decisions and issue orders. In most recreational boating situations, a loose assignment of command is acceptable.

After pointing out the location of safety equipment on board and explaining to guests and crew what is expected of them, the skipper can become a laissez-faire leader. A weekend outing is not a Naval exercise with the captain barking orders and the crew smartly carrying out his commands.

But during times of crisis, this changes.

Suddenly, there is a need for a strong and clear command. If you are the boat operator, even if it is not your personality, you must strongly assert yourself as the leader. You are responsible for the vessel and the people on board.

Think through your situation, make decisions and issue orders. Use all the resources available to you. You can seek input from other crew members, but in the end you must formulate and implement the plan.

Even when the situation is life threatening and you are truly afraid, you must project an image of confidence. Controlling yourself is the first step toward controlling passengers and crew members and ultimately controlling the outcome of the emergency.

To deal with any emergency, you must first be prepared, have proper equipment on board and know how to use it.

Next you must form a plan — know what to do if something goes wrong.

Be prepared

I remember an incident some years ago that involved a young ranger who had just completed his basic boat training and was dispatched to assist a vessel that had gone aground during a storm. The ranger knew this was beyond his ability and requested another patrol boat take the call. Unfortunately, his supervisor insisted that he take the assignment.

The grounded boat was on a rocky leeward beach and a rescue would have been a tough job for an experienced operator with a deckhand.

But this ranger had neither experience nor help. He got the towline to the grounded boat, but before he could pull away, the line wrapped around the propeller. Without power, his boat went aground.

This ranger needlessly had to attempt something beyond his capabilities. As a boat operator you must stay within the limits of your ability and the limits of your equipment. You should also endeavor to expand your capabilities.

- Take safe boating classes.
- Learn CPR and First Aid.
- Practice emergency procedures.
- Learn from others.
- Read widely about boating and boaters.

Boating can be a lifelong learning opportunity and sharpening your skills will certainly improve your response to a real emergency.

Maintain a shipshape vessel

It is the operator's responsibility to make sure the boat is in good repair and that PFDs and other safety equipment are stowed properly on board. If you know there is a mechanical problem, don't take the boat out until it has been repaired. This is simple, common sense. Unfortunately, some boaters ignore their common sense.

And never, never leave the dock without a properly fitting PFD for each person in the boat. Not having adequate PFDs on board is illegal.

On May 19, 1995, two men went fishing on Lake Fannie, Florida, in a 12-foot aluminum boat powered by an electric motor. They had fished only about half an hour when they were suddenly hit by a powerful storm with winds of 35 miles per hour. The small craft swamped and sank in a matter of minutes and there was only one PFD in the boat. The operator made it to shore with the aid of the PFD. The other man drowned.

Since operating a vessel without the minimum-required Coast Guard safety equipment on board is against the law, this operator has been charged with one count of Culpable Negligence.

Have a plan

How a boat operator and crew handle themselves in an emergency is a true test of competency. Most experienced boaters in a seaworthy vessel can successfully navigate three- or four-foot seas without serious problems.

But throw in an emergency and the situation changes. Many boaters suddenly find themselves in serious trouble.

When things go wrong, you can still maintain control if you know what to do. The outcome of almost every emergency can be altered.

In this book, I have presented heavy weather emergencies and discussed methods of responding to them. But you alone will have to implement these procedures.

When a problem occurs you (the captain) must take control:

- Size up the problem.
- Formulate a plan.
- Execute the plan.
- Evaluate the results.

I recounted a tragic capsizing incident in Chapter 5 in which two people died of hypothermia. This accident occurred several years ago when a family of four became separated from the rest of their boating group and their vessel capsized in moderately heavy weather. Even though they were wearing PFDs and managed to climb onto the overturned hull of the boat, the wife and youngest child died of hypothermia before rescuers arrived more than six hours later.

Researching this accident, I talked to Philip Rennert, who helped rescue the survivors. Philip pointed out that these boaters might have saved themselves if they had not made some unfortunate decisions.

It was his opinion that they didn't properly size up the problem. When Philip asked the husband why they had remained with the boat instead of leaving the vessel and letting the wind drift them to shore, the man explained that his wife's purse was in the boat. Philip remembers the man said that, his wife's major concern was the boat and staying with the boat because her purse was in it.

This did not make sense to Philip, who went on to offer this advice to anyone in a similar situation, "You're responsible for everybody on that boat. Stop and take a breath and think clearly: Okay, what is my objective? My objective is to stay alive. It's not to worry about the boat I just bought, how much it cost, who I owe, where my wallet is or where the purse is. First and foremost is life. Save the life of my children, save my wife's life. Where is the shore? Get to shore."

Second, Philip believes they did not formulate a plan. "It is really important for people to have a plan ahead of time. They hadn't really planned if this were to happen, what would we do. It seemed like they said, 'We have something that's floating, so let's stick with it.'"

As I've pointed out, staying with the boat is normally the right choice. However, in this case, the anchor, which fell out of the boat when it capsized, had caught on a sand bar as the vessel drifted toward shore. These people were close to shore and wearing life jackets, and the wind was blowing toward the land.

Philip Rennert points out that the water was shallow. The victim later reported that he could see the anchor caught on the sand reef. This has caused Philip to wonder why they didn't cut the anchor line or dive down and dislodge the anchor.

I believe these victims may have been trying to execute the plan — stay with the boat. But staying with the boat was not keeping them alive.

The last step in solving a problem is to evaluate the results. If, as in this case, no help arrives, and you and your family begin to suffer from hypothermia, certainly when your wife dies — you should realize you are not achieving your objective. This is when you should reevaluate the situation and implement another plan.

Philip sums up the situation by saying, "There were a number of things that could have been done.... It seems to me that you ought to have a contingency plan — rather than just get one idea and go brain dead."

Summary

The captain's duty:

- Obtain an up-to-date weather forecast before casting off.
- Make sure the vessel is shipshape, in good repair and is equipped with safety gear.
- Operate within your limits and the limits of your vessel. If you lack experience or your boat is small don't go out on a bad weather day.
- Maintain full authority during a crisis.
- Consider existing conditions and anticipate the results of actions. A good leader does not allow the problem to drive him. He or she is proactive, not reactive.
- Prepare for emergencies.

There are many things that can go wrong during heavy weather. They can be minor annoyances, such as spilled coffee in the galley, or major disasters including capsizing and sinking. Whatever the problem, you have to take control.

Although the time you have to react may vary, the mental steps are the same: size up the problem, formulate a plan and then execute it.

Take this advice, like everything else in this book, and add to it.

Your experiences will provide new answers to old problems.

Twenty- to 30-foot cabin cruiser. This seaworthy vessel has decked over bow, enclosed cockpit, bilge pumps and backup pumps, marine electronics and a powerful marine engine.

This is the boater's boat. The captain of this vessel is proud of his or her "ship" and enjoys taking it out on the water. Typically the skipper is safety concious and has a good background of nautical information.

EPILOGUE

Small boats are better designed, stronger and safer than ever. The boating equipment available today is excellent. State and federal boating regulations have been tightened, and boating education and safety campaigns are being promoted.

At the present time, 20 states require some form of boater education for young boat operators. There have been tremendous improvements in all areas of boating safety, yet people are still getting into trouble on the water.

Many of the problems are the result of heavy weather. I know, because while I'm no longer a patrol ranger, I'm still actively involved in water search and rescue.

Usually when I get a call, it is on a gray, foul day. I believe inland boaters could avoid most heavy weather accidents, or at least the tragic results of these accidents, if skippers were better prepared and trained.

Every year hundreds of storms cross the United States and in their wake they often leave destruction and sometimes death. While the storms inflict havoc on some boaters, for others the big blow is just an adventure.

Why is bad weather a disaster for one boater and not another? Luck may play some part, but I believe the real difference is in knowing what to do.

I train rangers to operate in heavy weather and how to conduct search-and-rescue missions. I have been doing this for years. It is my hope that this book will reduce the need for my search-and-rescue work by providing inland powerboaters with options for avoiding emergencies and handling life-threatening crises.

BIBLIOGRAPHY

Andrews, Howard L. and Russell, Dr. Alexander L. *Basic Boating*. Englewood Cliffs, NJ: Prentice-Hall, Inc., 1964.

Battye, James K. *Toward Safer Boating*. Stevensville, MD: James K. Battye, 1992.

Bottomley, Tom. *Boatman's Handbook*. NY: Hearst Marine Books, 1988.

Bree, Marlin. *Call of the North Wind*. St. Paul, MN: Marlor Press, 1996.

Bree, Marlin. *In the Teeth of the Northeaster*. Hardcover edition, New York: Clarkson N. Potter, 1988. Trade paperback edition, St. Paul, MN: Marlor Press, 1993.

Henderson, Richard. *Essential Seamanship*. Centerville, MD: Cornell Maritime Press, 1994.

Kotsch, William J. *Weather for the Mariner*. Annapolis, MD: Naval Institute Press, 1983.

Larkin, Frank J. *Basic Coastal Navigation*. Dobbs Ferry, NY: Sheridan House, 1995.

Laskin, David. *Braving the Elements*. NY: Doubleday, 1996.

Maloney, Elbert S. *Chapman Piloting: Seamanship & Small Boat Handling*. NY: Hearst Marine Books, 61st edition,1994.

Markell, Jeff. *Coastal Navigation for the Small Boat Sailor*. Blue Ridge Summit, PA: TAB Books Inc., 1984.

Ratigan, William. *Great Lakes Shipwrecks & Survivals*. Grand Rapids, MI: Wm. B. Eerdmans Publishing Co., 3rd edition, 1980.

Riley, Denis and Spolton, Lewis. *World Weather and Climate*. Cambridge, NY: Cambridge University Press, 1983.

Schroeder, Mark J. and Buck, Charles C. *Fire Weather*. U.S. Dept. of Agriculture -- Forest Service, Agriculture Handbook 360, 1977.

Smith, David S. and Smith, Sara J. *Water Rescue, Basic Skills for Emergency Responders*. St. Louis, MO: Mosby Lifeline, 1994.

Spiess, Gerry and Bree, Marlin. *Alone Against the Atlantic*. Minneapolis, MN: Control Data Publishing, 1981.

Stapleton, Sid. *Emergencies at Sea*. NY: Hearst Marine Books, 1991.

U.S. Coast Guard Auxiliary. *Boating Skills and Seamanship*. Washington, D.C.: 1990.

Vihlen, Hugo and Kimberlin, Joan. *The Stormy Voyage of Father's Day*. St. Paul, MN: Marlor Press Inc., 1997.

Waters, John M., Jr. *A Guide to Small Boat Emergencies*. Annapolis, MD: Naval Institute Press, 1993.

Williams, Margaret. *The Boater's Weather Guide*. Centerville, MD: Cornell Maritime Press, 1990.

OTHER RESOURCES

Where to find boating organizations, equipment, charts and helpful information

American Red Cross
431 18th St. NW
Washington, D.C. 20002 - 202

One of the largest humanitarian organizations in the United States and has more than 1,200 local chapters. It offers health and safety services, which include training in CPR, first aid, aquatics and water safety.

U.S. Army Corps of Engineers
Mississippi Valley Division
P.O. Box 80
Vicksburg, MS 39181 - 0080
Telephone: 601 - 631 - 5042

Dedicated to improving navigation and stabilizing the Mississippi River and its tributaries. It provides information about the river and is a source for regional maps and river charts.

Boats/US
884 S. Pickett St.
Alexandria, VA 22304
Telephone: 703-823-9550

Major boating organization with annual membership dues offering discounts on boating supplies and equipment. Sells from large, helpful color catalog and direct from 45 marine stores throughout the U.S. Offers many specialized services for boaters, including charts, books, engine parts, discount outfitting, and boat insurance.

Coast Guard Auxiliary
2100 Second St. SW
Washington, D.C. 20593
Telephone: 1 - 800 - 368 - 5647

A civilian organization of volunteer boaters which assists the U.S.

Coast Guard. Members, who have received specialized training, conduct courtesy checks of boating safety equipment, assist search-and-rescue patrols and teach classes in boating safety. In addition, members may participate in outings, cruises and rendezvous.

Federal Communications Commission
1919 M Street NW
Washington, D.C. 20554

Federal agency provides information concerning laws regulating the use of marine radios. FCC publications give general information about types of radios, licensing requirements and operating procedures.

NOAA Distribution Service (N/CG33)
National Ocean Service
Riverdale, MD 20737 - 1199
Telephone: 301 - 436 - 6990
800 - 638 - 8972

A source of NOAA charts, and Coast Pilots used on the Great Lakes and the lower Mississippi River. Offers pamphlets which list locations of local weather service radio stations as well as publications which detail the dangers of storms and give weather tips for boaters.

Superintendent of Documents
U.S. Government Printing Office
Washington, D.C. 20402
Telephone: 202 - 512 - 1800

The government printer is the source of the latest edition of the Rules of the Road and U.S. Coast Guard regulations concerning boating equipment requirements and navigation lights. Also a source for Light Lists, The American Nautical Almanac and information on weather broadcasts.

Quimby's Cruising Guide
Waterways Journal
319 N 4th St., Suite 650
St. Louis, MO 63102
Telephone: 314 - 241 - 7354

A guide for the Great Lakes, Mississippi River and connecting waterways. It presents information about harbors, locks, dams, services and attractions. Presents useful information for navigation of the Mississippi River.

U.S. Coast Guard
2100 Second St. SW
Washington, D.C. 20593
Telephone: 202 - 267 - 2229
U.S. Coast Guard Customer Infoline:
Telephone 800 - 368 - 5647
Web site: http://www.navcen.uscg.mil

An agency of the Department of Transportation responsible for the maintenance of navigation aids and water search and rescue in coastal waters, the Great Lakes and Mississippi River. Publishes a variety of free materials on recreational boating safety. Contact this agency for information about laws, equipment requirements and safety recommendations.

US Power Squadron
P.O. Box 30423
Raleigh, NC 27622
Telephone: 919 - 821 - 0281

Civilian organization of recreational boaters dedicated to boating safety education. U.S. Power Squadron headquarters details requirements for membership and also provides addresses and telephone numbers of local units which offer boating safety classes.

West Marine
P.O. Box 50070
Watsonville, CA 95077-0070
Telephone: 800 - 538 - 0775

Largest marine supply retailer offers boating equipment at more than 200 stores and from a large, colorful catalog. A trained staff can answer questions and "The West Advisor" sections of the catalog presents information on the newest technology as well as helpful advice to boaters.

CANADIAN

Canadian Coast Guard
Office of Boating Safety
344 Slater St., 9th Floor
Ottawa, Ontario K1A 0N7
Telephone: 613 - 990 - 3116

Characterized as the boater's friend, this organization's primary objective is to guide mariners in safe navigation. Publishes the monthly edition of Notices of Mariners and various other publications. Notices to Mariners can be ordered by mail or telephone or accessed at this web site: http://www.notmar.com.

Hydrographic Chart Distribution Office
Department of Fisheries and Oceans
PO Box 8080
1675 Russell Road
Ottawa, Ontario K1G 3H6
613 - 998 - 4931
Fax: 613 - 998 - 1217
E-mail: chs_sales@dfo-mpo.gc.ca
Web site: http://www.chshq.dso.cal

A source of Canadian charts for the Great Lakes, regulations and the annual edition of Notices to Mariners and Light List.

NOTES

INDEX

at night, 182

bridle, 174, diagram of, 175

dangers of, 147, 166-170, 179

equipment, 172-175

  kicker hook, diagram of, 177

in fog, 182

in step, 181, diagram of 181

procedure, 147-148, 170-184

safety precautions, 179-180

side tow, 183-184,

  diagram of, 183

trim, 63, 79-80

Truman Lake, MO, 95

turning, 88

twin engine, 225-226

U

United States Coast Guard, 40, 41, 50, 54, 56, 61, 114, 116, 134, 135, 147, 148, 168, 172, 190, 196, 199-200, 207, 217, 232, 233, 236, 239, 242, 243, 244, 246-247, 254, 259-261, 265

  advice of, 50, 176

  Cleveland Rescue Coordination

    Center, 41, 260

  minimal equipment standards, &

    requirements, 51-54, 107,

      209, 212, 228, 249, 265

United States Coast Guard Auxiliary, 48, 49, 150, 201-202

United States Power Squadron, 48, 49, 112, 150, 202

Upton, Roger, 202

utility boats, 231-232

V

vessel maintenance, 59-60, 98, 136

check list, 59, 60

vessel protection, 66-67

vessel seaworthiness, 50-51, 103

vessel survivability, 227-230

W

waterspout, 44

water survival, 133

  See cold water survival

Waterways Journal, 258

waves, action of wind on, 70

  described by, 70

  diagram of, 71

  estimating height of, 72

  types of, 71

weather forecast, 20, 26, 27-28, 60, 267

  chart of indicators, 34

  warning flags, 20-21, 255-256

    sidebar, 22

Westford, 235

Whaley, Bob, 236, 249-250, 254, 255

Williams, Don, 257

Wilson, Bob, 16

wind, causes of, 32-33, gusty, 43-44

windage, 223-224

Y

yaw, 76

yawing of towed vessel, 181

BOOKS FOR BOATERS

Heavy Weather Boating Emergencies Boaters! This book can save a life. Here is the *first* emergency survival guide for powerboat skippers on fresh water. A veteran search-and-rescue specialist tells all a sailor really needs to know about heavy weather seamanship (including how to maneuver the boat in waves and survive freshwater storms.) Plus much more. Fascinating reading. A must for any boater's library and an important on-board reference manual. Only $19.95

Call of the North Wind. Here's an inspiring true tale of seafaring on the largest expanse of freshwater in the world. Join best-selling author Marlin Bree as he sets sail in his home-built wooden sailboat to retrace voyages of lost ships, brave captains and early explorers on Lake Superior. This is the author's second book about Lake Superior, based on a voyage from the Apostle Islands eastward along the Shipwreck Coast into Canada. "It captures the feel and wild spirit of one of the most beautiful but treacherous bodies of water in the world." — *Star Tribune.* Only $16.95

Guest Afloat. Anyone who has ever had a guest on board who didn't know what to do and acted as if he or she were a paying guest at a B & B will want this book. *Guest Afloat* is the essential guide to being a welcome guest on board a boat. Tells how to use the boat's equipment, including the head, how to steer the boat and how to become a really useful and valued member of the crew. Lots on all-important boating etiquette and safety afloat. Written by veteran boaters Barbara Bradfield and Sally Slater, who saw the need for such a book on their own boats. Nicely done with many illustrations. Great to leave out in the main stateroom for guests afloat or to loan before a cruise. "A light-hearted approach to offering tips every boater should know (197) whether at the helm or not. Easy reading and well illustrated." — *Mariner's Log.* Only $14.95

Boat Log & Record. The most complete book of its kind! Here's every serious boater's long-needed permanent record to keep everything about a boat and its voyages. Includes daily logs, equipment and maintenance records, galley gear, emergency procedures, plans, and important insurance information. Plus important safety, layup checklists. All with lots of salty nautical sayings, advice. More! Every boater can use and enjoy this book. "...the boatowner's answer to a Filofax." — *Boating.* Only $17.95

In the Teeth of the Northeaster: A solo voyage on Lake Superior. For one summer, Marlin Bree sailed alone on Lake Superior in a 20-foot wooden sailboat he built in his backyard. He writes about kind-hearted waterfront people, early voyageurs, shipwrecks, storms, and an island of silver that once was the world's largest mine. Great tales of seafaring and surprises on the world's largest lake. His gripping adventures as he encounters heavy weather will thrill readers. This is the author's first book of sailing adventures on Superior, beginning in Bayfield, WI, through the Apostle Islands to Duluth, MN, and then up the unforgiving North Shore into Canada, where he meets the mother of all inland summer storms. "Fascinating" — *Sail* magazine. $17.95

The Stormy Voyage of Father's Day. On June 14, 1993, Hugo Vihlen set out alone to cross the North Atlantic Ocean in a homebuilt sailboat measuring only five feet, four inches long. At sea, the 61-year-old ex-aviator faced fierce storms, mountainous waves, near capsizes and many close calls. After 105 days, he triumphantly sailed his *Father's Day* into Falmouth, England to capture a new world record. Here is inspiring real-life adventure. "A good, well-written read about an amazing 105-day voyage" — *Cruising World*. Only $16.95

Alone Against the Atlantic, by Gerry Spiess with Marlin Bree. This is the classic tale of one man against the sea in a home-built plywood boat. In 1979, Gerry Spiess set sail in a ten-foot-long sailboat of his own design in an attempt to cross the North Atlantic to set a new world record, west to east. Fifty-four days later, after battling intense loneliness, raging storms, physical pain and the never-ending motion of the waves, Gerry pulled into the English port of Falmouth, England. *Yankee Girl* had carried him safely across nearly 3,800 miles of the treacherous North Atlantic. This is far more than an ordinary adventure tale: it is an intimate portrait of a modern American sailing hero. This book became a national best seller and went on to become a selection in *Readers Digest Books* around the world. A modern classic that has thrilled and inspired countless sailors! A good read. Only $12.95

You can buy these fine books at many book or marine stores, on book-selling sites on the internet, or order them by mail directly from Marlor Press, 4304 Brigadoon Dr., St. Paul, MN 55126, or by calling toll free 800 - 669 - 4908. Visa and Master Card orders are accepted by telephone during business hours. Include $3 for shipping and handling for the first book, 75 cents for each additional book.

Chuck Luttrell is at the helm of a National Park Service boat he uses for heavy weather search and rescue. The author is a Department of the Interior certified instructor in motorboat operation and has more than 14 years of professional boating experience. He has worked as a boat patrol ranger in Kentucky, Texas and at Lake Mead, Nevada. As a District Boating Officer, he developed and taught training courses in heavy weather boat handling. This book, which he wrote with his mother, Jean Luttrell, was developed from his National Park Service training courses. Chuck and his wife, Eileen, a Las Vegas attorney, live in Boulder City, Nevada.